The Theory of Learning in Games

MIT Press Series on Economic Learning and Social Evolution
General Editor
Ken Binmore, Director of the Economic Learning and Social Evolution Centre, University College London.

1. *Evolutionary Games and Equilibrium Selection*, Larry Samuelson, 1997

2. *The Theory of Learning in Games*, Drew Fudenberg and David K. Levine, 1998

The Theory of Learning in Games

Drew Fudenberg
and
David K. Levine

The MIT Press
Cambridge, Massachusetts
London, England

This book was set in Palatino on the Monotype "Prism Plus" PostScript Imagesetter by
Asco Trade Typesetting Ltd., Hong Kong.

Printed and bound in the United States of America.

Library of Congress Cataloging-in-Publication Data

Fudenberg, Drew.
  The theory of learning in games / Drew Fudenberg and David K. Levine.
    p. cm.—(Economic learning and social evolution)
  Includes bibliographical references and index.
  ISBN 0-262-06194-5 (hc : alk. paper)
  1. Game theory. I. Levine, David K. II. Title. III. Series:
MIT Press series on economic learning and social evolution.
QA269.F83 1998
519.3—dc21   97-39957
                                                              CIP

To our wives, Geneen O'Brien and Joyce Davidson,
who have taught us much

Contents

Series Foreword

The MIT Press series on Economic Learning and Social Evolution reflects the widespread renewal of interest in the dynamics of human interaction. This issue has provided a broad community of economists, psychologists, philosophers, biologists, anthropologists, and others with a sense of common purpose so strong that traditional interdisciplinary boundaries have begun to melt away.

Some of the books in the series will be works of theory. Others will be philosophical or conceptual in scope. Some will have an experimental or empirical focus. Some will be collections of papers with a common theme and a linking commentary. Others will have an expository character. Yet others will be monographs in which new ideas meet the light of day for the first time. But all will have two unifying features. The first will be a rejection of the outmoded notion that what happens away from equilibrium can safely be ignored. The second will be a recognition that it is no longer enough to speak in vague terms of bounded rationality and spontaneous order. As in all movements, the time comes to put the beef on the table—and the time for us is now.

Authors who share this ethos and would like to be part of the series are cordially invited to submit outlines of their proposed books for consideration. Within our frame of reference, we hope that a thousand flowers will bloom.

Ken Binmore
Director
Economic Learning and Social Evolution Centre
University College London
Gower Street
London WC1E 6BT, England

Acknowledgments

As befits a book on learning, we have learned a great deal from our colleagues in the course of this project, so we have quite a number of people to thank. At the preliminary stages, Eddie Dekel and Glenn Ellison made useful suggestions about how to understand and organize the vast and growing literature that the book attempts to survey. Somewhat later, as we realized how little we knew about evolutionary game theory, Ken Binmore and Josef Hofbauer were very helpful in answering our questions and suggesting papers that we should include. On this topic, we also learned a great deal from Josef Hofbauer and Karl Sigmund's classic *The Theory of Evolution and Dynamical Systems*[1] and Jörgen Weibull's *Evolutionary Game Theory*.[2] Obviously the work discussed in chapters 4, 6, and 7 owes a great deal to David Kreps; we would like to give him a special thanks for many years of fascinating discussions and fruitful collaborations in the study of learning in games, and game theory more generally. Dean Foster and Rakesh Vohra introduced us to the computer science literature, much of which is referenced in chapter 8.

Once the first draft of the book was completed, we were fortunate to benefit from the comments and suggestions of many readers. Ken Binmore, Daniel Benjamin, Glenn Ellison, Dan Friedman, Sendhil Mullinaithan, and several anonymous reviewers suggested numerous improvements in the exposition of chapters 1 through 5. Dov Monderer identified some errors in an earlier draft of chapter 2. Josef Hofbauer, Klaus Nitzberger, Larry Samuelson, and Karl Schlag found mistakes in chapter 3; Larry also sent us detailed comments on that chapter and on the book as a whole. Michel Benaim, Glenn Ellison, George Mailath, and Peyton Young

---

1. English translation published by Cambridge University Press, 1988.
2. MIT Press, 1995.

helped us correct errors in chapter 5. Mathias Erlei caught some mistakes and suggested expositional improvements, especially in chapter 7. Leat Yarriv read chapter 8 very carefully; her suggestions led to many improvements and corrections. The discussion of stimulus-response models and experimental evidence benefited from a number of conversations and correspondence with Ken Binmore, Tilman Börgers, Al Roth, Larry Samuelson, and John Van Huyck, and correspondence with Gary Bolton and Ido Er'ev. We would also like to thank Stefano Dellarigna for careful proofreading.

We would like to thank MIT Press for producing and distributing this book; we especially thank Dana Andrus for her careful copyediting and Terry Vaughn for his encouragement. We are grateful to the UCLA Academic Senate and National Science Foundation grants SBR-93-20695 and SBR-94-24013 for financial support. Most of all, we thank our wives for their forbearance and support those nights when revising a chapter temporarily took priority over spending time with our families.

The Theory of Learning
in Games

1   Introduction

1.1   Introduction

This book is about the theory of learning in games. Most of non-cooperative game theory has focused on equilibrium in games, especially Nash equilibrium and its refinements such as perfection. This raises the question of when and why we might expect that observed play in a game will correspond to one of these equilibria. One traditional explanation of equilibrium is that it results from analysis and introspection by the players in a situation where the rules of the game, the rationality of the players, and the players' payoff functions are all common knowledge. Both conceptually and empirically, these theories have many problems.[1]

    This book develops the alternative explanation that equilibrium arises as the long-run outcome of a process in which less than fully rational players grope for optimality over time. The models we will discuss serve to provide a foundation for equilibrium theory. This is not to say that learning models provide foundations for all of the equilibrium concepts in the literature, nor does it argue for the use of Nash equilibrium in every situation; indeed, in some cases most learning models do not lead to any equilibrium concept beyond the very weak notion of rationalizability.

---

1. First, a major conceptual problem occurs when there are multiple equilibria, for in the absence of an explanation of how players come to expect the same equilibrium, their play need not correspond to any equilibrium at all. While it is possible that players coordinate their expectations using a common selection procedure such as Harsanyi and Selten's (1988) tracing procedure, left unexplained is how such a procedure comes to be common knowledge. Second, we doubt that the hypothesis of exact common knowledge of payoffs and rationality apply to many games, and relaxing this to an assumption of almost common knowledge yields much weaker conclusions. (See, for example, Dekel and Fudenberg 1990 and Borgers 1994.) Third, equilibrium theory does a poor job explaining play in early rounds of most experiments, although it does much better in later rounds. This shift from non-equilibrium to equilibrium play is difficult to reconcile with a purely introspective theory.

Nevertheless, learning models can suggest useful ways to evaluate and modify the traditional equilibrium concepts. Learning models lead to refinements of Nash equilibrium; for example, considerations of the long run stochastic properties of the learning process suggest that risk dominant equilibria will be observed in some games. They lead also to descriptions of long-run behavior weaker than Nash equilibrium; for example, considerations of the inability of players in extensive form games to observe how opponents would have responded to events that did not occur suggests that self-confirming equilibria that are not Nash may be observed as the long-run behavior in some games.

We should acknowledge that the learning processes we analyze need not converge, and even when they do converge, the time needed for convergence is in some cases quite long. One branch of the literature uses these facts to argue that it may be difficult to reach equilibrium, especially in the short run. We downplay this antiequilibrium argument for several reasons. First, our impression is that there are some interesting economic situations in which most of the participants seem to have a pretty good idea of what to expect from day to day, perhaps because the social arrangements and social norms that we observe reflect a process of thousands of years of learning from the experiences of past generations. Second, although there are interesting periods in which social norms change so suddenly that they break down, such as during the transition from a controlled economy to a market one, the dynamic learning models that have been developed so far seem unlikely to provide much insight about the medium-term behavior that will occur in these circumstances.[2] Third, learning theories often have little to say in the short run, making predictions that are highly dependent on details of the learning process and prior beliefs; the long-run predictions are generally more robust to the specification of the model. Finally, from an empirical point of view, it is difficult to gather enough data to test predictions about short-term fluctuations along the adjustment path. For this reason we will focus primarily on the long-run properties of the models we study. Learning theory does, however, make some predictions about rates of convergence and behavior in the medium run, and we will discuss these issues as well.

Even given the restriction to long-run analysis, there is a question of the relative weight to be given to cases where behavior converges and

---

2. However, Boylan and El-Gamal (1993), Crawford (1995), Roth and Er'ev (1995), Er'ev and Roth (1996), Nagel (1993), and Stahl (1994) use theoretical learning models to try to explain data on short-term and medium-term play in game theory experiments.

cases where it does not. We chose to emphasize the convergence results, in part because they are sharper but also because we feel that these are the cases where the behavior that is specified for the agents is most likely to be a good description of how the agents will actually behave. Our argument here is that the learning models that have been studied so far do not do full justice to the ability of people to recognize patterns of behavior by others. Consequently, when learning models fail to converge, the behavior of the model's individuals is typically quite naive; for example, the players may ignore the fact that the model is locked in to a persistent cycle. We suspect that if the cycles persist long enough, the agents will eventually use more sophisticated inference rules that detect them; for this reason we are not convinced that models of cycles in learning are useful descriptions of actual behavior. However, this does not entirely justify our focus on convergence results: As we discuss in chapter 8, more sophisticated behavior may simply lead to more complicated cycles.

We find it useful to distinguish between two related but different kinds of models that are used to model the processes by which players change the strategies they are using to play a game. In our terminology a "learning model" is any model that specifies the learning rules used by individual players and examines their interaction when the game (or games) is played repeatedly. In particular, while Bayesian learning is certainly a form of learning, and one that we will discuss, learning models can be far less sophisticated and include, for example, stimulus-response models of the type first studied by Bush and Mosteller in the 1950s and more recently taken up by economists.[3] As will become clear in the course of this book, our own views about learning models tend to favor those in which the agents, while not necessarily fully rational, are nevertheless somewhat sophisticated; we will frequently criticize learning models for assuming that agents are more naïve than we feel is plausible.

Individual-level models tend to be mathematically complex, especially in models with a large population of players. Consequently there has also been a great deal of work that makes assumptions directly on the behavior of the aggregate population. The basic assumption here is that some unspecified process at the individual level leads the population as a whole to adopt strategies that yield improved payoffs. The standard practice is to call such models "evolutionary," probably because the first examples of such processes came from the field of evolutionary biology.

---

3. Examples include Cross (1983), and more recently the Borgers and Sarin (1995), Er'ev and Roth (1996), and Roth and Er'ev (1995) papers discussed in chapter 3.

However, this terminology may be misleading, since the main reason for interest in these processes in economics and the social sciences is not that the behavior in question is thought to be genetically determined but rather that the specified "evolutionary" process corresponds to the aggregation of plausible learning rules for the individual agents. For example, chapter 3 discusses papers that derive the standard replicator dynamics from particular models of learning at the individual level.

Often evolutionary models allow the possibility of mutation, that is, the repeated introduction (either deterministically or stochastically) of new strategies into the population. The causes of these mutations are not explicitly modeled, but as we will see, mutations are related to the notion of experimentation, which plays an important role in the formulation of individual learning rules.

1.2 Large Populations and Matching Models

This book is about learning, and if learning is to take place, players must play either the same or related games repeatedly so that they have something to learn about. So far most of the literature on learning has focused on repetitions of the same game and not on the more difficult issue of when two games are "similar enough" that the results of one may have implications for the other.[4] We too will avoid this question, even though our presumption that players *do* extrapolate across games they see as similar is an important reason to think that learning models have some relevance to real-world situations.

To focus our thinking, we will begin by limiting attention to two-player games. The natural starting point for the study of learning is to imagine two players playing a two-person game repeatedly and trying to learn to anticipate each other's play by observation of past play. We refer to this as the *fixed-player model*. However, in such an environment players ought to consider not only how their opponent will play in the future but also the possibility that their current play will influence the future play of their opponents. For example, players might think that if they are nice, they will be rewarded by their opponent being nice in the future, or that they can "teach" their opponent to play a best response to a particular action by playing that action over and over.

---

4. Exceptions that develop models of learning from similar games are Li Calzi (1993) and Romaldo (1995).

	L	R
U	1, 0	3, 2
D	2, 1	4, 0

Figure 1.1
Player 1 would like to "teach" player 2 that she is playing D

Consider, for example, the game in figure 1.1. In almost any learning model a player 1 who ignores considerations of repeated play will play D, since D is a dominant strategy and thus maximizes 1's current expected payoff for any beliefs about opponents. If, as seems plausible, player 2 eventually learns 1 plays D, the system will converge to (D, L), where 1's payoff is 2. But if 1 is patient, and knows that 2 "naively" chooses each period's action to maximize that period's payoff given 2's forecast of 1's action, then player 1 can do better by always playing U, since this eventually leads 2 to play R. Essentially a "sophisticated" and patient player facing a naive opponent can develop a "reputation" for playing any fixed action and thus in the long run obtain the payoff of a "Stackelberg leader."

Most of learning theory abstracts from such repeated game considerations by explicitly or implicitly relying on a model in which the incentive to try to alter the future play of opponents is small enough to be negligible. One class of models of this type is one in which players are locked in their choices, and the discount factors are small compared to the maximum speed at which the system can possibly adjust. However, this is not always a sensible assumption. A second class of models that makes repeated play considerations negligible is that of a large number of players who interact relatively anonymously, with the population size large compared to the discount factor.

We can embed a particular two- (or N-) player game in such an environment by specifying the process by which players in the population are paired together to play the game. There are a variety of models, depending on how players meet and what information is revealed at the end of each round of play:

Single-pair model Each period a single pair of players is chosen at random to play the game. At the end of the round, their actions are revealed to everyone. Here, if the population is large, it is likely that the players who play today will remain inactive for a long time. Even for players who are patient, it will not be worth their while to sacrifice current payoff to influence the future play of their opponents if the population size is sufficiently large compared to the discount factor.

Aggregate statistic model Each period all players are randomly matched. At the end of the round, the population aggregates are announced. If the population is large, each player has little influence on the population aggregates and consequently little influence on future play. Once again, players have no reason to depart from myopic play.

Random-matching model Each period all players are randomly matched. At the end of each round, each player observes only the play in his own match. The way a player acts today will influence the way his current opponent plays tomorrow, but the player is unlikely to be matched with his current opponent or anyone who has met the current opponent for a long time. Once again, myopic play is approximately optimal if the population is finite but large compared the players' discount factors.[5] This is the treatment most frequently used in game theory experiments.

The large population stories provide an alternative explanation of "naive" play; of course they do so at the cost of reducing its applicability to cases where the relevant population might plausibly be thought to be large.[6] We should note that experimentalists often claim to find that a "large" population can consist of as few as six players. Some discussion of this issue can be found in Friedman (1996).

From a technical point of view, there are two commonly used models of large populations: *finite populations* and *continuum populations*. The continuum model is generally more tractable.

Another, and important, modeling issue concerns how the populations from which the players are drawn relate to the number of "player roles" in the stage game. Let us distinguish between an *agent* in the game, corresponding to a particular player role, and the actual player taking on the role of the agent in a particular match. If the game is symmetric, we can imagine that there is a single population from which the two agents are drawn. This is referred to as the *homogeneous population* model. Alter-

---

5. The size of the potential gain depends on the relationship between the population size and the discount factor. For any fixed discount factor, the gain becomes negligible if the population is large enough. However, the required population size may be quite large, as shown by the "contagion" arguments of Ellison (1993).

6. If we think of players extrapolating their experience from one game to a "similar" one, then there may be more cases where the relevant population is larger than there appear to be at first sight.

natively, we could assume that each agent is drawn from a distinct population. This case is referred to as an *asymmetric population*. In the case of an aggregate statistic model where the frequency of play in the population is revealed and the population is homogeneous, there are two distinct models depending on whether individual players are clever enough to remove their own play from the aggregate statistic before responding to it. There seems little reason to believe that they cannot, but in a large population it makes little difference; it is frequently convenient to assume that all players react to the same statistic.

Finally, in a symmetric game, in addition to the extreme cases of homogeneous and heterogeneous populations, one can also consider intermediate mixtures of the two cases, as in Friedman (1991), in which each player has some chance of being matched with an opponent from a different population and some chance of being matched with an opponent from the same population. This provides a range of possibilities between the homogeneous and asymmetric cases.

1.3   Three Common Models of Learning and/or Evolution

Three particular dynamic adjustment processes have received the most attention in the theory of learning and evolution. In *fictitious play*, players observe only the results of their own matches and play a best response to the historical frequency of play. This model is frequently analyzed in the context of the fixed-player (and hence asymmetric population) model, but the motivation for that analysis has been the belief that the same or similar results obtain with a large population. (Chapter 4 will discuss the extent to which that belief is correct.) In the *partial best-response* dynamic, a fixed portion of the population switches each period from its current action to a best response to the aggregate statistic from the previous period. Here the agents are assumed to have all the information they need to compute the best response, so the distinctions between the various matching models are unimportant; an example of this is the Cournot adjustment process discussed in the next section. Finally, in the *replicator* dynamic, the share of the population using each strategy grows at a rate proportional to that strategy's current payoff, so strategies giving the greatest utility against the aggregate statistic from the previous period grow most rapidly, while those with the least utility decline most rapidly. This dynamic is usually thought of in the context of a large population and random matching, though we will see in chapter 4 that a similar process can be derived as the result of boundedly rational learning in a fixed-player model.

The first part of this book will examine these three dynamics, the connection between them, and some of their variants in the setting of one-shot simultaneous-move games. Our focus will be on the long-run behavior of the systems in various classes of games, in particular, on whether the system will converge to a Nash equilibrium and, if so, which equilibrium will be selected. The second part of the book will examine similar questions in the setting of general extensive form games. The concluding chapter of the book will examine more sophisticated and far-sighted alternatives to these simple learning models.

1.4   Cournot Adjustment

To give the flavor of the type of analyses the book considers, we now develop the example of Cournot adjustment by firms, which is perhaps the oldest and most familiar nonequilibrium adjustment model in game theory. While the Cournot process has many problems as a model of learning, it serves to illustrate a number of the issues and concerns that recur in more sophisticated models. This model does not have a large population but only one "agent" in the role of each firm. Instead, as we explain below, the model implicitly relies on a combination of "lock-in" or inertia and impatience to explain why players don't try to influence the future play of their opponent.

Consider a simple duopoly whose players are firms labeled $i = 1, 2$. Each player's strategy is to choose a quantity $s^i \in [0, \infty)$ of a homogeneous good to produce. The vector of both strategies is the strategy profile denoted by $s \in S$. We let s^{-i} denote the strategy of player i's opponent. The utility (or profit) of player i is $u^i(s^i, s^{-i})$, where we assume that $u^i(\cdot, s^{-i})$ is strictly concave. The best response of player i to a profile, denoted $BR^i(s^{-i})$, is

$$BR^i(s^{-i}) = \arg\max_{\bar{s}^i} u^i(\bar{s}^i, s^{-i}).$$

(The assumption that utility is strictly concave in the player's own action implies that the best response is unique.)

In the Cournot adjustment model, time periods $t = 1, 2, \ldots$, are discrete. There is an initial state profile $\theta_0 \in S$. The adjustment process itself is given by assuming that in each period the player chooses a pure strategy that is a best response to the previous period; that is, at each date t player i chooses a pure strategy $s^i_t = BR_i(s^{-i}_{t-1})$. In other words, the Cournot pro-

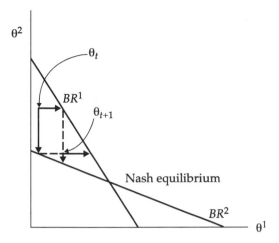

Figure 1.2
Cournot adjustment dynamic

cess is $\theta_{t+1} = f^C(\theta_t)$, where $f_i^C(\theta_t) = BR_i(\theta_t^{-i})$. A steady state of this process is a state $\hat{\theta}$ such that $\hat{\theta} = f^C(\hat{\theta})$; once $\theta_t = \hat{\theta}$, the system will remain in this state forever.

The crucial property of a steady state is that by definition it satisfies $\hat{\theta}^i = BR_i(\hat{\theta}_{-i})$, so every steady state is a Nash equilibrium.

1.5 Analysis of Cournot Dynamics[7]

We can analyze the dynamics of the two-player Cournot process by drawing the reaction curves corresponding to the best-response function, as illustrated in figure 1.2. As drawn, the process converges to the intersection of reaction curves, which is the unique Nash equilibrium.

In this example the firms' output levels change each period. Therefore, even if they start out thinking that their opponent's output is fixed, they should quickly learn that it is not. However, we will see later that there are variations on the Cournot process in which players' beliefs are less obviously wrong.

In figure 1.2 the process converges to the unique Nash equilibrium from any initial conditions; that is, the steady state is *globally stable*. If there are multiple Nash equilibria, we cannot really hope that where we end up is

---

7. The appendix at the end of this chapter reviews basic facts about stability conditions in dynamical systems.

independent of the initial condition, so we cannot hope that any one equilibrium is globally stable. What we can do is ask whether the play converges to a particular equilibrium once the state gets sufficiently close to it. The appendix reviews the relevant theory of the stability of dynamical systems for this and other examples.

1.6 Cournot Process with Lock-In

We argued above that interpreting Cournot adjustment as a model of learning supposes that the players are not particularly sharp-witted: They choose their actions to maximize against the opponent's last-period play as if they expect that today's play will be the same as yesterday's. In addition each player assigns probability 1 to a single strategy of the opponent, so there is no subjective uncertainty. Although the players have such strong belief that their opponent's play is constant, their opponent's actual play can vary quite a bit. Under these circumstances it seems likely that as players learn that their opponent's play changes over time, they will alter their play.[8]

One response to this criticism is to consider a different dynamic process with alternating moves: Suppose that firms are constrained to take turns, with firm 1 moving in periods 1, 3, 5, and firm 2 in periods 2, 4, 6. Each firm's decision is "locked in" for two periods: Firm 1 is constrained to set its second-period output s_2^1 to be the same as its first-period output s_1^1.

Suppose further that each firm's objective is to maximize the discounted sum of its per-period payoffs $\sum_{t=1}^{\infty} \delta^{t-1} u^i(s_t)$, where $\delta < 1$ is a fixed common discount factor. There are two reasons why a highly rational firm 1 would not choose its first-period output to maximize its first-period payoff. First, since the output chosen must also be used in the second period, firm 1's optimal choice for a fixed time path of outputs by firm 2 should maximize the weighted sum of firm 1's first- and second-period profit, as opposed to maximizing first-period profit alone. Second, as in the discussion of Stackelberg leadership in section 1.2, firm 1 may realize that its choice of first-period output will influence firm 2's choice of output in the second period.

---

8. Selten's (1988) model of anticipatory learning models this by considering different degrees of sophistication in the construction of forecasts. The least sophisticated is to assume that opponents will not change their actions; next is to assume that opponents believe that *their* opponents will not change their actions, and so forth. However, no matter how far we carry out this procedure, in the end players are always more sophisticated than their opponents imagine.

However, if firm 1 is very impatient, then neither of these effects matters because both pertain to future events, and then it is at least approximately optimal for firm 1 to choose at date 1 the output that maximizes its current-period payoff. This process, in which firms take turns setting outputs that are the static best response to the opponent's output in the previous period, is called the *alternating-move Cournot dynamic.* It has qualitatively the same long-run properties as the simultaneous-move adjustment process, and it is in fact the process that Cournot studied.[9]

There is another variant on the timing of moves that is of interest: Instead of firms taking turns, suppose that each period one firm is chosen at random and given the opportunity to change its output, while the output of the other remains locked in. Then, once again, if firms are impatient, the equilibrium behavior is to choose the action that maximizes the immediate payoff given the current output of the opponent. There is no need to worry about predictions of future because the future does not matter. Note that this model has exactly the same dynamics as the alternating-move Cournot model, in the sense that if a player gets to move twice or more in a row, his best response is the same as it was last time; thus he does not move at all. In other words, the only time movement occurs is when players switch roles, in which case the move is the same as it would be under the Cournot alternating-move dynamic. While the dating of moves is different, and random to boot, the condition for asymptotic stability is the same.

What do we make of this? Stories that make myopic play optimal require that discount factors be very small, and in particular small compared to the speed that players can change their outputs: The less locked-in the players are, the smaller the discount factor needs to be. So the key is to understand why players might be locked in. One story is that choices are capital goods like computer systems that are only replaced when they fail. This makes lock-in more comprehensible but limits the applicability of the models. Another point is that under the perfect foresight interpretation, lock-in models do not sound like a story of learning. Rather they are a story of dynamics in a world where learning is irrelevant because players know just what they need to do to compute their optimal actions.[10]

---

9. Formally the two processes have the same steady states, and a steady state is stable under one process if and only if it is stable under the other.
10. Maskin and Tirole (1988) study the Markov-perfect equilibria of this game with alternating moves and two-period lock-in.

1.7 Review of Finite Simultaneous-Move Games

1.7.1 *Strategic-Form Games*

Although we began by analyzing the Cournot game because of its famil-
iarity to economists, this game is complicated by the fact that each player
has a continuum of possible output levels. Throughout the rest of the
book, we are going to focus on finite games in which each player has only
finitely many available alternatives. Our basic setting will be one in which
a group of players $i = 1, \ldots, I$ plays a *stage game* against one another.

The first half of the book will discuss the simplest kind of stage game,
namely *one-shot simultaneous-move games*. This section reviews the basic
theory of simultaneous-move games and introduces the notation we use
to describe them. The section is not intended as an introduction to game
theory; readers who would like a more leisurely or detailed treatment
should look elsewhere.[11] Instead, we try to highlight those aspects of
"standard" game theory that will be of most importance in this book, and
we focus on those problems in game theory for which learning theory has
proved helpful in their analysis.

In a one-shot simultaneous-move game, each player i simultaneously
chooses a strategy $s^i \in S^i$. We refer to the vector of players' strategies as a
strategy profile, denoted by $s \in S \equiv \times_{i=1}^{I} S^i$. As a result of these choices by
the players, each player receives a *utility* (also called a payoff or reward)
$u^i(s)$. The combination of the player set, the strategy spaces, and the payoff functions is called the *strategic* or *normal* form of the game. In two-
player games the strategic form is often displayed as a matrix, where rows
index player 1's strategies, columns index player 2's, and the entry corresponding to each strategy profile (s^1, s^2) is the payoff vector

$$(u^1(s^1, s^2), u^2(s^1, s^2)).$$

In "standard" game theory, that is, analysis of Nash equilibrium and its
refinements, it does not matter what players observe at the end of the
game.[12] When players learn from each play of the stage game how to
play in the next one, what the players observe makes a great deal of difference to what they can learn. Except in simultaneous-move games,
though, it is not terribly natural to assume that players observe their

---

11. For example, Fudenberg and Tirole (1991) or Myerson (1991).
12. However, what players observe at the end of each stage game in repeated games does
play a critical role even without learning. See for example Fudenberg, Levine, and Maskin
(1994).

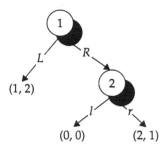

Figure 1.3
Observability in the extensive form

opponent's strategies because in general extensive-form games a strategy specifies how the player will play at every one of his information sets. For example, suppose that the extensive form is as shown in figure 1.3 and player 1 plays L. Then player 2 does not actually get to move. In order for player 1 to observe 2's strategy, player 1 must observe how player 2 would have played had 1 played R. We could make this assumption. For example, player 2 could write down his choice on a piece of paper and hand it to a third party, who would implement the choice if 2's information set is reached and at the end of the period 1 get to see the piece of paper. This sounds rather farfetched. Consequently, when we work with strategic-form games and suppose that the chosen strategies are revealed at the end of each period, the interpretation is that we are looking at a simultaneous-move game, that is, a game where each player moves only once and all players choose their actions simultaneously. This is the case we will consider in the first part of the book.

In addition to pure strategies, we allow the possibility that players use random or "mixed" strategies. The space of probability distributions over a set is denoted by $\Delta(\cdot)$. A randomization by a player over his pure strategies is called a *mixed strategy* and is written $\sigma^i \in \Sigma^i \equiv \Delta(S^i)$. Mixed-strategy profiles are denoted $\sigma \in \Sigma = \times_{i=1}^I \Sigma^i$. Players are expected to be utility maximizers, so their payoff to a mixed-strategy profile σ is the expected value $u^i(\sigma) \equiv \sum_s u^i(s) \prod_{j=1}^I \sigma^j(s^j)$. Notice that the randomization of each player is independent of other players' play.[13]

---

13. We will not take time here to motivate the use of mixed strategies, but two motivations will be discussed later on in the book, namely (1) the idea that the randomization corresponds to the random draw of a particular opponent from a population each of which is playing a pure strategy, and (2) the idea that what looks like randomization to an outside observer is the result of unobserved shocks to the player's payoff function.

As in the analysis of the Cournot game, it is useful to distinguish between the play of a player and his opponents. We will write s^{-i}, σ^{-i} for the vector of strategies (pure and mixed, respectively) of player i's opponents.

In the game each player attempts to maximize his own expected utility. How he should go about doing this depends on how he thinks his opponents are playing, and the major issue addressed in the theory of learning is how he should form those expectations. For the moment, though, suppose that player i believes that the distribution of his opponents' plays corresponds to the mixed-strategy profile σ^{-i}. Then player i should play a *best response*, that is, a strategy $\hat{\sigma}^i$ such that $u^i(\hat{\sigma}^i, \sigma^{-i}) \geq u^i(\sigma^i, \sigma^{-i})$, $\forall \sigma^i$. The set of all best responses to σ^{-i} is denoted by $BR^i(\sigma^{-i})$, so $\hat{\sigma}^i \in BR^i(\sigma^{-i})$. In the Cournot adjustment process, players expect that their opponents will continue to play as they did in the last period, so they will play the corresponding best response.

In the Cournot process, and in many related processes, such as fictitious play, which we will discuss later in the book, the dynamics are determined by the best-response correspondences, in the sense that two games with the same best-response correspondences will give rise to the same dynamic learning process. For this reason it is important to know when two games have the same best-response correspondences. If two games have the same best-response correspondence for every player, we say that they are *best-response equivalent*.

A simple transformation that leaves preferences, and consequently best responses, unchanged is a linear transformation of payoffs. The following proposition gives a slight generalization of this idea:

Proposition 1.1   Suppose that $\tilde{u}^i(s) = au^i(s) + v^i(s^{-i})$ for all players i. Then $\tilde{u}$ and u are best-response equivalent.

This result is immediate, since adding a constant that depends only on another player's action does not change what is best for the player in question.

One important class of games is zero-sum games, which are two-player games whose payoff to one player is the negative of the payoff to the other player.[14] Zero-sum games are particularly simple and have been extensively studied. The following result relates best-response correspondences of general two-player, two-action games to those of two-player, two-action, zero-sum games.

---

14. Note that the "zero" in "zero-sum" is unimportant; what matters is that the payoffs have a constant sum.

Proposition 1.2 Every 2 × 2 game for which the best-response correspondences have a unique intersection that lies in the interior of the strategy space is best-response equivalent to a zero-sum game.

Proof Denote the two strategies A and B, respectively. There is no loss
of generality in assuming that A is a best response for player 1 to A and
that B is a best response for player 2 to A. (If A was also a best response
to A for 2, then the best-response correspondences intersect at a pure-
strategy profile, which we have ruled out by assumption.) Let σ^i denote
player i's probability of playing A. Then the best-response correspondences of the two players are determined by the intersection point, as
diagrammed in figure 1.4. The trick is to show that this intersection point
can be realized as the intersection of best responses of a zero-sum game.
To do this, consider the zero-sum game displayed in figure 1.5. Notice
that if $a < 1$, the best response for player 1 to A is A and the best response of player 2 to A is B. Moreover player 1 is indifferent between A
and B when $\sigma^2 = a\sigma^2 + b(1 - \sigma^2)$, while player 2 is indifferent between A
and B when $\sigma^1 + a(1 - \sigma^1) = b(1 - \sigma^1)$. Fixing the intersection point
σ^1, σ^2, we can solve these two linear equations in two unknowns to find

$$a = \frac{\sigma^2 - \sigma^1}{1 + \sigma^1\sigma^2}.$$

Since $\sigma^2 - \sigma^1 < 1$, we see that $a < 1$, as required. ■

σ^2

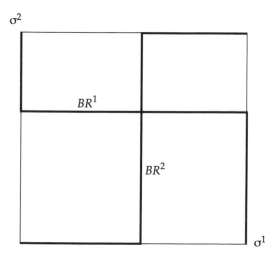

Figure 1.4
Best-response correspondences in a 2 × 2 game with a unique mixed-strategy equilibrium

	A	B
A	1, −1	0, 0
B	a, −a	b, −b

Figure 1.5
Equivalent zero-sum game

	A	B
A	3, 3	1, 5
B	5, 1	2, 2

Figure 1.6
Prisoner's dilemma

1.7.2 Dominance and Iterated Dominance

The most primitive notion in game theory is that of dominance. Roughly a strategy is dominated if another strategy does better no matter how the player expects his opponents to play. The general idea is that we should not expect dominated strategies to be played.[15] The strongest notion of dominance is that of *strict dominance*.

Definition 1.1 Strategy σ^i is *strictly dominated for player i* if there is some other $\tilde{\sigma}^i \in \Sigma^i$ such that $u^i(\tilde{\sigma}^i, \sigma^{-i}) > u^i(\sigma^i, \sigma^{-i})$ for all $\sigma^{-i} \in \Sigma^{-i}$.

(This condition is equivalent to $u^i(\tilde{\sigma}^i, s^{-i}) > u^i(\sigma^i, s^{-i})$ for all pure-strategy profiles s^{-i} of i's opponents because i's payoff, when his opponents play a mixed profile, is a convex combination of the corresponding pure-strategy payoffs.)

A famous example of a game where dominant strategies play a role is the one-shot prisoner's dilemma game in figure 1.6. In this game the strategy B does better than A no matter what the opponent does. If we eliminate the strategy A, then there is a unique prediction that both players play B. Note, however, that (A, A) Pareto dominates (B, B), which is why there is a dilemma.

In this example both the dominated strategy and the dominating one are pure strategies. Neither of these are general properties. More pre-

---

15. But note that in nonsimultaneous-move games, strategies may differ in how much information they generate about opponents' play. When learning is considered, low payoff strategies may be played to acquire information.

	A	B
A	5, 0	0, 0
B	0, 0	5, 0
C	2, 0	2, 0

Figure 1.7
A pure strategy dominated by a mixed strategy

	A	B
A	1, −100	1, 1
B	2, 2	2, 1

Figure 1.8
B dominates A for player 1

cisely, a pure strategy s^i can be strictly dominated by a mixed strategy σ^i and yet not dominated by any pure strategy, as in figure 1.7. Here the strategy C is not dominated by either A or B for player 1, but it is dominated by a 50-50 mixture over A and B. Moreover, although any mixed strategy that assigns positive probability to a strictly dominated pure strategy is strictly dominated, a mixed strategy can also be strictly dominated even if it assigns probability 0 to every dominated pure strategy.

If a strategy of player 1's is strictly dominated, then there are several reasons why player 2's beliefs might come to assign that strategy probability 0. The first, traditional, argument is that if player 2 knows player 1's payoff function, and knows that 1 is rational, then player 2 should be able to deduce that player 1 will not use a strictly dominated strategy. Second, from the viewpoint of learning theory, if the strategy is strictly dominated, then[16] player 1 will have no reason to play it, and so player 2 should eventually learn that the dominated strategy is not being played.

Either story leads to the idea of *iterated strict dominance*, in which the deletion of some strategies for one player permits the deletion of some strategies for others, and so on. (It can be shown that the order in which strategies are deleted does not matter so long as the deletion process continues until no more deletions are possible.) We will not give a formal definition of iterated strict dominance here, but the example shown in figure 1.8 should make the idea clear: Here no strategy is dominated for

16. We presume that there are not extensive-form complications of the type mentioned in note 15.

```
      A      B
B [ 2, 2  | 2, 1 ]
```

Figure 1.9
Figure 1.8 after reduction by strict dominance

player 2, but the strategy A is strictly dominated for player 1. Eliminating that strategy results in the game shown in figure 1.9. In this game, B is strictly dominated for player 2, so the unique survivor of iterated strict dominance is (B, A). Note, however, that player 2 must be quite sure that player 1 is not playing A, since (A, A) results in a large loss for him. Consequently the prediction of (B, A) might be overturned if there is some small probability that player 1 has played A. (Perhaps there is some chance that player 1 has different payoffs than those given here or that player 1 makes a "mistake.")

Related to strict dominance is the notion of *weak dominance*.

Definition 1.2 Strategy σ^i is *weakly dominated for player i* if there is some $\tilde{\sigma}^i \in \Sigma^i, \tilde{\sigma}^i \neq \sigma^i$, such that $u^i(\tilde{\sigma}^i, \sigma^{-i}) \geq u^i(\sigma^i, \sigma^{-i})$ for all $\sigma^{-i} \in \Sigma^{-i}$, with strict inequality for at least one σ^{-i}.

Again, there seems to be no reason to play a weakly dominated strategy, and indeed weakly dominated strategies will not be played in models in which agents "tremble" or, more generally, in models where agents' beliefs about their opponent's strategies correspond to a completely mixed strategy. However, the notion of *iterated weak dominance* is problematic and will not play a role in this book.

1.7.3 Nash Equilibrium

One of the problems with dominance is that in many games of interest, the process of iterated dominance does not lead to strong predictions. This has encouraged the application of equilibrium theory in which all players simultaneously have correct beliefs about each others play while playing best responses to their own beliefs.

Definition 1.3 A *Nash Equilibrium* is a strategy profile $\hat{\sigma}$ such that $\hat{\sigma}^i \in BR^i(\hat{\sigma}^{-i}), \forall i$.

It follows from the Kakutani fixed-point theorem that a Nash equilibrium exists in finite games so long as mixed strategies are permitted. (Many

	A	B
A	2, 2	0, 0
B	0, 0	2, 2

Figure 1.10
Coordination game

simple games, e.g., "matching pennies," have no pure-strategy equilibria.)
A game may have several Nash equilibria, as in the example of a *coordination game* shown in figure 1.10: Here player 1 picks the row, and player 2 the column. Each player has two pure strategies A and B. The numbers in the table denote the utilities of player 1 and player 2, respectively. There are two pure strategy Nash equilibria at (A, A) and (B, B). There is also one mixed-strategy Nash equilibrium where both player randomize with a 1/2 chance of A and a 1/2 chance of B.

What would we expect to happen in this game? Both players prefer either of the two pure-strategy Nash equilibria to the mixed-strategy Nash equilibrium, since the expected utility to each player at the pure equilibrium is 2 while the expected utility at the mixed equilibrium is only 1. But in the absence of any coordinating device, it is not obvious how the two players can guess which equilibrium to go to. This might suggest that they will play the mixed equilibrium. But at the mixed equilibrium each player is indifferent, so while equilibrium requires that they give each strategy exactly the same probability, there is no strong reason for them to do so. Moreover, if player 1, say, believes that player 2 is even slightly more likely to play A than B, then player 1 will want to play A with probability one. From an intuitive point of view, the stability of this mixed-strategy equilibrium seems questionable.

In contrast, it seems easier for play to remain at one of the pure equilibria because here each player strictly prefers to play his part of the Nash equilibrium profile as long as he believes there is a high probability that his opponent is playing according to that equilibrium. Intuitively this type of equilibrium seems more robust. More generally, this is true whenever equilibria are "strict" equilibria in the following sense:

Definition 1.4   A Nash equilibrium s is *strict* if for each player i, s^i is the unique best response to s^{-i}; that is, player i strictly prefers s^i to any other response. (Note that only pure-strategy profiles can be strict equilibria, since if a mixed strategy is a best response to the opponents' play, then so is every pure strategy in the mixed strategy's support.)

This coordination game example, although simple, illustrates the two main questions that the theory of learning in games has tried to address, namely: When and why should we expect play to correspond to a Nash equilibrium? And, if there are several Nash equilibria, which ones should we expect to occur?

These questions are closely linked. Absent an explanation of how the players coordinate their expectations on the same Nash equilibrium, we are faced with the possibility that player 1 expects the equilibrium (A, A) and so plays A, while player 2 expects (B, B) and plays B, with the result of the nonequilibrium outcome (A, B). Briefly, the idea of learning-based explanations of equilibrium is that the fact that the players share a history of observations can provide a way for them to coordinate their expectations on one of the two pure-strategy equilibria. Typical learning models predict that this coordination will eventually occur, with the determination of which of the two equilibria arise left either to (unexplained) initial conditions or to random chance.

However, for the history to serve this coordinating role, the sequence of actions played must eventually become constant or at least readily predictable by the players, and there is no presumption that this is always the case. Perhaps rather than going to a Nash equilibrium, the result of learning is that the strategies played wander around aimlessly, or perhaps play lies in some set of alternatives larger than the set of Nash equilibria.

Because of the extreme symmetry of the coordination game above, there is no reason to think that any learning process will favor one of its strict equilibria over the other. The coordination game in figure 1.11 is more interesting. Here there are two strict Nash equilibria, (A, A) and (B, B); both players would prefer the Nash equilibrium (A, A) with payoffs $(2, 2)$, since it Pareto dominates the equilibrium at $(1, 1)$. Will players learn to play the Pareto-efficient equilibrium? One consideration lies in the risk that they face. That is, if a is very large, guessing that your opponent is going to play $(2, 2)$ is very risky because you suffer a large loss if you are wrong. One might expect that in a learning setting it would be unlikely for play to converge to a very risky equilibrium, even if the equi-

	A	B
A	2, 2	$-a, 0$
B	0, $-a$	1, 1

Figure 1.11
(A, A) Pareto-dominates (B, B), but (B, B) is risk-dominant if $1 + a > 2$

librium is Pareto efficient. A notion that captures this idea of risk is the Harsanyi-Selten criterion of *risk dominance*.[17] In symmetric 2×2 games the risk-dominant strategy can be found by computing the minimum probability of A that makes A the best response and comparing it to the minimum probability of B required to make B the best response. In this example A is optimal if there is probability at least $(a + 1)/(3 + a)$ that the opposing player plays A, while B is optimal if the probability that the opponent plays B is at least $2/(3 + a)$; thus A is risk dominant if $a < 1$. Alternatively, risk dominance in 2×2 games is equivalent to a simple concept called 1/2-dominance. An strategy is 1/2-*dominant* if it is optimal for all players to play the strategy whenever their opponents are playing that strategy with probability at least 1/2. Thus A is risk dominant if $2 - a > 1$ or $a < 1$.

In both of the examples above there is a finite number of Nash equilibria. Although some strategic-form games have a continuum of equilibria (e.g., if each player's payoff function is a constant), generically this is not the case. More precisely, for a fixed-strategy space S, the set of Nash equilibria is finite (and odd) for an open and dense set of payoff functions (Wilson 1971).[18] In particular, for generic strategic-form payoffs each Nash equilibrium is locally isolated, a fact that will be very useful in analyzing the stability of learning processes. However, this fact is really only applicable to one-shot simultaneous-move games, since in a general extensive-form generic assignments of payoffs to *outcomes* or *terminal nodes* do not generate generic strategic-form payoffs: For example, in the strategic form of the game in figure 1.3, (L, l) and (L, r) lead to the same outcome and so must give each player the same payoff.

1.7.4 Correlated Equilibrium

There is a second important noncooperative equilibrium concept in simultaneous-move games, namely Aumann's (1974) notion of a *correlated equilibrium*. This assumes that players have access to randomization devices that are privately viewed, but the randomization devices are correlated with each other. In this case, if each player chooses a strategy based on observations of his own randomization device, the result is a proba-

---

17. The use of the word "risk" here is different than the usual meaning in economics. Actual risk aversion by the players is already incorporated into the utility functions.
18. For a fixed-strategy space S, the payoff functions of the I players correspond to a vector in the euclidean space of dimension $I \cdot \#S$; a set of payoff functions is "generic" if it is open and dense in this space.

bility distribution over strategy profiles, which we denote by $\mu \in \Delta(S)$. Unlike a profile of mixed strategies, such a probability distribution allows play to be correlated.

As in the theory of Nash equilibrium, suppose that players have figured out how their opponents' play depends on their private randomization device and they know how the randomization device works. Since each player knows what pure strategy he is playing, he can work out the conditional probability of signals received by his opponents and the conditional probabilities of their play. Let $\mu^{-i}(s^i) \in \Delta(S^{-i})$ denote the probability distribution over opponents play induced by μ conditional on s^i, and let μ^i be the marginal for player i. Then, if $\mu^i(s^i) > 0$ so that player i is willing to play s^i, it must be a best response to $\mu^{-i}(s^i)$. Formally, if $\mu^{-i} \in \Delta(S^{-i})$, we can calculate the expected utility $u^i(\sigma^i, \mu^{-i})$ and define the best response $\hat{\sigma}^i \in BR^i(\mu^{-i})$ if $u^i(\hat{\sigma}^i, \mu^{-i}) \geq u^i(\sigma^i, \mu^{-i}), \forall \sigma^i$. A *correlated equilibrium* is a correlated strategy profile μ such that $\mu^i(s^i) > 0$ implies that $s^i \in BR^i(\mu^{-i}(s^i))$.

Jordan's (1993) simple three-person matching-pennies game illustrates the idea of a correlated equilibrium. This game is a variant on matching pennies, where each player simultaneously chooses H or T, and all entries in the payoff matrix are either $+1$ (win) or -1 (lose). Player 1 wins if he plays the same action as player 2, player 2 wins if he matches player 3, and player 3 wins by *not* matching player 1. The payoffs are given in figure 1.12, where the row corresponds to player 1 (up for H, down for T), the column to player 2, and the matrix to player 3. This game has a unique Nash equilibrium, namely for each player to play $(1/2, 1/2)$. However, it also has many correlated equilibria: One is the distribution over outcomes in which each of the profiles (H, H, H), (H, H, T), (H, T, T), (T, T, T), (T, T, H), (T, H, H) has equal weight of $1/6$. Notice that in this distribution each player has a 50% chance of playing H. However, no weight is placed on (H, T, H), so the play of the players is not independent. (It is "correlated.") Taking player 1, for example, we notice that when he plays H, he faces a $1/3$ chance each of his opponents playing

	H	T
H	$+1, +1, -1$	$-1, -1, -1$
T	$-1, +1, +1$	$+1, -1, +1$

	H	T
H	$+1, -1, +1$	$-1, +1, +1$
T	$-1, -1, -1$	$+1, +1, -1$

Figure 1.12
Jordan's three-player matching pennies

(H, H), (H, T), and (T, T). Since his goal is to match player 2, he wins two-thirds of the time by playing H, and only one-third of the time if he plays T. So H is a best response to the distribution of opponents play given H. Similarly, when he plays T, his opponents are equally likely to play (T, T), (T, H), and (H, H). Now tails wins two-thirds the time, as against heads which wins only one-third the time. The idea of correlated play is important in the theory of learning for two reasons. First, the types of learning models players are assumed to use are usually relatively naive, such as in the Cournot adjustment model. In the Cournot model it is possible for play to cycle endlessly. One consequence of this is that play viewed over time is correlated. In more sophisticated models we still have to face the possibility that players incidentally correlate their play using time as a correlation device, and in some instances this results in learning procedures converging to correlated rather than Nash equilibrium. Indeed, this is in a sense what happens if the Cournot adjustment procedure is used in the Jordan game. If we begin with (H, H, H) player 3 will want to switch, leading to (H, H, T). Then player 2 switches to (H, T, T), then player 1 to (T, T, T). Now 3 wants to switch again, leading to (T, T, H), 2 switches to (T, H, H), and finally 1 to (H, H, H), completing the cycle. In other words, in this example Cournot best-response dynamics lead to cycling, and if we observe the frequency with which different profiles occur, each of the 6 profiles in the correlated equilibrium is observed 1/6 the time. That is, play in the best-response dynamic resembles a correlated equilibrium.

We should note, however, that the fact that Cournot adjustment leads to correlated equilibrium in this particular game is actually a coincidence. If we modify the payoffs so that when (H, T, T) is played, player 1 gets -100 rather than -1, then the best-response cycle remains unchanged. However, it is no longer optimal for player 1 to play H against a 1/3 chance of his opponents playing (H, H), (H, T), and (T, T) with equal probability. It turns out that for some more sophisticated learning procedures the long run actually will be a correlated equilibrium to a good approximation.[19]

A second reason correlation is important is that during the process of learning, players will have beliefs about the mixed strategies that opponents are using. This takes the form of a probability distribution over opponents' mixed profiles. Such a probability distribution is always

---

19. This is true for consistent procedures discussed in chapters 2 and 4 because the game has only two actions. However, the even more sophisticated calibrated procedures discussed in chapter 8 give rise to correlated equilibrium in all games.

equivalent to a correlated distribution over opponents' pure-strategy profiles but need not be equivalent to a profile of mixed strategies for the
opponents. Suppose, for example, that there are two opponents, each with
two alternatives A and B. Player 1 believes that there is a 50% chance that
both opponents are playing A and a 50% chance that both are playing B.
If he plays against them for a while, he hopes to learn which of these
alternatives is correct; that is, he does not think that they are correlating
their play. In the meantime, however, he will wish to optimize against the
correlated profile 50%(A, A)–50%(B, B).

Appendix: Dynamical Systems and Local Stability

In general, at any moment of time t, certain players are playing particular
strategies and have available certain information on which they base their
decisions. We refer to all the variables relevant to determining the future
of the system as the *state* and denote it by $\theta_t \in \Theta$. In the Cournot adjustment model the current state is simply the output levels chosen currently
by the two firms. More generally, the variables that are represented in θ_t
will depend on the particular model we are studying. In addition to discrete time models where $t = 1, 2, \ldots$, such as Cournot adjustment, we will
also consider some continuous-time models where $t \in [0, \infty)$. In discrete
time the state variable will evolve over time according to the determin-
istic *law of motion* $\theta_{t+1} = f_t(\theta_t)$ or according to the *stochastic* (Markovian)
law of motion $\Pr(\theta_{t+1} = \theta) = \phi_t(\theta|\theta_t)$. In continuous time the deterministic
law of motion will be $\dot{\theta}_t = f_t(\theta_t)$. Although we will discuss some results in
the case of stochastic continuous time, the notation for these models is
complicated and will be introduced when appropriate.

We begin with some basic definitions and results about stability in
dynamic processes; a good reference for this material is Hirsch and Smale
(1974). We let $F_t(\theta_0)$ denote the value assumed by the state variable
at time t when the initial condition at time 0 is θ_0. In discrete time
$F_{t+1}(\theta_0) = f_t(F_t(\theta_0))$, in continuous time $D_t F_t(\theta_0) = f(F_t(\theta_0))$, and in both
cases $F_0(\theta_0) = \theta_0$; the map F is called the *flow* of the system.

Definition 1.5   A *steady state* $\hat{\theta}$ of a flow satisfies $F_t(\hat{\theta}) = \hat{\theta}, t > 0$.

Definition 1.6   A steady state $\hat{\theta}$ of a flow is *stable* if for every neighborhood U of $\hat{\theta}$ there is a neighborhood U_1 of $\hat{\theta}$ in U such that if $\theta_0 \in U_1$
$F_t(\theta_0) \in U, t > 0$; that is, if the system starts close enough to the steady
state, it remains nearby. If a steady state is not stable, we say that it is
unstable.

Definition 1.7 A steady state $\hat{\theta}$ of a flow is *asymptotically stable* if it is stable, and in addition if $\theta_0 \in U_1$, then $\lim_{t \to \infty} F_t(\theta_0) = \hat{\theta}$. The *basin (of attraction)* of an asymptotically stable steady state is the set of all points θ_0 such that $\lim_{t \to \infty} F_t(\theta_0) = \hat{\theta}$. If there is a unique steady state with basin equal to the entire state space Θ, it is called *globally stable*.

Definition 1.8 A steady state $\hat{\theta}$ is *locally isolated* if it has an open neighborhood in which there are no other steady states.

Note that an asymptotically stable steady state must be locally isolated but that a stable steady state need not be.

Definition 1.9 A steady state $\hat{\theta}$ is called *hyperbolic* if $Df(\hat{\theta})$ has no eigenvalues on the unit circle (discrete time) or no eigenvalues with zero real parts (continuous time). If the eigenvalues all lie inside the unit circle (discrete time) or have negative real parts (continuous time), the steady state is called a *sink*; if the eigenvalues all lie outside the unit circle (discrete time) or have positive real parts (continuous time), it is called a *source*. Otherwise, a hyperbolic steady state is called a *saddle*.

The critical aspect of a hyperbolic steady state in a nonlinear dynamical system is that it behaves locally like the linear system $\theta_{t+1} = \hat{\theta} + Df(\hat{\theta})(\theta_t - \hat{\theta})$ (discrete time) or $\dot{\theta} = Df(\hat{\theta})\theta$ (continuous time). The precise meaning of this can be found in the smooth linearization theorem of Hartmann (see Irwin 1980), which says that there is a smooth local coordinate system that maps the trajectories of the nonlinear system exactly onto the trajectories of the linear system.

Proposition 1.3 A sink is asymptotically stable.

In the two-player Cournot process we can check for asymptotic stability by computing the appropriate eigenvalues. Denoting the slopes of the best-response functions $BR_i(s_{-i})$ by $BR_i'(s_{-i})$, we have

$$Df = \begin{pmatrix} 0 & BR_1' \\ BR_2' & 0 \end{pmatrix},$$

with corresponding eigenvalues $\lambda = \pm\sqrt{BR_1' \cdot BR_2'}$. Consequently the absolute value of λ is smaller than 1 if slope BR_2 is less than the slope of BR_1, in which case the process is asymptotically stable.[20]

---

20. Recall that because s_2 is on the vertical axis, the "slope" of player 1's best-response function is $1/BR_1'$.

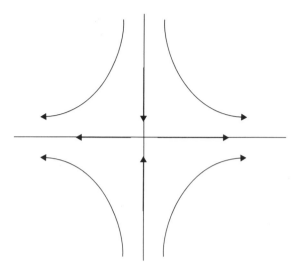

Figure 1.13
A saddle point

To the extent that we accept the adjustment process, we can argue that sources will not be observed. However, the case of saddles is more complicated; a flow corresponding to a saddle is illustrated in figure 1.13. In the figure at the origin there are paths that approach close to the steady state but eventually move away. However, once the system moves close to the steady state, the actual speed of movement becomes very slow, so the system will remain near the steady state for a long time before leaving. Consequently a saddle may be a good model of the "intermediate run," even though it is not a good model of the "long run." This point is emphasized in Binmore and Samuelson (1995), who argue that saddles may be a sensible model of actual behavior over long periods of time.

Even if a game has stable equilibria, it may have more than one of them. Consequently stability analysis will not in general yield a unique prediction, although it can help reduce the set of possible outcomes. Moreover the fact that a system has one or more stable equilibria does not imply that the state will approach any of the equilibria. As a result we will sometimes have need of the following more general concepts in characterizing the long-run behavior of dynamic systems:

Definition 1.10 The set of *ω-limit points of the flow F* are the points θ such that for some θ_0, and sequence of times $t_n \to \infty$, $\lim_{n \to \infty} F_{t_n}(\theta_0) = \theta$. That is, θ is an ω-limit point if there is an initial condition from which θ is approached infinitely often. A set $\Theta' \subseteq \Theta$ is *invariant* if $\theta_0 \in \Theta'$ implies that $F_t(\theta_0) \in \Theta'$ for all t. An invariant set $\Theta' \subseteq \Theta$ is an *attractor* if it has a compact invariant neighborhood Θ'' such that if $\theta_0 \in \Theta''$, and there is a sequence of times $t_n \to \infty$ for which $\theta = \lim_{n \to \infty} F_{t_n}(\theta_0)$ exists, then $\theta \in \Theta'$.

In addition to containing steady states, the set of ω-limit points can contain *cycles* or even other limit sets known as *strange attractors*. There has been a limited amount of work on strange attractors in the theory of learning, such as that of Skyrms (1992, 1993). So far, however, the existence of strange attractors, and the *chaotic* trajectories that surround them, have not played a central role in the theory of learning in games.

References

Aumann, R. 1974. Subjectivity and correlation in randomized strategies. *Journal of Mathematical Economics* 1: 67−96.

Binmore, K., and L. Samuelson. 1995. Evolutionary drift and equilibrium selection. Mimeo. University College London.

Binmore, K., L. Samuelson, and R. Vaughan. 1995. Musical chairs: Modelling noisy evolution. *Games and Economic Behavior* 11: 1−35.

Borgers, T. 1994. Weak dominance and approximate common knowledge. *Journal of Economic Theory* 4: 265−76.

Boylan, R., and M. El-Gamal. 1993. Fictitious play: A statistical study of multiple economic experiments. *Games and Economic Behavior* 5: 205−22.

Crawford, V. (1995). Adaptive dynamics in coordination games. *Econometrica* 63: 103−43.

Cross, J. 1983. *A Theory of Adaptive Economic Behavior*. Cambridge: Cambridge University Press.

Dekel, E., and D. Fudenberg. 1990. Rational behavior with payoff uncertainty. *Journal of Economic Theory* 52: 243−67.

Ellison, G. 1993. Learning, local interaction, and coordination. *Econometrica* 61: 1047−71.

Er'ev, I., and A. Roth. 1996. On the need for low rationality cognitive game theory: Reinforcement learning in experimental games with unique mixed strategy equilibria. Mimeo. University of Pittsburgh.

Friedman, D. 1991. Evolutionary games in economics. *Econometrica* 59: 637−66.

Friedman, D. 1996. Equilibrium in evolutionary games: Some experimental results. *Economic Journal*, 106: 1−25.

Fudenberg, D., and J. Tirole. 1991. *Game Theory*. Cambridge: MIT Press.

Fudenberg, D., D. K. Levine, and E. Maskin. 1994. The folk theorem with imperfect public information. *Econometrica* 62: 997−1039.

Harsanyi, J., and R. Selten. 1988. *A General Theory of Equilibrium Selection in Games.* Cambridge: MIT Press.

Hirsch, M., and S. Smale. 1974. *Differential Equations, Dynamical Systems, and Linear Algebra.* New York: Academic Press.

Irwin, M. C. 1980. *Smooth Dynamical Systems.* New York: Academic Press.

Jordan, J. 1993. Three problems in learning mixed-strategy equilibria. *Games and Economic Behavior* 5: 368–86.

Li Calzi, M. 1993. Fictitious play by cases. Mimeo. Istituo di Matemataica E. Levi, Univeristà di Parma.

Maskin, E., and J. Tirole. 1988. A theory of dynamic oligopoly. 1: Overview and quantity competition with large fixed costs. *Econometrica* 56: 549–70.

Myerson, R. 1991. *Game Theory.* Cambridge: Harvard University Press.

Nagel, R. 1994. Experimental results on interactive competitive guessing. Mimeo, D.P. B-236. Universität Bonn.

Romaldo, D. 1995. Similarities and evolution. Mimeo.

Roth, A., and I. Er'ev. 1995. Learning in extensive form games: Experimental data and simple dynamic models in the intermediate run. *Games and Economic Behavior* 8: 164–212.

Selten, R. 1988. Anticipatory learning in two-person games. Mimeo. University of Bonn.

Skyrms, B. 1992. Chaos in dynamic games. *Journal of Logic, Language and Information* 1: 111–30.

Skyrms, B. 1993. Chaos and the explanatory significance of equilibrium: Strange attractors in evolutionary game theory. Mimeo. University of California at Irvine.

Stahl, D. 1994. Evolution of smart n players. *Games and Economic Behavior* 5: 604–17.

Wilson, R. 1971. Computing equilibria of n-person games. *SIAM Journal of Applied Mathematics* 21: 80–87.

2 Fictitious Play

2.1 Introduction

One widely used model of learning is the process of fictitious play and its variants. In this process agents behave as if they think they are facing a stationary, but unknown, distribution of opponents' strategies. In this chapter we examine whether fictitious play is a sensible model of learning and what happens in games when players all use fictitious play learning rules.

We will begin our discussion of fictitious play in a two-player setting. After introducing fictitious play in section 2.2, we will discuss conditions under which fictitious play converges in section 2.3. Although the assumption of stationarity that underlies fictitious play is a reasonable first hypothesis in many situations, we might expect players eventually to reject it given sufficient evidence to the contrary. In particular, if the system in which the agents are learning fails to converge, then the assumption of stationarity does not make much sense. As we will see in section 2.4, most of the problems with the long-run behavior of fictitious play arise in this case of nonconvergence.

We then move on to the multiplayer case in section 2.5. Here a key issue is the whether players form estimates of the joint distribution of opponents' play by taking the product of independent marginal distributions or whether they instead form these estimates in ways that allow for either objective or subjective correlation.

Another important issue in studying any learning process is whether it succeeds in learning. Section 2.6 discusses the notion of payoff consistency. Since fictitious play only tracks information about the frequency that each strategy is played, it is natural to ask under what conditions fictitious play successfully enables players to learn these frequencies, in the sense that they do as well (as measured by the time average of their payoffs) as if the limiting frequencies were known. We refer to this property as "consistency" and show in section 2.6 that if the course of fictitious play involves less "infrequent" switching between strategies, then fictitious play is consistent in this sense. In chapter 4 we show that a randomized version of fictitious play can give rise to universal consistency, meaning that they do as well asymptotically as if the frequencies were known in advance no matter what strategies are used by opponents.

What can be said about the course of play when players use fictitious play rules? We take up this topic in section 2.8 where we show that fictitious play has dynamics very similar to the partial best-response dynamic discussed in chapter 1. In chapter 3 we will consider more closely the behavior of best-response and related dynamics.

For the purpose of modeling short-run behavior in experiments, fictitious play can be improved by allowing for larger weights on more recent observations and player "inertia" in the sense of a probability of repeating the most recently chosen action. These and other variants on fictitious play are discussed in section 2.9; extensions to random versions of fictitious play are considered in chapter 4.

One important observation is that the process of fictitious play supposes that players do not try to influence the future play of their opponents. As we discussed in the introduction, there are several models of interactions in a large population in which such "naive" or unsophisticated behavior is sensible. We should point out that many of the formal results on fictitious play deal with a small finite population, so when the models are taken literally naïve play is problematic. More interesting from an economic point of view is the case of a continuum population, since here it is legitimate to ignore strategic interactions. In the most interesting case, with a large but finite population and anonymous random matching, the matching process adds a source of randomness to the evolution of the system even if the play of each individual agent is a deterministic function of his observations. However, as we will see in the next chapter, this and other sources of randomness turn out not to have much impact on the qualitative conclusions derived in models with one agent per player role.

2.2   Two-Player Fictitious Play

To keep the formalities reasonably simple, we will start out with the case of a two-player simultaneous-move game, with finite strategy spaces S^1, S^2 and payoff functions u^1, u^2. The model of fictitious play supposes that players choose their actions in each period to maximize that period's expected payoff given their prediction or *assessment* of the distribution of opponent's actions in that period, and this assessment takes the following special form:

Player i has an exogenous initial weight function $\kappa_0^i: S^{-i} \to \mathscr{R}_+$. This weight is updated by adding 1 to the weight of each opponent strategy each time it is played so that

$$\kappa_t^i(s^{-i}) = \kappa_{t-1}^i(s^{-i}) + \begin{cases} 1 & \text{if } s_{t-1}^{-i} = s^{-i}, \\ 0 & \text{if } s_{t-1}^{-i} \neq s^{-i}. \end{cases}$$

The probability that player i assigns to player $-i$ playing s^{-i} at date t is given by

$$\gamma_t^i(s^{-i}) = \frac{\kappa_t^i(s^{-i})}{\sum_{\tilde{s}^{-i} \in S^{-i}} \kappa_t^i(\tilde{s}^{-i})}.$$

Fictitious play itself is then defined as any rule $p_t^i(\gamma_t^i)$ that assigns $p_t^i(\gamma_t^i) \in BR^i(\gamma_t^i)$. Note that there is not a unique fictitious play rule, since there may be more than one best response to a particular assessment. Traditional analyses suppose that the player chooses a pure-strategy best response when indifferent between several pure strategies. Since exact indifference will not occur for generic payoffs and priors, which specification is used is unimportant. Note also that the behavior prescribed by fictitious play is a discontinuous function of the player's assessment, since there does not in general exist a continuous selection from the best-response correspondence.

One way to interpret this method of forming an assessment is to note that it corresponds to Bayesian inference when player i believes that his opponents' play corresponds to a sequence of i.i.d. multinomial random variables with a fixed but unknown distribution, and player i's prior beliefs over that unknown distribution take the form of a Dirichlet distribution.[1] In this case player i's prior and posterior beliefs correspond to a distribution over the set $\Delta(S^{-i})$ of probability distributions on S^{-i}. The distribution over opponent's strategies γ_t^i is the induced marginal distribution over pure strategies. In particular, if beliefs over $\Delta(S^{-i})$ are denoted by μ^i, then we have $\gamma_t^i(s^{-i}) = \int_{\Sigma^{-i}} \sigma^{-i}(s^{-i})\mu_t^i[d\sigma^{-i}]$. The hypothesis

---

1. The Dirichlet distribution and multinomial sampling form a "conjugate family," meaning that if the prior over the probability distributions belongs to the Dirichlet family, and the likelihood function is multinomial, then posterior is also in the Dirichlet family. See the appendix to this chapter for details.

to emphasize here is not the Dirichlet functional form but rather the implicit assumption that the player treats the environment as stationary. In section 2.8 we will discuss the possibility of weighting current observations more heavily than past observations, which is one way that players might respond to the possibility that the environment is nonstationary.

We also define the marginal empirical distribution of j's play as

$$d_t^j(s^j) = \frac{\kappa_t(s^j) - \kappa_0(s^j)}{t}.$$

The assessments γ_t^i are not quite equal to the marginal empirical distribution d_t^j (recall that there are only two players, so $j = -i$) because of the influence of player i's prior. This prior has the form of a "fictitious sample" of data that might have been observed before play began. However, as observations are received over time, they will eventually outweigh the prior, and the assessments will converge to the marginal empirical distributions.

Compared to the updating rule in the myopic adjustment process, fictitious play has the advantage that as long as all of the initial weights are positive, there is no finite sample to which the beliefs assign probability zero. The beliefs reflect the conviction that the opponent's strategy is constant and unknown, and this conviction may be wrong along the path of the process, for example, if the process cycles. But any finite string of what looks like cycles is consistent with the belief that the world is constant and the observations are a fluke. If cycles persist, we might expect the player to eventually notice them, but at least his beliefs will not be falsified in the first few periods as they are in the Cournot process.

2.3 Asymptotic Behavior of Fictitious Play

One key question about fictitious play is whether or not play converges. If it does, then the stationarity assumption employed by players makes sense, at least asymptotically; if it does not, then it seems implausible that players will maintain that assumption. In this section we examine some sufficient conditions under which fictitious play converges. The discussion here, and propositions 2.1 and 2.2, are based on Fudenberg and Kreps (1990).

The state of the fictitious play process is the vector of the player's assessments, and not the strategies played at date t, since the latter is not sufficient to determine the future evolution of the system. Nevertheless, in a slight abuse of terminology, we will say that a strategy profile is a steady state if it is played in every period after some finite time T.

	H	T
H	1, –1	–1, 1
T	–1, 1	1, –1

Figure 2.1
Matching pennies

Proposition 2.1   (1) If s is a strict Nash equilibrium, and s is played at date t in the process of fictitious play, s is played at all subsequent dates.[2] That is, strict Nash equilibria are absorbing for the process of fictitious play. (2) Any pure-strategy steady state of fictitious play must be a Nash equilibrium.

Proof   First, suppose that players' assessments γ_t^i are such that their optimal choices correspond to a strict Nash equilibrium $\hat{s}$. Then, when the strict equilibrium is played, each player i's beliefs in period $t+1$ are a convex combination of γ_t^i and a point mass on $\hat{s}^{-i}$: $\gamma_{t+1}^i = (1 - \alpha_t)\gamma_t^i + \alpha_t \delta(\hat{s}^{-i})$. Since expected utilities are linear in probabilities, $u^i(\hat{s}^i, \gamma_{t+1}^i) = \alpha_t u^i(\hat{s}^i, \delta(\hat{s}^{-i})) + (1 - \alpha_t)u^i(\hat{s}^i, \gamma_t^i)$, and so if $\hat{s}^i$ is a best response for player i for γ_t^i, it is a strict best response for γ_{t+1}^i. Conversely, if play remains at a pure-strategy profile, then eventually the assessments will become concentrated at that profile, and so if the profile is not a Nash equilibrium, one of the players would eventually want to deviate.   ■

Since the only pure-strategy profiles that fictitious play can converge to are those that are Nash equilibria, fictitious play cannot converge to a pure-strategy profile in a game all of whose equilibria are mixed. Consider, for example, the game "matching pennies" illustrated in figure 2.1 with initial weights $(1.5, 2)$ and $(2, 1.5)$. Then fictitious play cycles as follows: In the first period, 1 and 2 play T, so the weights the next period are $(1.5, 3)$ and $(2, 2.5)$. Then 1 plays T and 2 plays H for the next two periods, after which 1's weights are $(3.5, 3)$ and 2's are $(2, 4.5)$. At this point 1 switches to H, and both players play H for the next three periods, at which point 2 switches to T, and so on.

It may not be obvious, but although the actual play in this example cycles, the empirical distribution over player i's strategies d_t^i are converging to $(1/2, 1/2)$, so the product of the two empirical marginal

---

2. Recall from section 1.6.3 that a strategy profile is a strict Nash equilibrium if each player's strategy is a strict best response to the opponents' play; that is, every other choice for the player gives a strictly lower payoff.

	L	M	R
T	0, 0	1, 0	0, 1
M	0, 1	0, 0	1, 0
D	1, 0	0, 1	0, 0

Figure 2.2
Shapley's example where fictitious play does not converge

distributions, namely $\{(1/2, 1/2), (1/2, 1/2)\}$, is the mixed-strategy equilibrium of the game. The fact that the limiting marginal distributions correspond to a Nash equilibrium is a general property of fictitious play:

Proposition 2.2 Under fictitious play, if the empirical distributions d_t^i over each player's choices converge, the strategy profile corresponding to the product of these distributions is a Nash equilibrium.

Proof The proof is the same as before: If the product of the empirical distributions converges to some profile $\hat{\sigma}$, then the beliefs converge to $\hat{\sigma}$, and hence if $\hat{\sigma}$ were not a Nash equilibrium, some player would eventually want to deviate. In fact it should be clear that this conclusion does not require that the assessments take the specific form given in fictitious play; it suffices that they are "asymptotically empirical," in the sense that in the limit of a great many observations, they become close to the empirical frequencies.   ∎

Proposition 2.3 Under fictitious play the empirical distributions converge if the stage has generic payoffs[3] and is 2×2 (Robinson 1951), or zero sum (Miyasawa 1961), or is solvable by iterated strict dominance (Nachbar 1990), or has strategic complements and satisfies another technical condition (Krishna and Sjostrom 1995).

The empirical distributions, however, need not converge. The first example of this is due to Shapley (1964) who considered a game equivalent to the one illustrated in figure 2.2. This game has a unique Nash equilibrium, namely for each player to use the mixed strategy $(1/3, 1/3, 1/3)$. Shapley

---

3. By "generic" we mean for a set of payoff vectors that have full Lebesgue measure in the relevant payoff space, which here is $\mathscr{R}^8$. (See section 1.7.3 for a brief discussion of genericity in strategic form games.) Generic 2×2 games have either one or three Nash equilibria, but for nongeneric payoffs the set of Nash equilibria may be a connected interval of strategy profiles. In this case, whether fictitious play converges can depend on the precise rule used to determine a player's choice when indifferent. See Monderer and Sela (1996) for a discussion of the importance of tie-breaking rules.

showed that if the initial weights lead players to choose (T, M), then the fictitious play follows the cycle $(T, M) \rightarrow (T, R) \rightarrow (M, R) \rightarrow (M, L) \rightarrow (D, L) \rightarrow (D, M) \rightarrow (T, M) \ldots$, which is the path of Cournot's alternating-move best-response process. In particular, the three "diagonal profiles" (T, L), (M, M), and (D, R) are never played. Moreover the number of consecutive periods that each profile in the sequence is played increases sufficiently quickly that the empirical distributions d_t^1, d_t^2 do not converge but instead follow a limit cycle. Shapley's proof of this latter fact explicitly computes the time spent in each stage of the sequence. Monderer, Samet, and Sela (1995) have an easier proof of nonconvergence which we present in section 2.6.

If the payoffs along the diagonal are increased to $(1/2, 1/2)$, then the example above becomes the zero-sum game "rock-scissors-paper" in which rock smashes scissors, scissors cuts paper, and paper wraps the rock. This game has the same, unique, Nash equilibrium, namely for each player to play $(1/3, 1/3, 1/3)$. This also is the unique *correlated* equilibrium of the game. Note for future reference that since rock-scissors-paper is a zero-sum game, the empirical distributions generated by fictitious play must converge to the Nash equilibrium. However, the outcomes played will follow the same best-reply cycle as in the Shapley example; the empirical distributions converge here because the time spent playing each profile increases sufficiently slowly. The rock-scissors-paper game and its modifications have been very useful in understanding learning and evolution in games, and we will be referring to it again in the next chapter.

2.4   Interpretation of Cycles in Fictitious Play

The early literature on fictitious play viewed the process as describing preplay calculations players might use to coordinate their expectations on a particular Nash equilibrium (hence the name "fictitious" play.) From this viewpoint, or when using fictitious play as a means of calculating Nash equilibria, the identification of a cycle with its time average is not problematic, and the early literature on fictitious play accordingly focused on finding conditions that guaranteed the empirical distributions converge.

However, this notion of convergence has some problems as a criterion for whether players have learned to play the corresponding strategies, for it supposes that the players ignore the persistence of cycles and that their opponents' play corresponds to i.i.d. draws from a fixed distribution. Moreover, because of these cycles, the empirical *joint* distribution of the two players' play (formed by tracking the empirical frequency of strategy

	A	B
A	0, 0	1, 1
B	1, 1	0, 0

Figure 2.3
Fudenberg and Kreps's example of persistent miscoordination

profiles, as opposed to the empirical *marginal* frequencies tracked by the d_t^i) can be correlated. Consider figure 2.3 from Fudenberg and Kreps (1990, 1993).[4] Suppose that the game is played according to the process of fictitious play, with initial weights $(1, \sqrt{2})$ for each player. In the first period both players think the other will play B, so both play A. The next period the weights are $(2, \sqrt{2})$, and both play B; the outcome is the alternating sequence (B, B), (A, A), (B, B), and so on. The empirical frequencies of each player's choices converge to $1/2$, $1/2$, which is the Nash equilibrium. The realized play is always on the diagonal, however, and both players receive payoff 0 each period. Another way of putting this is that the empirical joint distribution on pairs of actions does not equal the product of the two marginal distributions, so the empirical joint distribution corresponds to correlated as opposed to independent play.

From the standpoint of players learning how their opponents behave, such an example where the joint distribution is correlated does not seem to give a very satisfactory notion of "converging to an equilibrium." More generally, even if the empirical joint distribution does converge to the product of the empirical marginals so that the players end up getting the payoffs they would expect to get from maximizing against i.i.d. draws from the long-run empirical distribution of their opponents' play, one might still wonder if players would ignore persistent cycles in their opponents' play.

One response to this is to use a more demanding convergence notion so that a player's behavior only converges to a mixed strategy if his intended actions *in each period* converge to that mixed strategy. The standard fictitious play process cannot converge to a mixed strategy in this sense for generic payoffs, so we postpone our discussion of this response until chapter 4.

An alternative response is to decide that the players' ignoring the cycles is not problematic because players keep track only of data on opponents' frequency of play. We explore this response more fully in section 2.7.

---

4. Young (1993) gives a similar example.

2.5   Multiplayer Fictitious Play

We now turn to an important modeling issue that arises in extending fictitious play to games with three of more players: In a three-player game, say, should player 1's assessment γ^1 about the play of his opponents have range $\Sigma^2 \times \Sigma^3$, with $\gamma^1(s^2, s^3) = \gamma^1(s^2)\gamma^1(s^3)$, so that the assessment always corresponds to a mixed-strategy profile, or should the range of the assessment be the space $\Delta(S^2 \times S^3)$ of all the probability distributions over opponents' play, including the correlated ones?

To answer this, we rely on the interpretation of fictitious play as the result of Bayesian updating, with the assessments corresponding to the marginal distribution over the opponents' current period strategies that is derived from the players' current beliefs. From this viewpoint player 1's current assessment of his opponents' play can correspond to a correlated distribution even if player 1 is certain that the true distribution of his opponents' play in fact corresponds to independent randomizations. Formally the assumption that 2 and 3 randomize independently implies that

$$\gamma_t^1(s^2, s^3) = \int_{\Sigma^{-i}} \sigma^2(s^2)\sigma^3(s^3)\mu_t^1[d(\sigma^2, \sigma^3)];$$

the assumption of independent mixing is reflected in the fact that the integrand uses the product of $\sigma^2(s^2)$ and $\sigma^2(s^3)$. Despite this, the assessment γ_t^1 need not be a product measure, and indeed it typically will not be a product measure unless player 1's subjective uncertainty about his opponents is also uncorrelated; that is, unless μ_t^1 is a product measure.

To make this more concrete, suppose, for example, that there is a 1/2 chance that both opponents are playing A and a 1/2 chance that both are playing B. Thus the support of player 1's beliefs is concentrated on uncorrelated (in fact, pure-) strategy profiles of the opponents, but his current assessment corresponds to the correlated profile $1/2\ (A, A) - 1/2\ (B, B)$.

Consequently we see that there is no strong reason to suppose that the players' initial assessments correspond to uncorrelated randomizations. A deeper question is whether the support of the players' *prior beliefs* should be the set of opponents' mixed-strategy profiles, as in the calculation of the marginal above, or whether the prior should allow for the possibility that the opponents do manage to consistently correlate their play. If the support is the set of mixed strategies, then over time each player will become convinced that the distribution of opponents' play corresponds to the product of the empirical marginal distribution of each opponent's action, so persistent correlation will be ignored.

To see the difference this makes, consider a three-player variant of the rock-scissors-paper game discussed above, where players 1 and 2 have exactly the same actions and payoffs as before and player 3 has the option of betting on the play of the other two. More precisely, if player 3 chooses Out, 3 gets 0; if 3 chooses In, she gets 10 if 1 and 2 play on the diagonal, and −1 if 1 and 2 play on the off-diagonal; player 3's action has no effect on the payoffs of the others. It is easy to see that this game has a unique Nash equilibrium: Players 1 and 2 play the mixed strategy $(1/3, 1/3, 1/3)$, and player 2 chooses In. Moreover this is the unique correlated equilibrium of the game.

As observed above, the play of players 1 and 2 in this game will cycle through the off-diagonal elements, the empirical distributions over the individual payers' actions will converge to $(1/3, 1/3, 1/3)$. If player 3 estimates separate distributions for player 2 and player 3, then her beliefs will eventually converge to the empirical distributions, leading her to choose In; yet doing so will result in a payoff of −1 in every period, which is below player 3's reservation utility. If, on the other hand, player 3 instead keeps track of the frequencies of each strategy profile (s^1, s^2) (e.g., by having a Dirichlet prior over the strategy profiles of the opponents), then she will learn to play Out, so the play converges to an outcome that is not a Nash nor even a correlated equilibrium. Moreover player 3 is recognizing the correlation in the actions of players 1 and 2 that those players themselves ignore.

In our opinion this example shows that there are problems with either formulation of multiplayer fictitious play whenever play *in each period* fails to converge to a fixed-strategy profile. This is an additional argument against using the convergence of the empirical distributions as the convergence criterion.

In the introduction we used Jordan's (1993) simple three-person matching pennies game to illustrate the idea of a correlated equilibrium. Here we show how fictitious play leads to a robust cycle in this game, similar to the best-response cycle we discussed in the introduction.

Recall that the game in question is a variant on matching pennies, where each player simultaneously chooses H or T, and all entries in the payoff matrix are either +1 (win) or −1 (lose). Player 1 wins if he plays the same action as player 2, player 2 wins if he matches player 3, and player 3 wins by *not* matching player 1. The payoffs are given in figure 2.4, where the row corresponds to player 1 (up for H, down for T), the

	H	T
H	+1, +1, −1	−1, −1, −1
T	−1, +1, +1	+1, −1, +1

	H	T
	+1, −1, +1	−1, +1, +1
	−1, −1, −1	+1, +1, −1

Figure 2.4
Jordan's three-player matching pennies

column to player 2, and the matrix to player 3. This game has a unique Nash equilibrium, namely for each player to play $(1/2, 1/2)$, but we observed that the distribution over outcomes in which each of the profiles (H, H, H), (H, H, T), (H, T, T), (T, T, T), (T, T, H), and (T, H, H) have equal weight of $1/6$ is a correlated equilibrium.

Jordan specifies that players estimate a separate marginal distribution for each opponent as in two-player fictitious play and that the players' assessments be the product of these marginals; this corresponds to the case where players believe that their opponents randomize independently and where the subjective prior γ^i of each player is a product measure. However, each player cares only about the play of one of the two opponents, so the particular assumptions about how the opponents' play is correlated are irrelevant. Jordan improves on Shapley's example by providing a game where the empirical distributions fail to converge for all initial conditions outside of a one-dimensional stable manifold, thus showing that the failure to converge is very robust to the initial conditions. The cycle is similar to the best-response cycle we discussed above: If players start with assessments that lead them to play (H, H, H), eventually player 3 will want to switch to T. After playing (H, H, T) for a long time, eventually player 2 will want to switch, and so forth. As in Shapley's example, the cycle takes longer and longer as time goes on; however, unlike the Shapley example, the joint distribution of player's play converges to the correlated equilibrium putting equal weight on the six strategies the cycle passes through.[5] We will see below that it is not a coincidence that the cycle passes through profiles in the same order as the best-response dynamic, nor that the joint distribution converges to a correlated equilibrium.

2.6 Payoffs in Fictitious Play

In fictitious play, players keep track only of data about the frequency of opponents' play. In particular, they do not keep track of data on condi-

---

5. This assertion is not meant to be obvious; we provide a proof in section 2.7.

tional probabilities and so may not recognize that there are cycles.[6] Given this limitation, we can still ask whether fictitious play accomplishes its purpose. That is, if fictitious play successfully "learns" the frequency distribution, then it ought, asymptotically at least, yield the same utility that would be achieved when the frequency distribution is known in advance. This section examines the extent to which fictitious play satisfies this property, which we call "consistency."

In this section we will suppose that if there are more than two players, their assessments track the joint distribution of opponents' strategies. We denote the empirical distribution over player i's opponents by D_t^{-i}, denote the best payoff against the empirical distribution by $\hat{U}_t^i = \max_{\sigma^i} u^i(\sigma^i, D_t^{-i})$, denote by $U_t^i = (1/t)\sum_{\tau=1}^{t} u^i(s_\tau^i, s_\tau^{-i})$ the time average of player i's realized payoffs.

Definition 2.1 Fictitious play is ε-consistent along a history if there exists a T such that for any $t \geq T$, $U_t^i + \varepsilon \geq \hat{U}_t^i$ for all i.

Note that this is an ex post form of consistency, in contrast to consistency in the sense of classical statistics. Chapter 4 discusses behavior rules that are "universally ε-consistent" in the sense of being ε-consistent along every possible history.

It is useful to consider not only how well the player actually does against his opponents' empirical play but also how well he does relative to the utility he expects to get. Since the expected payoffs are linear in the probabilities, a player whose assessment over an opponent's date-t actions is γ_t^i believes that his expected date-t payoff is $U_t^{i^*} = \max_{\sigma^i} u^i(\sigma^i, \gamma_t^i)$. Since the distance between γ_t^i and D_t^{-i} converges to 0 whether or not play converges, and the payoff function is continuous in the opponents' mixed strategies, $\|\hat{U}_t^i - U_t^*\|$ converges to 0 asymptotically. Consequently consistency means that not only does a player do as well as he might if he knew the frequencies in advance, but he does as well as he expects to do. For example, if, as in the example of the last section, U_t^i remains less than $\hat{U}_t^i$, player i should eventually realize that something is wrong with his model of the environment. This provides an alternative motivation for the notion of consistency.

Our main result concerns the connection between how frequently a player changes strategies and the consistency of his play. For any time t we define the *frequency of switches* η_t^i to be the fraction of periods $\tau \leq t$ in which $s_\tau^i \neq s_{\tau-1}^i$.

---

6. Of course real players may keep track of this information; we discuss the consequences of this more fully in chapter 8.

Definition 2.2 Fictitious play exhibits *infrequent switches along a history* if for every $\varepsilon > 0$ there exists a T and for any $t \geq T$, $\eta_t^i \leq \varepsilon$ for all i.

Proposition 2.4 If fictitious play exhibits infrequent switches along a history, then it is it is ε-consistent along that history for every $\varepsilon > 0$.

This result was established independently by Fudenberg and Levine (1994) and by Monderer, Samet, and Sela (1994); we present the Monderer-Samet-Sela proof, since it is shorter and more revealing.[7]
    Intuitively, once there are enough data to swamp the prior, at each date t player i's action will be a best response to the empirical distribution through date $t - 1$. On the other hand, if player i is not on average doing as well as the best response to the empirical distribution, there must be a nonnegligible fractions of dates t at which the action i chooses at date t is not a best response to the distribution of opponents' play through that date. But at such dates player i will switch and choose a different action at date $t + 1$; conversely, infrequent switches imply that most of the time i's date-t action is a best response to the empirical distribution at the end of date t.
    In what follows it is convenient to let $\hat{\sigma}_t^i$ denote the argmax specified by the fictitious play.

Proof of Proposition 2.4   Let $k = \sum_{s^{-i}} \kappa_0^i(s^{-i})$ be the length of the "fictitious history" implicit in the initial beliefs γ_0^i, and let $\hat{\sigma}_t^i$ denote a best response to γ_t^i. Observe that

$$U_t^{i*} = u^i(\hat{\sigma}_t^i, \gamma_t^i) \geq u^i(\hat{\sigma}_{t+1}^i, \gamma_t^i)$$

$$= \frac{((t + k + 1)u^i(\hat{\sigma}_{t+1}^i, \gamma_{t+1}^i) - u^i(\hat{\sigma}_{t+1}^i, s_t^{-i}))}{(t + k)}$$

$$= \frac{((t + k + 1)U_{t+1}^{i*} - u^i(\hat{\sigma}_{t+1}^i, s_t^{-i}))}{(t + k)},$$

so

$$U_{t+1}^{i*} \leq \frac{t + k}{t + k + 1} U_t^{i*} + \frac{u^i(\hat{\sigma}_{t+1}^i, s_t^{-i})}{t + k + 1},$$

$$U_{t+1}^{i*} - U_t^{i*} \leq \frac{-1}{t + k + 1} U_t^{i*} + \frac{u^i(\hat{\sigma}_{t+1}^i, s_t^{-i})}{t + k + 1}.$$

---

7. Monderer, Sela, and Samet only present the case of fictitious play with a null prior, whereby the player's beliefs (at every period after the first one) are exactly equal to the empirical distribution so that $\varepsilon = 0$, but their proof extends immediately to general priors.

Consequently

$$U_t^{i*} \leq \frac{\sum_{\tau=0}^{t-1} u^i(\hat{\sigma}_{\tau+1}^i, s_\tau^{-i})}{t+k} + \frac{U_0^{i*}}{t+k}$$

$$= \frac{\sum_{\tau=0}^{t-1} u^i(\hat{\sigma}_\tau^i, s_\tau^{-i})}{t+k} + \frac{\sum_{\tau=0}^{t-1} u^i(\hat{\sigma}_{\tau+1}^i, s_\tau^{-i}) - u^i(\hat{\sigma}_\tau^i, s_\tau^{-i})}{t+k} + \frac{U_0^{i*}}{t+k}.$$

The first quotient in this expression converges to player i's realized average payoff U_t^i. The second sums terms that are zero except when player i switches; so it converges to 0 on any path with infrequent switches, and the third is an effect of the prior beliefs that converges to 0 along any path. ∎

Proposition 2.5 For any initial weights there is a sequence $\varepsilon_t \to 0$ such that along any infinite horizon history $U_t^{i*} \geq U_t^i + \varepsilon_t$. That is, once there are enough data to outweigh the initial weights, players believe that their current period's expected payoff is at least as large as their average payoff to date.

Proof Take

$$U_t^{i*} = u^i(\hat{\sigma}_t^i, \gamma_t^i) \geq u^i(\hat{\sigma}_{t-1}^i, \gamma_t^i) = \frac{u^i(\hat{\sigma}_{t-1}^i, s_{t-1}^{-i}) + (t+k-1)u^i(\hat{\sigma}_{t-1}^i, \gamma_{t-1}^i)}{t+k},$$

where the inequality comes from the fact that $\hat{\sigma}_t^i$ is a best response to γ_t^i. Expanding $u^i(\hat{\sigma}_{t-1}^i, \gamma_{t-1}^i)$ shows that

$$U_t^{i*} \geq \frac{u^i(\hat{\sigma}_{t-1}^i, s_{t-1}^{-i}) + (t+k-1)(u^i(\hat{\sigma}_{t-2}^i, s_{t-2}^{-i}) + (t+k-2)u^i(\hat{\sigma}_{t-2}^i, \gamma_{t-2}^i))/(t+k-1)}{t+k}$$

$$= \frac{u^i(\hat{\sigma}_{t-1}^i, s_{t-1}^{-i}) + (u^i(\hat{\sigma}_{t-2}^i, s_{t-2}^{-i}) + (t+k-2)u^i(\hat{\sigma}_{t-2}^i, \gamma_{t-2}^i))}{t+k};$$

proceeding iteratively, we have

$$U_t^{i*} \geq \frac{\sum_{\tau=1}^{t-1} u^i(\hat{\sigma}_\tau^i, s_\tau^{-i}) + (k+1)u^i(\hat{\sigma}_1^i, \gamma_1^i)}{t+k}$$

$$= \frac{(t-1)U_t^i + (k+1)u^i(\hat{\sigma}_1^i, \gamma_1^i)}{t+k}.$$

By taking $\varepsilon_t > (1/t)\max u^i$, we complete the proof. Note that this proof does not use the "infrequent switches" property. ∎

The Fudenberg and Kreps example above fails the infrequent switch test because players change their strategies every period. On the other hand, the nonconvergent paths in both the Shapley and the Jordan examples are easily seen to have infrequent switches. Moreover, as noted by Monderer, Samet, and Sela (1994), proposition 2.5 can be used to provide an easy proof that the empirical distributions do not converge in those examples. In the Shapley cycle, for instance, the sum of the realized payoffs is 1 in every period, so by proposition 2.5 the sum of the payoffs $U_t^{i^*}$ that the players expect to receive is at least 1 for large t. If, however, the empirical distributions were to converge, they would need to converge to the Nash equilibrium distributions (from proposition 2.2); thus the players' beliefs would converge to the Nash equilibrium distributions as well, so their expected payoffs would converge to the Nash equilibrium payoffs, which sum to 2/3.

2.7   Consistency and Correlated Equilibrium in Games with Two Strategies

In the Jordan game each player has only two actions. As a result consistency has an interesting consequence: It implies that the long-run average of action profiles resembles a correlated equilibrium.

Specifically, suppose that the outcome of play is ε-*consistent* in the sense of the previous section, with $\varepsilon = 0$. Let $D_t^{-i}[s^i]$ denote the distribution over the play of i's opponents derived from the joint distribution over profiles D_t by conditioning on player i playing s^i, and recall that d_t^i is the marginal distribution of i's play. In particular, $D_t^{-i} = \sum_{s^i} d_t^i(s^i) D_t^{-i}[s^i]$. Note also that $\max_{\sigma_i} u^i(\sigma_i, D_t^{-i}) = \max_{s_i} u^i(s_i, D_t^{-i})$.

Consistency then is equivalent to the condition that $u^i(D_t) \geq u^i(s_i, D_t^{-i})$ for all s^i. Supposing that player i has only two actions, we write

$$d_t^i(s^i)u^i(s^i, D_t^{-i}[s^i]) + d_t^i(r^i)u^i(r^i, D_t^{-i}[r^i]) = u^i(D_t)$$

$$\geq u^i(s^i, d_t^i(s^i)D_t^{-i}[s^i] + d_t^i(r^i)D_t^{-i}[r^i])$$

$$= d_t^i(s^i)u^i(s^i, D_t^{-i}[s^i]) + d_t^i(r^i)u^i(s^i, D_t^{-i}[r^i])$$

from which we conclude by subtraction that

$$d_t^i(r^i)u^i(r^i, D_t^{-i}[r^i]) \geq d_t^i(r^i)u^i(s^i, D_t^{-i}[r^i])$$

for all s^i. This says that r^i is a best response to the conditional distribution of opponents' actions given r^i whenever it is played with positive probability. We conclude that whenever each player has only two strategies, if D_t is consistent, it is a correlated equilibrium as well.

2.8   Fictitious Play and the Best-Response Dynamic

We observed in the Jordan example that the sequence of pure-strategy profiles generated by fictitious play (but not the number of times each profile occurs) is the same as that in the alternating-move best-response dynamic. (This is true also in the Shapley example.) It is easy to see that these two processes cannot be the same in general games, for under the alternating-move best-response dynamic players only choose strategies that are best replies to some *pure* strategy of their opponents, whereas under fictitious play a player may choose a strategy that is not a best response to any pure-strategy profile but is a best response to some mixed-strategy profile. However, the asymptotic behavior of fictitious play is closely related to the continuous-time version of the best-response dynamic, which also describes the asymptotic behavior of the "partial best-response dynamic" discussed in the introduction if the fraction of the population that adjusts its play each period is sufficiently small.

We will first explain the relationship between the partial- and continuous-time best-response dynamics. Suppose that there is a continuum population of each type of player, and take the state variable θ_t^i to be the frequency distribution over strategies played by type i. That is, $\theta_t^i(s^i)$ is the fraction of type i's that are playing s^i. In discrete time, if a fraction of the population λ is picked at random and switches to the best response to their opponents' current play, and the rest of the population continues their current play, then the partial best-response dynamic is given by

$$\theta_{t+1}^i = (1-\lambda)\theta_t^i + \lambda BR^i(\theta_t^{-i}) = \theta_t^i + \lambda(BR^i(\theta_t^{-i}) - \theta_t^i),$$

where each BR^i is a (discontinuous) function corresponding to some selection from the best-response correspondence for that player. If the time periods are very short, and the fraction of the population adjusting is very small, this may be approximated by the continuous-time adjustment process

$$\dot{\theta}_t^i = \beta(BR^i(\theta_t^{-i}) - \theta_t^i).$$

Notice that this dynamic is time homogeneous as is the discrete-time version of the process, so the former does not "converge" to the latter as the process evolves. Rather, the shift from the discrete-time system to the continuous-time one was justified by considering a change in the system's underlying parameters.

In contrast, the fictitious play process moves more slowly over time because every new observation becomes relatively less important as

evidence accumulates. Suppose that when there are more than two players, population averages of opponents are viewed as independent so that
asymptotically beliefs γ_t^i are approximately given by the product of marginal empirical distributions $\prod_{j \neq i} d_t^j$. Recalling that d_{t-1}^{-i} is the vector of
marginal empirical distributions of the play of players other than player i,
the marginal empirical distributions in fictitious play evolve approximately (ignoring the prior) according to

$$d_t^i = \frac{t-1}{t} d_{t-1}^i + \frac{1}{t} BR^i(d_{t-1}^{-i}).$$

This is of course very much like the partial best-response dynamic, except
that the weights on the past is converging to one and the weight on the
best response to zero.

Moreover we can make the fictitious play system seem stationary by
changing the units in which time is measured. Specifically, let $\tau = \log t$, or
$t = \exp \tau$. Suppose that there are infrequent switches so that play remains
more or less constant between τ and $\tau + \Delta$. Observing that

$$\exp(\tau + \Delta) - \exp \tau = (\exp(\Delta) - 1)\exp \tau \approx \Delta \exp \tau = \Delta t,$$

and letting $\tilde{d}_\tau^i = d_{\exp \tau}^i$, we can write

$$\tilde{d}_{\tau+\Delta}^i = d_{t+\Delta t}^i = \frac{t - \Delta t}{t} d_t^i + \frac{\Delta t}{t} BR^i(d_t^{-i})$$

$$= (1 - \Delta) d_t^i + \Delta BR^i(d_t^{-i})$$

$$= (1 - \Delta) \tilde{d}_\tau^i + \Delta BR^i(\tilde{d}_\tau^{-i}).$$

In the continuous-time limit for large t and small Δ, this can be approximated by

$$\dot{\tilde{d}}_\tau^i = BR^i(\tilde{d}_\tau^{-i}) - d_\tau^i,$$

which is of course the same as the continuous-time best-response
dynamic.

The conclusion is that with an appropriate time normalization, discrete-
time fictitious play asymptotically is approximately the same as the
continuous-time best-response dynamic. More precisely, the set of
limit points of discrete-time fictitious play is an invariant subset for
the continuous-time best-response dynamics. Moreover the path of the
discrete-time fictitious play process starting from some large T remains
close to that of the corresponding continuous-time best-response process

until some time $T + T'$, where T' can be made arbitrarily large by taking T arbitrarily large (Hofbauer 1995). Note well, though, that the discrete- and continuous-time processes can tend toward different long-run limits from the same initial conditions. This sort of relationship between discrete- time and continuous-time solutions is fairly typical and recurs in the study of the replicator dynamic, as we will see in the next chapter. Subsequently we will consider fictitious playlike systems with noise. The theory of sto- chastic approximation studies the exact connection between discrete-time stochastic dynamical systems and their continuous-time limits, and we will have much more to say on this subject in chapter 4.

2.9   Generalizations of Fictitious Play

As one might expect, many of the results about the asymptotic behavior of fictitious play continue to hold for processes that might prescribe dif- ferent behavior in the early periods but "asymptotically converge" to fictitious play. Following Fudenberg and Kreps (1993), we say that the player's beliefs are *asymptotically empirical* if $\lim_{t\to\infty}\|\gamma_t^i - D_t^{-i}\| = 0$ along every sequence of infinite histories. It is easy to verify that proposition 2.1 continues to hold (strict equilibria are absorbing, and pure-strategy steady states are Nash) when fictitious play is generalized to allow any asymptotically empirical forecasts. If in addition γ_t^i are the product of marginal beliefs, Fudenberg and Kreps show that propositions 2.2 (con- vergence of the marginal distributions of play implies Nash equilibrium) continues to hold when fictitious play is generalized to allow any asymp- totically empirical beliefs.[8] In a similar vein Jordan (1993) shows that his example of nonconvergent empirical distributions converges to the same limit cycle for any beliefs that (1) satisfy a "uniform" version of asymp- totic empiricism (i.e., for any ε the distance between the forecasts and the empirical distribution should become less than ε for *all* histories of at least some $T(\varepsilon)$ length) and (2) depend on the history only through the empiri- cal distribution.

Milgrom and Roberts (1991) use a still weaker condition on forecasts: They say that forecasts are *adaptive* if the forecasts assign very low prob- ability to any opponent's strategy that has not been played for a long time. Formally, a forecast rule is adaptive if for every $\varepsilon > 0$ and for every t, there is a there is $T(\varepsilon, t)$ such that for all $t' > T(\varepsilon, t)$ and all histories of

---

8. As the example in section 2.5 showed, in the multiplayer case, if it is not a priori thought that opponents play independently, this result can fail even for fictitious play.

play up to date t', the forecast γ_t^i assigns probability no more than ε to the set of pure strategies of i's opponent that were not played between times t and t'. Since this condition restricts only the support of the forecasts but not the relative weights of strategies in the support, it is clearly inappropriate for modeling situations where the player's forecasts converge to a mixed distribution. However, as Milgrom and Roberts (1991) show, the condition is strong enough to preserve the second part of proposition 2.1: If forecasts are adaptive, and play converges to a pure-strategy profile, that profile must be a Nash equilibrium.

One example of an adaptive forecasting rule is the "exponentially weighted fictitious play" under which the forecast probability of strategy s^j at date t is

$$\frac{1 - \beta^t}{1 - \beta} \sum_{\tau=1}^{t-1} \beta^\tau I(s_\tau^j = s^j),$$

where I is the indicator function and $\beta > 1$. By this rule the weight given to the most recent observation never vanishes, so if the opponent's play is a fixed mixed-strategy, then the assessments do not converge. (If the weight β is allowed to shrink to 1 as t goes to infinity, perhaps to reflect the greater weight given a lengthier past history, then the rule is asymptotically empirical.) We will discuss the properties of this type of exponential weighting scheme in chapter 4, along with some evidence that exponential weights do a better job than standard fictitious play of describing learning behavior in the experimental play of games. Since these experiments are not run for very large horizons, the implications of this for our purposes are not clear.

Finally many asymptotic properties of fictitious play are preserved if the assumption that actions are chosen to maximize current payoffs given current forecasts is weakened to only hold asymptotically. Fudenberg and Kreps (1993) say that a behavior rule ρ^i (a map from histories to actions) is *strongly asymptotically myopic with respect to forecast rule* γ^i if for some sequence of positive numbers $\{\varepsilon_t\}$ converging to 0, for every t and every time-t history, every pure strategy s^i that has positive probability under ρ^i is an ε_t-optimal response given forecast γ^i.[9] Proposition 2.1 holds for all behavior rules that are strongly asymptotically myopic with respect to some asymptotically empirical forecast rule, and proposition 2.2 holds if beliefs are the product of independent marginals.

---

9. That is, each s^i in the support must satisfy $u^i(s^i, \gamma^i) + \varepsilon_t \geq \max_{\hat{s}^i} u^i(\hat{s}^i, \gamma^i)$.

Appendix: Dirichlet Priors and Multinomial Sampling

Our summary follows DeGroot (1970).

1. *Multinomial distribution.* Consider a sequence of n i.i.d. trials where each period one of k outcomes occurs, with p_z denoting the probability of outcome z. Denote the outcome of the n trials by the vector κ, where κ_z is the number of the outcomes of type z. (Think of the outcomes as being the opponent's choice of an action in a simultaneous-move game.) Then the distribution of the κ's, called the *multinomial distribution with parameters n, and $p = (p_1, \ldots, p_k)$*, is given by

$$f(\kappa) = \frac{n!}{\kappa_1! \ldots \kappa_k!} p_1^{\kappa_1} \ldots p_k^{\kappa_k}$$

for κ such that $\sum_{z=1}^{k} \kappa_z = n$.

2. *Dirichlet distribution.* Let Γ denote the gamma function. A random vector p has the Dirichlet distribution with parameter vector α ($a_z > 0 \forall z$) if its density is given by

$$f(p) = \frac{\Gamma(\alpha_1 + \cdots + \alpha_k)}{\Gamma(\alpha_1) \ldots \Gamma(\alpha_k)} p_1^{\alpha_1 - 1} \ldots p_k^{a_k - 1}$$

for all $p > 0$ such that $\sum_{z=1}^{k} p_z = 1$. This is sometimes called the *multivariate beta distribution* because, if p has a Dirichlet distribution, the marginal distribution of p_z is the beta distribution with parameters α_z and $\sum_{w \neq z} \alpha_z$. In particular, if p has the Dirichlet distribution, the expected value of p_z is $\alpha_z / \sum_{w=1}^{k} \alpha_w$.

3. *Dirichlet distributions as a conjugate family for multinomial sampling.* A family of distributions is said to be a conjugate family for a likelihood function if whenever the prior distribution lies in the family, the posterior distribution will lie in the same family for any sample drawn according to the specified form of likelihood function. One classic example is the normal distribution: If samples are drawn according to a normal distribution with unknown mean, and the prior is itself a normal distribution, then the posterior distribution will also be a normal distribution. Likewise the Dirichlet distribution is a conjugate family for multinomial sampling.

To see this, suppose that the prior distribution over the probability vector p has a Dirichlet distribution with parameter α so that the density function $f(p)$ at each p is proportional to

$$\prod_{z=1}^{k} p_z^{\alpha_z - 1}.$$

For each value of p the likelihood of the vector κ of outcomes is proportional to

$$\prod_{z=1}^{k} p_z^{\kappa_z}.$$

To compute the posterior distribution over p, we use Bayes's rule:

$$f(p|\kappa) = \frac{f(\kappa|p)f(p)}{\int f(\kappa|p)f(p)\, dp} \propto \prod_{z=1}^{k} p_z^{\alpha_z - 1} \prod_{z=1}^{k} p_z^{\kappa_z} = \prod_{z=1}^{k} p_z^{\alpha_z + \kappa_z - 1}$$

so that the posterior is Dirichlet with parameter α', where $\alpha'_z = \alpha_z + \kappa_z$.

If player i's date-t beliefs about $-i$'s mixed strategy have a Dirichlet distribution, player i's assessment of the probability that $-i$ plays s^{-i} in period t is

$$\gamma_t^i(s^{-i}) = \int_{\Sigma^{-i}} \sigma^{-i}(s^{-i}) \mu_t^i[d\sigma^{-i}],$$

which is simply the expected value of the component of σ^{-i} corresponding to s^{-i}; from our remark above, if $z = s^{-i}$, this is just $\alpha_z / \sum_{w=1}^{k} \alpha_w$. Therefore, after observing sample κ, player i's assessment of the probability that the next observation is strategy z is

$$\frac{\alpha'_z}{\sum_{w=1}^{k} \alpha'_w} = \frac{\alpha_z + \kappa_z}{\sum_{w=1}^{k} (\alpha_w + \kappa_w)},$$

which is the formula for fictitious play.

References

Brown, G. W. 1951. Iterative solutions of games by fictitious play. In *Activity Analysis of Production and Allocation*, ed. by T. C. Koopmans. New York: Wiley.

DeGroot, M. 1970. *Optimal Statistical Decisions*. New York: McGraw-Hill.

Ellison, G. 1994. Learning with one rational player. Mimeo. Massachusetts Institute of Technology.

Fudenberg, D., and D. K. Levine. 1995. Consistency and cautious fictitious play. *Journal of Economic Dynamics and Control* 19: 1065–90.

Fudenberg, D., and D. Kreps. 1990. Lectures on learning and equilibrium in strategic-form games. Mimeo. CORE Lecture Series.

Fudenberg, D., and D. Kreps. 1993. Learning mixed equilibria. *Games and Economic Behavior* 5: 320–67.

Hofbauer, J. 1995. Stability for the best response dynamic. Mimeo. University of Vienna.

Jordan, J. 1993. Three problems in learning mixed-strategy equilibria. *Games and Economic Behavior* 5: 368–86.

Krishna, V., and T. Sjostrom. 1995. On the convergence of fictitious play. Mimeo. Harvard University.

Milgrom, P., and J. Roberts. 1991. Adaptive and sophisticated learning in normal-form games. *Games and Economic Behavior* 3: 82–100.

Miyasawa, K. 1961. On the convergence of learning processes in a 2 × 2 non-zero-person game. Research Memo 33. Princeton University.

Monderer, D., and A. Sela. 1996. A 2 × 2 game without the fictitious play property. *Games and Economic Behavior* 68: 200–11.

Monderer, D., D. Samet, and A. Sela. 1994. Belief affirming in learning processes. Mimeo. Technion.

Nachbar, J. 1990. "Evolutionary" selection dynamics in games: Convergence and limit properties. *International Journal of Game Theory* 19: 59–89.

Robinson, J. 1951. An iterative method of solving a game. *Annals of Mathematics* 54: 296–301.

Shapley, L. 1964. Some topics in two-person games. In *Advances in Game Theory*, ed. by M. Drescher, L. S. Shapley, and A. W. Tucker. Princeton: Princeton University Press.

Young, P. 1993. The Evolution of Conventions. *Econometrica* 61: 57–84.

3

Replicator Dynamics and Related Deterministic Models of Evolution

3.1 Introduction

At this point we shift from models that are explicitly based on learning to models based on the idea of evolution. These models originated in the field of evolutionary biology, but such models have become very popular among game theorists in the last few years.[1]

There are three main reasons for this interest. First, although the archetypal evolutionary model, that of the replicator dynamics, was originally motivated by a (simplified version of) biological evolution, the process can also describe the result of some types of "emulation" by economic agents. Second, some of the properties of the replicator dynamic extend to various classes of more general processes that may correspond to other sorts of learning or emulation. Finally, the study of evolutionary models has proved helpful (if controversial) in understanding animal behavior, and while this does not imply that the models have economic interest, it is still an interesting use of the theory of games.

Our discussion begins with the two concepts that have been central to the study of evolutionary models: the replicator dynamic and the idea of an evolutionary stable strategy, or ESS. Section 3.2 begins with the case of a homogeneous population. The replicator dynamic assumes that the population playing a particular strategy grows in proportion to how well that strategy is doing relative to the mean population payoff. Every Nash equilibrium is a steady state in the replicator dynamic, and every stable steady state is a Nash equilibrium. The major question posed in this literature is the extent to which the stability of a steady state leads to a refinement of Nash equilibrium. One major result is that in a homogeneous

---

1. See, for example, the symposium issues in the *Journal of Economic Theory* (1992) and *Games and Economic Behavior* (1993).

population a stable steady state must be isolated and trembling hand perfect.

Section 3.4 introduces the notion of an ESS, which is a static concept that was inspired by, but not derived from, considerations of evolutionary dynamics. ESS requires that the strategy be robust when it is invaded by a small population playing a different strategy. Every ESS is Nash, so ESS is a refinement of Nash equilibrium. One goal of the literature on evolution is to establish more closely the connection between replicator (and related) dynamics and the ESS concept. In the homogeneous population case, an ESS is stable in the replicator dynamic, but not every stable steady state is an ESS.

After examining the homogeneous case, we turn to the case of a heterogeneous population and the asymmetric replicator dynamic in section 3.5. One major result is that in the asymmetric case mixed profiles cannot be asymptotically stable.

Our interest in this book is primarily about the consequences of learning by individual players. Evolutionary models are generally cast in terms of the behavior of an entire population and are vague about the individual behavior that leads to this population dynamic. However, the work discussed in section 3.6 shows that it is possible to give stories of learning that lead to replicator like dynamics. One such story we consider is the emulation dynamic in which new players ask an old player what strategy that player used and how well it did. This leads to a model in which it is the deviation from the median rather than mean that determines how rapidly the population playing a strategy grows. There is also a reinforcement model of learning that leads to a dynamic closely related to the replicator. We introduce this model here, but postpone a discussion of its merits to chapter 4, so that we can compare it to variations on fictitious play.

The replicator dynamic is very specific and may not be a good description of many economic situations. Indeed, the learning models that lead to the replicator can lead also to other "replicatorlike" dynamics, in addition to the replicator itself. As a result much attention has focused on the extent to which results obtained for the replicator dynamic extend to other dynamics with a more concrete economic foundation. Section 3.8 discusses the class of monotonic processes, which incorporate various versions of the idea that strategies that do better grow faster. A weak version of monotonicity is sufficient to assure that strategies that are strictly dominated by pure strategies can be iteratively eliminated; under the stronger condition of convex monotonicity, this conclusion extends to all strictly dominated strategies.

Section 3.8 discusses another generalization of the replicator dynamic called myopic adjustment. This class of processes, which includes the best-response dynamic, also is sufficiently strong to yield useful results. In 2×2 symmetric games with a single population, if there is a unique mixed-strategy equilibrium, it is stable. If there is a mixed-strategy equilibrium but there are also two pure-strategy equilibria, the two pure-strategy equilibria are stable.

In addition to point-valued equilibrium notions, it can also be interesting to consider set-valued stability notions such as strategic stability and their relationship to components of steady states in the evolutionary dynamics. One useful result is that attractors in the myopic adjustment process (which may or may not exist) contain a strategically stable set, a rather strong refinement.

Section 3.9 examines the relationship between unmodeled "drift" or "mutation" terms and the possibility that equilibria (or equilibrium components) that do not satisfy strong refinements may nevertheless persist. Section 3.10 examines a set-valued concept of stability due to Gilboa and Matsui (1991) that effectively incorporates the idea of drift, and shows how it can be used to eliminate certain mixed-strategy equilibria in cheap-talk games.

Most of this chapter, like most of the evolutionary literature, considers continuous-time dynamical systems. Section 3.11 examines discrete-time versions of the replicator dynamic. Unlike the continuous-time version, the discrete-time dynamic need not remove dominant strategies. In addition, where the continuous-time dynamic has a center, the discrete-time dynamic instead cycles outward to the boundary.

3.2   Replicator Dynamics in a Homogeneous Population

Much of the work on evolution has studied the case of a single homogeneous population playing a symmetric stage game, so we begin our discussion with this case; we consider models of asymmetric populations later on in this chapter. The most basic evolutionary model is the replicator dynamic. Our goal in this section is to define this dynamic and discuss how it might be interpreted; we will also see how the steady states of the dynamic relate to the set of Nash equilibria.

To define the replicator dynamic, suppose that all agents use pure strategies and specialize to a homogeneous population. Let $\phi_t(s)$ be the measures of the set of players using pure strategy s at date t; let $\theta_t(s) = \phi_t(s)/\sum_{s'} \phi_t(s')$ be the fraction of players using pure strategy s at date t, and let the state variable θ_t be the vector of population fractions. Then the expected payoff to using pure strategy s at date t is $u_t(s) \equiv \sum_{s'} \theta_t(s')u(s,s')$, and the average expected payoff in the population is $\bar{u}_t = \sum_s \theta_t(s)u_t(s)$.

Suppose that each individual is genetically programmed to play some pure strategy, and that this programming is inherited. Finally suppose that the net reproduction rate of each individual is proportional to its score in the stage game. This leads to the continuous-time dynamic system:

$$\dot{\phi}_t(s) = \phi_t(s)u_t(s),\tag{3.1}$$

so that

$$\dot{\theta}_t(s) = \frac{\dot{\phi}_t(s)\sum_{s'}\phi_t(s') - \phi_t(s)\sum_{s'}\dot{\phi}_t(s')}{\left(\sum_{s'}\phi_t(s')\right)^2} = \theta_t(s)[u_t(s) - \bar{u}_t].\tag{3.2}$$

Equation (3.1) says that strategies with negative scores have negative net growth rates; if all payoffs are negative, the entire population is shrinking. There is no problem with this on the biological interpretation; in economic applications we tend to think of the number of agents playing the game as being constant. But note that even if payoffs are negative, the sum of the population shares is always 1. Note also that if the initial share of strategy s is positive, then its share remains positive: the share can shrink toward 0, but 0 is not reached in finite time.

Notice that the population share of a strategy that is not a best response to the current state is increasing whenever that strategy does better than the population average. This is a key distinction between the replicator dynamic and the best-response dynamic, and it also distinguishes the replicator dynamic from fictitious play. Despite this ability of suboptimal strategies to increase their share, there is still a close connection between steady states of the replicator dynamic and Nash equilibria. First, every Nash equilibrium is a steady state: In the state corresponding to a Nash equilibrium, all strategies being played have the same average payoff, so the population shares are constant. Interior steady states, where all actions have positive probability, must be Nash equilibria, but steady states on the boundary need not be Nash. For example, any state where all agents use the same strategy is a steady state, since the dynamic does not allow the "entry" of strategies that are "extinct." However, such non-Nash steady states cannot be asymptotically stable: If the state is perturbed by introducing a small weight on an improving deviation is introduced, the share playing that deviation it will grow.

Proposition 3.1 A stable steady state of the replicator dynamics is a Nash equilibrium; more generally, any steady state that is the limit of a path that originates in the interior is a Nash equilibrium. Conversely, for any non-Nash steady state there is a $\delta > 0$ such that all interior paths eventually move out of a δ-neighborhood of the steady state.

Proof Suppose that θ^* is a steady state, but the corresponding strategy profile σ^* is not a Nash equilibrium. Then, since payoffs are continuous, there exists a pure strategy $s \in \text{support}(\sigma^*)$, a pure strategy s', and an $\varepsilon > 0$ such that $u(s', \sigma^*) > u(s, \sigma^*) + 2\varepsilon$. There is moreover a δ such that $u(s', \sigma'') > u(s, \sigma'') + \varepsilon$ for all σ'' within δ of σ^*. Hence, if there is a path that remains in a δ-neighborhood of σ^*, the growth rate of strategy s' exceeds that of strategy s by an amount that is bounded away from zero. Thus the share of strategy s must converge to 0, which is a contradiction. ■

Note that this argument does not rely on the special structure of the replicator dynamics; it suffices that the growth rates are a strictly increasing function of the payoff differences. We discuss below another property that the replicator dynamics shares with a broad range of dynamic processes; namely the elimination of dominated and iterated elimination of dominated strategies.

3.3 Stability in the Homogeneous-Population Replicator Dynamic

We have already seen that stable steady states of the replicator must be Nash. We now examine dynamic stability more closely with an eye to answering the following questions: Does stability in the replicator dynamic refine Nash equilibrium? That is, can we narrow down the range of Nash equilibria through stability arguments? Does the replicator dynamic necessarily converge to a steady state, or are there other possible long-run outcomes? We will see that while it is possible to refine Nash equilibrium through stability arguments, it is also possible that the replicator does not converge to a steady state at all.

We begin with an example of an asymptotically stable steady state.

Example 3.1 Consider the game in figure 3.1. This game has two asymmetric Nash equilibria, (A, B) and (B, A), and a mixed equilibrium where both players randomize 1/2-1/2. Note that since a homogeneous population is assumed, there is no way to converge to the asymmetric equilibria because there are not separate populations of "player 1's" and

	A	B
A	0, 0	1, 1
B	1, 1	0, 0

Figure 3.1
An asymmetric coordination game

"player 2's." So the only possible steady state is the mixed equilibrium where all players randomize (1/2, 1/2). Moreover this mixed profile is a steady state even though no individual player uses a mixed strategy: When 1/2 of the population uses strategy A, and 1/2 uses strategy B, from an individual player's viewpoint the distribution of opponents' play looks like a mixed strategy. Furthermore it is easy to check that the mixed-strategy equilibrium is asymptotically stable: When fraction $\theta(A)$ of the population plays A, the payoff to A is $\theta(B) = 1 - \theta(A)$, while the payoff to B is $\theta(A)$. Consequently the average payoff in the population is $2\theta(A)(1 - \theta(A))$. Substituting into the replicator equation, we have the one-dimensional system

$$\dot{\theta}_t(A) = \theta_t(A)[(1 - \theta_t(A) - 2\theta_t(A)(1 - \theta_t(A))]$$
$$= \theta_t(A)[1 - 3\theta_t(A) + 2\theta_t(A)^2];$$

this expression is positive for $\theta_t(A) < 1/2$, exactly 0 at 1/2, and negative at larger values, so that the Nash equilibrium is asymptotically stable. (We will see below that the equilibrium is a saddle when there are distinct populations of player 1's and player 2's.)

Proposition 3.2 (Bomze 1986)   An asymptotically stable steady state in the homogeneous-population replicator dynamic corresponds to a Nash equilibrium that is trembling-hand perfect and isolated.

This result shows that asymptotic stability will be hard to satisfy in games with a nontrivial extensive form, for such games typically have connected sets of equilibria that differ only in their off-path play. For this reason evolutionary concepts need some modification to be applied to extensive-form games: Either a set-valued notion of stability must be used (e.g., as in Swinkels 1993) or the model is perturbed with "trembles" so that all information sets have positive probability of being reached.

As with most dynamical systems there is no guarantee that the replicator dynamics converge, and indeed, there are examples of games with

	R	S	P
R	0, 0	1, –1	–1, 1
S	–1, 1	0, 0	1, –1
P	1, –1	–1, 1	0, 0

Figure 3.2
Rock-paper-scissors

no asymptotically stable steady states. In particular, even a totally mixed equilibrium need not be asymptotically stable. This is significant because totally mixed equilibria satisfy the standard "equilibrium refinements" based on trembles, including such strong notions as Kohlberg and Mertens (1986) stability. A simple example in which there is no asymptotically stable steady state is the game "rock-scissors-paper."

Example 3.2   Consider the rock-scissors-paper game in figure 3.2. This may be reduced to a two-dimensional system by substituting $\theta(P) = 1 - \theta(R) - \theta(S)$. Making use of the fact that the average payoff is 0 at every state (because this is a zero-sum game), the resulting replicator dynamics are given by

$$\dot{\theta}_t(R) = \theta_t(R)[2\theta_t(S) + \theta_t(R) - 1]$$

$$\dot{\theta}_t(S) = \theta_t(S)[-2\theta_t(R) - \theta_t(S) + 1]$$

Linearizing at the equilibrium $(1/3, 1/3)$, we find that the Jacobian is

$$\begin{bmatrix} \dfrac{1}{3} & \dfrac{2}{3} \\[2ex] -\dfrac{2}{3} & -\dfrac{1}{3} \end{bmatrix}$$

The eigenvalues of this matrix are the solutions of $(1 - 3\lambda)(-1 - 3\lambda) + 4 = 0$, or $9\lambda^2 + 3 = 0$, and hence have zero real part. This means that the system is degenerate; it turns out that the steady state is surrounded by closed orbits so that it is a "center" and hence is stable but not asymptotically stable. The phase portrait for this system is illustrated below in figure 3.3. Since the real part of the eigenvalue equal to 0 (which means the steady state is not "hyperbolic") is a knife-edge case, we know that there are small changes to the system (i.e., small changes to the flow or vector field) that give the eigenvalues a positive real part. It turns out that such a change can be made simply by changing the payoffs slightly so

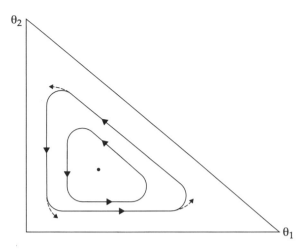

Figure 3.3
Phase portrait of the replicator dynamic for rock-paper-scissors

that each strategy gets a small $\varepsilon > 0$ when matched against itself.[2] Then
the unique Nash equilibrium is still $(1/3, 1/3, 1/3)$, but now the Nash equilibrium is an unstable steady state, and the trajectories of the replicator
dynamics spiral outward toward the boundary of the simplex without
reaching it, as shown by the dashed lines in figure 3.3.[3] Conversely, the
Nash equilibrium is an asymptotically stable steady state for small $\varepsilon < 0$.

3.4 Evolutionarily Stable Strategies

In applications, instead of working with explicit evolutionary dynamics,
analysts often use the static concept of an *evolutionary stable strategy* (ESS).
The idea of ESS is to require that the equilibrium be able to "repel invaders." After defining the static notion of ESS and showing that it is a

---

2. The fact that nonhyperbolic steady states are not robust to general perturbations of the
dynamics does not imply that they can be destroyed by small changes in the payoffs. Indeed,
in asymmetric-population models of 2×2 games, there are centers for a range of payoff
values, as we will see in section 3.5.

3. This was first shown by Zeeman (1980). See Hofbauer and Sigmund (1988) and Gaunersdorfer and Hofbauer (1995) for more discussion of variants of this game. If the system is
modified by a deterministic flow of "mutants" or new entrants, so that the boundary
becomes repelling, then for small $\varepsilon > 0$ there is a cycle (closed orbit) from the Poincaré-
Bendixson theorem. See Boylan (1994) for a discussion of the properties of steady states that
are robust (in the sense of an essential fixed point) to perturbations of the dynamics corresponding to such deterministic mutations.

refinement of Nash equilibrium, our goal is to relate it to the evolutionary dynamic. We will find that while every ESS is stable in the replicator dynamic, not every stable steady state needs to be an ESS.

To explain what is meant by "repelling invaders," suppose that the population is originally at some profile σ and then a small ε of "mutants" start playing σ'. ESS asks that the existing population gets a higher payoff against the resulting mixture $(1 - \varepsilon)\sigma + \varepsilon\sigma'$ than the mutants do. Specifically, we require that

$$u(\sigma, (1 - \varepsilon)\sigma + \varepsilon\sigma') > u(\sigma', (1 - \varepsilon)\sigma + \varepsilon\sigma') \qquad (3.3)$$

for all sufficiently small positive ε.

Using linearity of expected utility in probabilities, (3.3) is equivalent to

$$(1 - \varepsilon)u(\sigma, \sigma) + \varepsilon u(\sigma, \sigma') > (1 - \varepsilon)u(\sigma', \sigma) + \varepsilon u(\sigma', \sigma').$$

Since this needs only to hold for ε close to 0, it is equivalent to requiring that for all $\sigma' \neq \sigma$, either

$$u(\sigma, \sigma) > u(\sigma', \sigma) \qquad (3.4)$$

or

$$u(\sigma, \sigma) = u(\sigma', \sigma) \quad \text{and} \quad u(\sigma, \sigma') > u(\sigma', \sigma'). \qquad (3.5)$$

There is also a weaker notion of evolutionary stability: Profile σ is a *weak ESS* if every $\sigma' \neq \sigma$ either satisfies (3.4) or satisfies

$$u(\sigma, \sigma) = u(\sigma', \sigma) \quad \text{and} \quad u(\sigma, \sigma') \geq u(\sigma', \sigma'). \qquad (3.5')$$

This is a weaker condition because it allows for the case where the invader does just as well against the prevailing population as the population itself; then the invader is not driven out, but it does not grow, either.

Notice first that an ESS must be a Nash equilibrium; otherwise, the term on the left-hand side of (3.4) is smaller than the term on the right. Also any strict Nash equilibrium is an ESS. This follows since, by definition, strict equilibria satisfy (3.4) for all other strategies. But many games fail to have strict equilibria because, for example, mixed-strategy equilibria can never be strict.

While mixed-strategy equilibria can never be strict, they can, however, be ESS. Consider, in particular, example 3.1 above. In this example if both players play the same strategy, both get 0; if they play different strategies, both get 1. The unique mixed equilibrium is 1/2-1/2, and if either

	L	R
L	2, 2	−100, 0
R	0, −100	1, 1

Figure 3.4
A coordination game

player is playing this strategy, both players get an expected utility of 1/2. Examining (3.3), we see that if a player persists in playing 1/2-1/2 after an invasion, he gets 1/2. On the other hand, if he plays the invading strategy σ', he gets

$$u(\sigma', (1 - \varepsilon)\sigma + \varepsilon\sigma') = (1 - \varepsilon)u(\sigma', \sigma) + \varepsilon u(\sigma', \sigma')$$

$$= (1 - \varepsilon)\left(\frac{1}{2}\right) + \varepsilon u(\sigma', \sigma')$$

However, when both players play the same strategy, unless they play 1/2-1/2, they always get strictly less than 1/2. So $u(\sigma', (1 - \varepsilon)\sigma + \varepsilon\sigma')$ is strictly less than 1/2 unless $\sigma' = \sigma$, and the definition of an ESS is satisfied.

The cheap-talk games introduced by Crawford and Sobel (1982) provide a more economically interesting illustration of how ESS can reduce the equilibrium set. In these games players are allowed a period of costless and nonbinding communication prior to the actual play of the game. Consider, for example, the coordination game in figure 3.4.

In this game the outcome (L, L) is efficient, but the strategy R is risk dominant, so there are some grounds for expecting the outcome to be (R, R).[4] Suppose next that players can communicate. In the simplest version this means that there are two stages of play. In the first stage players simultaneously announce their "intended action" L or R; in the second stage they play the game. Talk is cheap in the sense that announcing an action has no direct effect at all on the realized payoffs, which depend only on the second-stage choices. Nevertheless, the ability to communicate can make a difference, since players can now signal their intention to play (L, L) by announcing this in the first-stage round. Formally, the two-stage game has a different extensive form than the original one and so, in principle, can lead to different conclusions. However, standard equilibrium notions such as subgame perfection, sequential equilibrium, or even Kohlberg-Mertens (1986) strategic stability generate the same predictions with or without cheap talk, in the sense that the sets of equilibrium pay-

---

4. See, for example, the stochastic perturbation results discussed in chapter 5.

offs and second-stage equilibrium outcomes of the two-stage game are the same as in the one-stage game without communication.

The ESS, on the other hand, does rule out some equilibria, and it suggests a tendency for meaningful communication to occur, as shown by Robson (1990), Warneryd (1991), Kim and Sobel (1991), and Blume, Kim, and Sobel (1993). The outcome (R, R) and a signal that is not sent cannot be evolutionary stable, since mutants can invade the population using the unused signal as a "secret handshake" to indicate to one another their intention to play the L equilibrium. Such invaders would not suffer against the existing players and would do even better when matched against one another.[5] Thus an ESS has more force here than do the standard equilibrium refinements. This is not to say that an ESS predicts that meaningful communication must occur in this game, for Schlag (1993) shows that the ESS is unique and involves sending every message with equal probability. This is a kind of "babbling" equilibrium; since every signal is already being sent with positive probability, there is no way for mutants to reveal their secret handshake. Section 3.10 discusses some attempts to strengthen the ESS concept to rule out this "babbling" equilibrium.

We turn next to the connection between ESS and the replicator dynamic.

Proposition 3.3 (Taylor and Jonker 1978; Hofbauer et al. 1979; Zeeman 1980)   Every ESS is an asymptotically stable steady state of the replicator dynamics.

Example 3.3 shows that the converse need not be true.

Proof   To see that an ESS implies asymptotic stability, suppose that σ is an ESS, and let $\sigma(s)$ denote the weight that σ assigns to the pure strategy s. Following the proof of Hofbauer and Sigmund (1988), we will show that the "entropy" function $E_\sigma(\theta) = \prod_s \theta_s^{\sigma(s)}$ is a strict local Lyapunov function at σ, that is, that E has a local (actually global here) maximum at σ and that it is strictly increasing over time along trajectories in some neighborhood of σ.

To see this, note that

$$\frac{\dot{E}_\sigma}{E_\sigma} = \frac{d}{dt}(\log E_\sigma) = \sum_s \sigma(s) \frac{d\log(\theta(s))}{dt}$$

$$= \sum_s \sigma(s)[u(s, \theta) - u(\theta, \theta)] = u(\sigma, \theta) - u(\theta, \theta).$$

---

5. Similar ideas have been used to explain why evolution might tend to select efficient equilibria in repeated games; see, for example, Binmore and Samuelson (1992) and Fudenberg and Maskin (1990).

	L	M	R
A	0, 0	1, −2	1, 1
B	−2, 1	0, 0	4, 1
C	1, 1	1, 4	0, 0

Figure 3.5
Game with a stable steady state that is not an ESS

Since σ is an ESS, it satisfies either inequality (3.4) or (3.5). Inequality (3.5) implies directly that the above expression is positive; (3.4) yields the same for all $\theta \neq \sigma$ in some neighborhood of σ by the continuity of u in its second argument. Hence E is an increasing function of time in this neighborhood as well. Finally it is well known that E is maximized at σ (e.g., E is the likelihood function for multinomial sampling, and the maximum likelihood estimate equals the sample probabilities[6]) so that E is a strict local Lyapunov function at s, and hence σ is asymptotically stable. ∎

The following example from van Damme (1987) shows that not every asymptotically stable steady state is an ESS.

Example 3.3   The payoff matrix is given in figure 3.5. This game has a unique symmetric equilibrium, namely (1/3, 1/3, 1/3), with equilibrium payoff 2/3.[7] This equilibrium is not an ESS, since it can be invaded by the strategy (0, 1/2, 1/2), which has payoff 2/3 when matched with the equilibrium strategy and payoff 5/4 when matched with itself. However, the Jacobian evaluated at the equilibrium is

$$\begin{bmatrix} -\dfrac{1}{9} & -\dfrac{1}{9} & -\dfrac{4}{9} \\ -\dfrac{7}{9} & -\dfrac{4}{9} & \dfrac{5}{9} \\ \dfrac{2}{9} & -\dfrac{1}{9} & -\dfrac{7}{9} \end{bmatrix}.$$

A computation shows that eigenvalues are $-1/3$ (twice) and $-2/3$, so the equilibrium is asymptotically stable.

The fact that asymptotically stable steady states need not be ESSs is linked to the fact that the replicator dynamics only allow for the inheritance of pure strategies. Bomze shows that if the dynamics are modified

---

6. A direct proof can be given by verifying that E is concave and using Jensen's inequality.
7. It also has asymmetric equilibria.

so that mixed strategies can be inherited as well, then the ESS is equivalent to asymptotic stability under the replicator dynamics. (Since this change in the dynamics does not change the definition of ESS, this statement is equivalent to saying that the change in dynamics renders unstable the non-ESSs that were stable previously.)

This raises the important issue of which replicator model, the pure- or mixed-strategy model, is more interesting. One of the drawbacks of the evolutionary approach is that because it starts at the aggregate level instead of modeling individual behavior, it cannot answer this question. The answer we would give (see also the discussion in the concluding section of this chapter) is that from an economic perspective neither replicator model should be taken to be precisely correct. Thus a primary motivation for our interest in the use of evolutionary models in economics comes from the fact that many of the results discussed later in this chapter, for example, about the elimination of dominated strategies, or set-valued notions of stability, hold for a wide range of "replicatorlike" dynamics. From this perspective it is troubling that the ESS does not have this robustness property: As noted by Friedman (1991), an ESS need not be asymptotically stable under the sort of monotone dynamics discussed in section 3.6. (We discuss an example that shows this in section 3.10.)

3.5 Asymmetric Replicator Models

We now turn to the case where there are distinct populations of player 1's, player 2's, and so forth. We consider first how the replicator should be defined in this case and, in particular, what to do if the populations of different player types are not the same size. We then show that in contrast to the symmetric case, mixed equilibria are never asymptotically stable. However, they can satisfy the weaker property of being a center.

How should replicator dynamics be defined if there are two populations that are not the same size? If there are three times as many player 1's, for example, then under a random matching interpretation of the model, each player 1 must on average be involved in only 1/3 as many interactions as each player 2, so the population of player 1's will evolve more slowly. Instead of examining the complications that stem from differential rates of adjustment, we will follow standard practice and consider only the dynamics

$$\dot{\theta}_t^i(s^i) = \theta_t^i(s^i)[u_t^i(s^i) - \bar{u}_t^i],$$

where the superscript i's refer to the various populations.[8] This dynamics corresponds to the random matching model provided that the two populations are always the same size. Alternatively, this equation can be viewed as describing a situation where agents know the distribution of opponents' strategies, and the evolution of the state variable reflects the agents' decisions about revising their choices, as opposed to a hardwired response to the payoffs obtained from play.

The most striking fact about the asymmetric case (in contrast to the homogeneous case) is that interior points, that is, strictly mixed profiles, cannot be asymptotically stable. Hofbauer and Sigmund (1988) gave a proof of this for two-player games based on the fact that the replicator dynamic "preserves volume," an observation of Akin's developed in Eshel and Akin (1983); Ritzberger and Weibull (1995) extended this result to n-player games. Rather than give a proof, we will settle for an example that suggests why interior points are less likely to be stable in the asymmetric-population model. The appendix provides a brief summary of volume-preserving maps and Liouville's formula.

Example 3.1 Revisited Consider again the game in example 3.1, only now with distinct populations of player 1 and player 2. Recall that if both players agree, they get 0; if they disagree, they get 1. It is easy to see that the two asymmetric equilibrium in which the players disagree are asymptotically stable. The mixed equilibrium, which was asymptotically stable in the homogeneous-population model, is now a saddle: If more than 1/2 of the player 1's play A, then the share of player 2's using B grows, and if more than 1/2 of the 2's use B, the share of 1's using A grows. So, starting from any point where more than half of the 1's play A and more than half of the 2's play B, the system converges to the state where all 1's play A and all 2's play B. Likewise, if more than half the 1's play B and more than half the 2's play A, the system converges to the other pure-strategy equilibrium. The phase portrait is shown in figure 3.6.

Since any open neighborhood of the mixed equilibrium contains points that converge to the two pure-strategy, asymmetric equilibria, the mixed equilibria is not stable. Note, though, that the trajectories that starting from any point on the "diagonal," where the share of A is the same in each population, do converge to the mixed equilibrium. This is a conse-

---

8. Hofbauer and Sigmund (1988, ch. 27) discuss an alternative due to Maynard Smith (1974) in which the relative speeds of adjustment of the two populations are scaled by their average payoffs, which may differ between the two populations, instead of by the population sizes.

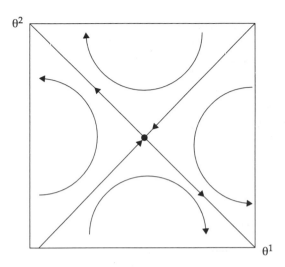

Figure 3.6
Phase portrait of the asymmetric coordination game with two populations

quence of the more general fact that in symmetric games, trajectories that start from symmetric initial positions remain symmetric and so follow the "same" path as in the one-population model. This also means that a symmetric point that is not stable in the homogeneous-population model is not stable with asymmetric populations.

This difference in conclusion with the one-population model should not be surprising: In the first case there is no asymmetry between the players that could allow them to coordinate on one of the pure-strategy equilibria; in the second game players can use their labels as a coordinating device.

Although the interior points cannot be asymptotically stable in asymmetric populations, they can satisfy a weaker condition. We say that a steady state is a *center* if it is surrounded by a family of closed orbits and all points that start near the equilibrium remain near it. From the viewpoint of general dynamical systems, being a center is a knife-edge property, meaning that small changes in the dynamics lead to abrupt changes in the asymptotic properties. Examples of small changes that can have this effect are the drift discussed in section 3.8, and the small probability of meeting a player from the same population as discussed in section 3.5. However, as usual with questions of robustness and genericity, a property that is not robust to a broad class of perturbations can be robust to a smaller one. In this case, centers are a robust property of the asymmetric-population replicator dynamics; that is, they can arise for a nonnegligible

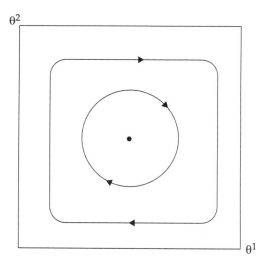

Figure 3.7
Phase portrait for 2 × 2 matching pennies

set of strategic-form payoffs. In particular, in 2 × 2 games the steady state
is a center whenever the game has no pure-strategy equilibria (Schuster
and Sigmund 1981).[9] Figure 3.7 depicts the center that arises in the 2 × 2
game "matching pennies."[10] In 3 × 3 games the asymmetric-population
replicator dynamics only has a center for a lower-dimensional set of
strategic-form payoffs (Hofbauer 1996).[11,12]

3.6   Interpretation of the Replicator Equation

3.6.1   Overview

Why should economists, or even game theorists more generally, be interested in the replicator dynamics? After all, we do not think that indi-

---

9. This shows that the sensitivity of the center in rock-scissors-paper to payoff perturbations
is not completely general—changing the payoff functions need not generate a sufficiently
large range of perturbations for structural stability arguments to apply.

10. To show that this figure is correct, one can note that the function $Q(\theta^1, \theta^2) = \theta^1(H)(1 - \theta^1(H))(\theta^2(H)(1 - \theta^2(H)))$ is a constant along any trajectory and then plot the
level curves of Q.

11. The proof of this is somewhat subtle, since even for these generic payoffs there can be
interior steady states where the linearized system has purely imaginary eigenvalues. Hofbauer
uses a second-order approximation to determine if the steady state is stable, unstable, or a center.

12. In a private communication, Hofbauer has conjectured that the result extends to games
with more than three actions.

viduals are genetically programmed to play certain strategies. For that matter, it is not clear that even monkeys are programmed directly for certain behaviors. And even behavior that we do think is inherited probably is not coded by a single gene, as this model suggests, but rather results from a complex interaction of genetic factors. Indeed, even a strict biological story does not lead directly to the replicator dynamic in cases where reproduction is not asexual.

How then could we explain this system in economics? Is there an underlying model of learning that gives rise to this dynamic? There are two types of learning stories that have been proposed to explain the replicator dynamic. One is a model of "asking around" or social learning, in which players can learn only from other players in the population. In order for the state of the resulting system to simply be the distribution of strategies currently played, as opposed to some function of the entire history, either the players must not remember their own past experience or the players must periodically be replaced so that only new players make choices.

Alternatively, replicatorlike dynamics may be explained by models of aspiration levels in which players "satisfice" rather than "optimize." There are many ways of formulating such models so that they generate a *payoff monotone* dynamic, that is, a system in which the growth rates of strategies are ordered by their expected payoff against the current population, so that strategies that are "doing better" grow faster. The replicator is the particular form of a payoff monotone dynamic in which the rates of growth are proportional to payoff differences with the mean, and particular specifications of these learning models can give rise to precisely the replicator dynamic. However, since there is typically not a compelling argument for that precise specification, we prefer to focus on the conclusion that a range of learning processes can give rise to payoff monotone dynamics.

3.6.2 Social Learning

Let us first examine the idea that the evolutionary model describes a process of social learning. The simplest such story is one in which each period, some fraction α of the agents leaves the system;[13] they are re-

---

13. This assumption serves to justify the agent's lack of memory. Alternatively, we could suppose that agents do not remember their past experience, or that agents revise their strategies so rarely that they consider their past experience to be irrelevant to the current situation.

placed by new agents, each of whom learns something about the prevailing state. To make things concrete, let us suppose that each new agent observes the strategy and payoff of one exiting agent and of one other agent drawn randomly from the same population.[14] The new agents then make a once-and-for-all choice of strategy, which they do by adopting the strategy with the higher observed payoff, or in case of a tie, the strategy they "inherited" from the exiting agent.[15] Moreover, if the agent they sample is using the same strategy that they "inherited," the agents do not switch, even if that strategy is performing poorly.

Intuitively, since a rule like "switch if the other strategy's payoff is higher" depends only on the ordinal rankings of the payoffs, and not on the size of the payoff difference, we would not expect it to lead to a dynamic like the replicator, where the speed of adjustment depends on the size of the payoff differences. Moreover, if agents observe the realized payoff of the agent they sample, as opposed to its average payoff against the current population, the resulting process need not even be payoff monotone. The point is that the rule "switch if the other strategy's observed payoff is higher" favors strategies with a high *median* payoff when matched with the distribution of opponents' play, as opposed to a high *average* payoff.[16]

To see this, consider the game in figure 3.8, where player 2 is a "dummy" whose payoffs are always 0: If 1/3 of the player 2's are playing L, then player 1's best response is U, but D has a higher median payoff. Consequently, whenever a player 1 using U samples a player 1 using D, and vice versa, fully 2/3 of them will choose the inferior response D. We call such "median-enhancing" dynamics *emulation dynamics*.

---

14. In other words the probability of sampling a strategy equals its share in the current population. This sort of "proportional" sampling is standard in the literature, but other sampling rules may be worth considering as well, as noted by Banerjee and Fudenberg (1995) in a related context of "social learning." For purposes of comparison with that paper, note that in process described here, each agent's sample size is 2.

15. If we think that agents forget, instead of being replaced, then this assumption would be that they stick with their own strategy unless they observe another one that does better.

16. This is essentially the same fact as the well-known "probability matching" in the mathematical psychology literature; see, for example, Norman (1972). More recently it is noted in Schlag (1994) in the context of learning in games, and in Ellison and Fudenberg (1993) in the context of agents learning about a move by Nature. The two contexts are the same as far as the response of one population to the play of the "opposing side"; the differences arise from the fact that in a game the distribution of strategies used by the player 2's evolves over time in response to the distribution in the population of player 1's, while the distribution over Nature's moves is usually supposed to be exogenous.

	L	R
U	9, 0	0, 0
D	2, 0	2, 0

Figure 3.8
Game with dummy player 2

To explore the properties of emulation dynamics, we consider a family of simple two-population models of play in the above game. Suppose that there is a large (continuum) population of each player type and that each period the agents are randomly matched with agents from the other population to play the stage game. Since player 2 is a dummy, we will fix the distribution of player 2 strategies, and to lighten notation, we will let $\bar{\theta}_2(L)$ denote the fraction of player 2's playing L. Under the simple emulation dynamics described above, new agents who sample someone using the same strategy as their "parent" do not switch; at date t, fraction $\theta_1^t(U)$ is using U, so a fraction $\theta_1^t(U)^2$ of the active agents is composed of agents with U parents who sample another agent using U. Agents with parents using U who sample someone using D stick with U if and only if their parent's payoff was 9; that is, if they were matched with strategy L last period; the fraction of such agents is $\bar{\theta}_2(L)\theta_1^t(U)\theta_1^t(D)$. Similarly agents whose parents used D switch to U if they meet a U-user whose last opponent played L; this corresponds to fraction $\bar{\theta}_2(L)\theta_1^t(U)\theta_1^t(D)$. Combining terms yields the difference equation

$$\theta_1^{t+1}(U) = (1 - \alpha)\theta_1^t(U) + \alpha(\theta_1^t(U)^2 + 2\bar{\theta}_2(L)\theta_1^t(U)\theta_1^t(D));$$

substituting $\theta_1^t(D) = 1 - \theta_1^t(U)$, simplifying, and passing to continuous-time yields the equation

$$\dot{\theta}_1^t = \theta_1^t(1 - \theta_1^t)(2\bar{\theta}_2(L) - 1).$$

Thus the system converges to $\theta_1^t = 0$ (all player 1's using D) whenever the fraction playing L is less than 1/2, even though U is a best response whenever $\theta_2^t(D) > 2/9$.[17]

In response to this, Schlag (1994) considers a discrete-time system in which agents observe the realized payoff of the agent they sample and then switch to the better strategy with a probability that grows linearly in

---

17. More generally, Ellison and Fudenberg show that if the probability p that U is better is i.i.d. instead of constant, the system is ergodic, with the long-run average of $\theta_1^t(U)$ equal to the probability that $\theta_1^t(U) > 1/2$.

the payoff difference. In the particular case that Schlag favors, this behavior rule has the following form: If the agent's parent's payoff is u, and
the agent samples an agent with payoff u', the agent switches with probability $\max\{0, b(u' - u)\}$.[18] One justification for this behavior is that there
is a distribution of switching costs in the population; another, due to
Binmore and Samuelson (1997), is that there is a distribution of "aspiration levels" and that agents only become active if their current payoff is
below their aspiration level. Schlag then shows that the trajectories of the
system converge to those of the continuous-time replicator dynamics as
the population grows.

For simplicity, we will present a large-population of his model for the
particular game described above. As previously, agents whose parents
used U and who are matched with L will not switch, and neither will
agents whose parents used D and who sample a U-user who is matched
with R. However, of the agents whose parents used D and sample a U-
user matched with L, only some fraction q will switch to U, while only a
fraction r of the agents who see D get a higher payoff than U switch from
U to D. (In Schlag's specification the parameters q and r are determined by
the payoff matrix of the game; we can treat them as fixed so long as we
consider a single payoff matrix. Moreover, with a more general payoff
matrix where the payoff to D depends on 2's strategy, there would be
four switching parameters to consider instead of two.) The equation of
motion is now

$$\theta_1^{t+1}(U) = (1 - \alpha)\theta_1^t(U) + \alpha\big(\theta_1^t(U)^2$$
$$+ [(\bar{\theta}_2(L)) + (1 - \bar{\theta}_2(L))(1 - r)]\theta_1^t(U)\theta_1^t(D)$$
$$+ [\bar{\theta}_2(L)q]\theta_1^t(U)\theta_1^t(D)\big),$$

and the corresponding continuous-time limit is

$$\dot{\theta}_1^t = \theta_1^t(1 - \theta_1^t)(z - 1),$$

where $z = \bar{\theta}_2(L)(q + r) + (1 - r)$.

Thus the system moves in the direction of increasing payoffs (is monotone) if and only if q and r are such that $z > 1$ whenever $\bar{\theta}_2(L) > 2/9$.
There are many combinations of q and r that satisfy this condition in
this game. Schlag's result shows that the "proportional" or linear imitation

---

18. Schlag also considers the more general formulation where agents sometimes switch to a
strategy with a lower payoff.

rate guarantees that the corresponding constraint is satisfied for any specification of the payoff matrix and that a particular proportional scheme
produces a discrete-time stochastic system that converges to the replicator dynamic in the limit of shorter and shorter time periods, where the
convergence is in the same (somewhat subtle) sense as in the Borgers-
Sarin model described later in this section.

Instead of supposing that agents observe the realized payoffs of other
players, Bjornerstedt and Weibull (1995) assume that agents receive possibly noisy statistical information about the current expected payoff of the
strategy they sample. They show that this assumption, together with the
assumption that the support of the noise is sufficiently large, leads to a
resulting process that is monotone.

To see this, suppose that the distribution of noise is such that the difference between any two noise terms has c.d.f. Φ_i. Then the probability
that a player i who is currently using s^i and who samples a player using $\tilde{s}^i$
will switch is the probability that the noise term is less than the payoff
difference $u_t^i(\tilde{s}^i) - u_t^i(s^i)$. This is equal to $\Phi_i(u_t^i(\tilde{s}^i) - u_t^i(s^i))$. Since under
proportional sampling the fraction that uses s^i and samples $\tilde{s}^i$, namely
$\theta^i(s^i)\theta_t^i(\tilde{s}^i)$, equals the fraction that uses $\tilde{s}^i$ and samples s^i, the population
evolves according to the dynamic

$$\dot{\theta}_t^i(s^i) = \theta_t^i(s^i)\left[\sum_{\tilde{s}^i}\theta_t^i(\tilde{s}^i)(\Phi_i(u_t^i(s^i) - u_t^i(\tilde{s}^i)) - \Phi_i(u_t^i(\tilde{s}^i) - u_t^i(s^i)))\right],$$

which is payoff monotone whenever the Φ_i are strictly increasing over
the range of all payoff differences; this will be the case whenever the support of the noise is big enough.

If moreover the noise has a uniform distribution over a sufficiently
large interval, and the distribution is the same for the various players,
then $\Phi(u) = a + bu$, $b > 0$, and the dynamic above simplifies to

$$\dot{\theta}_t^i(s^i) = \theta_t^i(s^i)\left[\sum_{\tilde{s}^i}\theta_t^i(\tilde{s}^i)(2b(u_t^i(s^i) - u_t^i(\tilde{s}^i)))\right]$$
$$= 2b\theta_t^i(s^i)(u_t^i(s^i) - \bar{u}_t^i),$$

which is the replicator dynamics (up to a time rescaling).

Bjornerstedt (1995) develops an alternative derivation of the replicator
based on the idea that only "dissatisfied" agents change their strategy,
with the probability of dissatisfaction depending on the agent's own payoff and on some function of the current state such as the current average
payoff in the population or the current lowest payoff. (These functions
describe the aggregate play of all agents currently using a given strategy;

in some cases they can be built up from behavior rules for individual agents in which each agent only observes the payoff of one other strategy.) Agents who are dissatisfied choose another agent at random (under proportional sampling) and copy that agent's choice regardless of its current payoff.[19] If agents with lower payoffs are more likely to be dissatisfied, the resulting dynamic is monotone; moreover Bjornerstedt shows that the result is exactly the replicator dynamics in the special case where the probability of dissatisfaction is a suitably scaled linear function of the payoffs. (The scaling must ensure that the revision probabilities stay between 0 and 1, and so depends on the payoff function of the particular game.)

One use that has been made of the replicator dynamic is in the study of experimental results, as in the Binmore and Samuelson (1995) paper discussed in section 3.9. However, the model of agents who forget and ask around does not really apply in this setting, since subjects are not permitted to "ask around" for information about the strategies and realized payoffs of other players. An alternative learning model that gives rise to replicator dynamics is a stimulus-response model that does not require that agents communicate with or observe one another, or even that there be many agents in each player role.

3.6.3 Stimulus-Response Model

An alternative justification for the replicator dynamic is drawn from the psychological stimulus-response model literature of learning. Basically it is a model of "rote" learning, in which it is assumed that actions that do well are "reinforced" and so are more likely to be used again in the future. Actions that do poorly receive "negative reinforcement" and are less likely to be used in the future. One example of how a stimulus-response-type model can lead to replicatorlike dynamics can be found in Borgers and Sarin (1995). In their paper each agent observes only his own realized action and the payoff that he receives. For simplicity, we specialize to two-player games. Agents at each date use a mixed strategy, and the state of the system at date t, denoted (θ_t^1, θ_t^2), is the vector of mixed actions played at time t by the two players. Payoffs are normalized to lie between

---

19. Similar models of "switch when dissatisfied" have been studied by Binmore and Samuelson (1997) among others. In the Binmore and Samuelson paper, agents become dissatisfied if their payoff is less than some exogenous aspiration level; dissatisfied agents choose what strategy to switch to according to a rule that, as in the example above, leads to greater switching to strategies with higher current payoffs.

zero and one so that they may be interpreted as probabilities. The state evolves in the following way: If player i plays s_t at date t, and the resulting payoff was $\tilde{u}_t^i(s_t)$, then

$$\theta_{t+1}^i(s) = (1 - \gamma\tilde{u}_t^i(s^t))\theta_t^i(s) + E(s_t, s)\gamma\tilde{u}_t^i(s_t),$$

$$E(s_t, s_t) = 1$$

$$E(s_t, s) = 0, \qquad s \neq s_t.$$

Here the reinforcement is proportional to the realized payoff, which is always positive by assumption; this implies that the action played always receives "positive reinforcement" in the sense that it is more likely to be played in the following period. Consequently in a stationary environment an agent using this rule has a positive probability of converging to a state where an inferior choice is played with probability 1.[20]

A simple calculation shows that expected increase in the probability that player i uses s equals the current probability multiplied by the difference between the strategy's expected payoff and the expected payoff of the player's current mixed strategy. In the limit as $\gamma \to 0$ Borgers and Sarin show that the trajectories of this stochastic process converge in probability to the continuous-time replicator dynamic. Note, however, that this does not imply that the replicator dynamic has the same asymptotic behavior as the stochastic system generated when the play of both agents follows the stimulus-response equation above, due to the possibility of "locking onto" a suboptimal choice which we noted above. For our example in matching pennies, the stochastic reinforcement model will eventually be absorbed by a pure-strategy profile, while the continuous-time replicator system does not converge to a pure-strategy profile. This discontinuity in the asymptotic behavior of discrete- and continuous-time systems is something we discuss in greater detail below.

3.7 Generalizations of the Replicator Dynamic and Iterated Strict Dominance

The replicator dynamic is very specific, and it seems difficult to justify the models of individual level adjustment that lead to precisely the replicator

---

20. This is similar to the "stochastic learning theory" of Bush and Mosteller (1955), in the case where all outcomes provide positive reinforcements; chapter 4 discusses related models of Borgers and Sarin (1996) and Er'ev and Roth (1996) that do accord more closely with experimental evidence but do not yield the replicator dynamic in the continuous-time limit.

dynamic at the aggregate level. Both the asking-around model and the stimulus-response model do, however, lead to dynamics that are payoff monotone, meaning that the number of people playing strategies that are doing well always grows. This leads the question of which properties of the replicator extend to other dynamics that retain this intuitive idea. Here we consider monotonicity and some if its variations, and we show how even relatively weak notions of monotonicity are sufficient to guarantee the iterated elimination of strictly dominated strategies.

Following Samuelson and Zhang (1992), say that an adjustment process (i.e., a flow on the state space $\Theta^1 \times \Theta^2 = \Sigma^1 \times \Sigma^2$) is *regular* if (1) it is Lipschitz continuous, (2) the sum of the flows in each population equals 0, and (3) strategies with 0 shares have nonnegative growth rates. The process is *payoff monotone* if strategies with higher current payoffs have higher current growth rates. [21]

Definition 3.1   A process is *payoff monotone* if at all interior points,

$$u_t^i(s^i) > (=)u_t^i(s^{i'}) \Rightarrow \frac{\dot{\theta}_t^i(s^i)}{\theta_t^i(s^i)} > (=) \frac{\dot{\theta}_t^i(s^{i'})}{\theta_t^i(s^{i'})}.$$

Although this condition is quite weak in some respects, the requirement that growth rates are strictly ordered by the corresponding payoffs does rule out the best-response dynamics, since under best response all strategies that are not best responses have identical growth rates of -1.

Recall the definition of strict dominance from chapter 1: A strategy σ^i is *strictly dominated* if there is some other (possibly mixed) strategy $\hat{\sigma}^i$ such that

$$u^i(\hat{\sigma}^i, \sigma^{-i}) > u^i(\sigma^i, \sigma^{-i})$$

for all profiles of opponents' strategies σ^{-i}. *Iterated strict dominance* is the process of first removing all strictly dominated strategies for each player, then removing all strategies that become strictly dominated once the dominated strategies are deleted, and so on, until no further deletions are possible. Following Samuelson and Zhang, define the process of *iterated pure-strategy strict dominance* to be the analogous iterative process when only dominance by pure strategies is considered. Obviously this process deletes fewer strategies, since a strictly dominated strategy may not be dominated by any pure strategy.

---

21. Samuelson and Zhang simply called these processes "monotone."

Proposition 3.4 (Samuelson and Zhang 1992)   Under any regular, monotone dynamics, if strategy s is eliminated by the process of iterated pure-strategy strict dominance, then the share of strategy s converges to 0 asymptotically irrespective of whether the state itself converges.[22]

Sketch of Proof   The easiest case is that of a strategy s that is strictly dominated by some other pure strategy $\hat{s}$. Then the growth rate of s is always some fixed amount less than the growth rate of $\hat{s}$, and so the share of s in the population must tend to 0 asymptotically. Once this is seen, it is not surprising that the result extends to iterative deletion. Intuitively we expect the adjustment process to run through the iterative deletion: Once the dominated strategies have shares close to 0, then strategies that are removed at the second round of iterated pure-strategy dominance must have lower payoffs than those of other strategies with nonnegligible shares, so their share starts to shrink to 0, and so on. Since the iterative deletion process stops in a finite number of rounds (in stage games with a finite number of actions), the adjustment process should eventually eliminate all of the strategies in question.

To make this intuition more precise, we adapt an argument that Hofbauer and Weibull (1996) used in their proof of proposition 3.5 below. Note first that the share of each strategy that is strictly dominated by a pure strategy is bounded above by a function that converges to 0 at an exponential rate. Since there are only a finite number of such dominated strategies, there is, for any positive ε, a finite time T such that at all $t > T$ every one of them has share less than ε.

Let $\bar{s}^i$ be a strategy for player i that is not strictly dominated by a pure strategy but is strictly dominated by some $\hat{s}^i$ once the first round of deletions is performed. Since payoff functions are continuous functions of the mixed strategies, $\hat{s}^i$ has a strictly higher payoff than $\bar{s}^i$ once the shares of all of the "pure-strategy–strictly dominated" strategies are less than some sufficiently small ε;[23] moreover, by taking ε small enough, we can ensure that this is true uniformly over all of the strategies removed at the second round of the iteration. Thus, after some finite time T', the shares of all of the strategies that are removed at the second round of iteration are bounded by a function that converges to 0 at an exponential rate. Hence

---

22. Nachbar (1990) has a similar result that applies only to "dominance-solvable" games where the iterated deletion process eliminates all but one strategy's profile. Milgrom and Roberts (1990) obtain a similar result for the class of supermodular games.
23. Note that this continuity argument does not apply to the concept of weak dominance.

1.00, 1.00	2.35, 0.00	0.00, 2.35	0.10, 1.10
0.00, 2.35	1.00, 1.00	2.35, 0.00	0.10, 1.10
2.35, 0.00	0.00, 2.35	1.00, 1.00	0.10, 1.10
1.10, 0.10	1.10, 0.10	1.10, 0.10	0.00, 0.00

Figure 3.9
Dekel and Scotchmer's rock-scissors-paper variant

the shares of these strategies become negligible at some finite time T'', and the argument continues on. Since the process of iteration ends in a finite number of rounds in finite games, only a finite number of iterations of the argument are required, and we conclude that there is a finite time T after which the shares of all strategies that are eliminated by iterated pure-strategy strict dominance converge to 0.   ∎

An example due to Bjornerstedt (1995) shows that monotone dynamics need not eliminate strategies that are strictly dominated by a mixed strategy. This example uses a version of the "sample-if-dissatisfied" dynamic.

Example 3.4 Consider the variant of the rock-scissors-paper game due to Dekel and Scotchmer (1992) shown in figure 3.9. Here the upper 3×3 matrix is a nonzero sum version of rock-scissors-paper, while the fourth strategy is strictly dominated by an equal mixture of the first three strategies but not by any pure strategy. However, the fourth strategy is a better-than-average response whenever it and one other strategy are scarce. Now consider a "sample-if-dissatisfied" dynamic where each player's propensity to sample depends on the current aggregate state as well as on the player's own payoff, and moreover this dependence takes the very special form that players with the lowest possible payoff given the current state are certain to sample. Then since the fourth strategy is typically not the worst-performing one, it can survive even in continuous time unless the system starts at exactly the Nash equilibrium.

Note, incidentally, that in this example the mixed Nash equilibrium is an ESS. Consequently this example also shows that ESS does not imply asymptotic stability for general monotone dynamics.

In order to eliminate strategies that are strictly dominated by a mixed strategy, Samuelson and Zhang introduce the condition of "aggregate monotonicity":

Definition 3.2 A system is *aggregate monotonic* if at all interior points

$$u_t^i(\sigma^i) > u_t^i(\hat{\sigma}^i) \Rightarrow \sum_{s^i}(\sigma^i(s^i) - \hat{\sigma}^i(s^i))\frac{\dot{\theta}_t^i(s^i)}{\theta_t^i(s^i)} > 0.$$

This says that if mixed strategy σ^i has a higher current payoff than mixed strategy $\hat{s}^i$, then the "growth rate" of σ^i is higher than that of $\hat{\sigma}^i$. It is easy to see that aggregate monotonicity implies monotonicity. Samuelson and Zhang show that the replicator dynamics is aggregate monotonic and that any aggregate monotonic system deletes all strategies deleted by iterated strict dominance.

Recently Hofbauer and Weibull (1996) have found a weaker sufficient condition which they call *convex monotonicity*.

Definition 3.3 A system is *convex monotonic* if at all interior points

$$u_t^i(\sigma^i) > u_t^i(s^i) \Rightarrow \sum_{s'^i}\sigma^i(s'^i)\frac{\dot{\theta}_t^i(s'^i)}{\theta_t^i(s'^i)} > \frac{\dot{\theta}_t^i(s^i)}{\theta_t^i(s^i)}.$$

In words, this says that if mixed strategy σ^i has a higher current payoff than pure strategy s^i, then the "growth rate" of σ^i is higher than that of s^i.

A convex monotonic system is clearly monotonic, so convex monotonicity rules out the best-response dynamics. However, there are approximations of the best-response dynamic that are convex monotonic. For example, Hofbauer and Weibull note that the following dynamics is convex monotone for any positive λ:

$$\dot{\theta}_t^i(s^i) = \theta_t^i(s^i)\left(\frac{\exp(\lambda u_t^i(s^i))}{\sum_{\hat{s}}\theta_t^i(\hat{s}^i)\exp(\lambda u_t^i(\hat{s}^i))} - 1\right).$$

As λ grows to infinity, this system converges to the best-response dynamics.

Proposition 3.5 (Hofbauer and Weibull 1996) Under any regular, convex monotone dynamics, if pure strategy s is eliminated by the process of iterated strict dominance, then the share of strategy s converges to 0 asymptotically, irrespective of whether the state converges. Moreover, if mixed strategy σ is removed by iterated strict dominance, then for all $\varepsilon > 0$ there is a time T such that for all $t > T$ the share of at least one of the pure strategies in the support of σ is less than ε.

Sketch of Proof As with the preceding proposition, the key step is showing that the dominated strategies are removed. To do this, suppose that strategy s^i of payer i is strictly dominated by strategy σ^i, and without loss of generality suppose that σ^i gives strictly positive probability to every strategy but s^i. Now consider the function P defined by $P^i_{\sigma^i}(\theta^i) = \theta^i(s^i) \prod_{\tilde{s}^i} \theta^i(\tilde{s}^i)^{-\sigma^i(\tilde{s}^i)}$; thus $P^i_{\sigma^i}(\theta^i) = \theta^i(s^i) E_{\sigma^i}(\theta^i)$, where $E_{\sigma^i}(\theta^i)$ is the inverse of entropy function used in the proof of proposition 3.3. Along any interior trajectory

$$\dot{P}_{\sigma^i}(\theta^i_t) = \dot{\theta}^i_t(s^i) E_{\sigma^i}(\theta^i_t) + \theta^i_t(s^i) \dot{E}_{\sigma^i}(\theta^i_t) = \left(\frac{\dot{\theta}^i_t(s^i)}{\theta^i_t(s^i)} + \frac{\dot{E}_{\sigma^i}(\theta^i_t)}{E_{\sigma^i}(\theta^i_t)} \right) P_{\sigma^i}(\theta^i_t)$$

$$= \left(\frac{\dot{\theta}^i_t(s^i)}{\theta^i_t(s^i)} - \sum_{\tilde{s}^i} \sigma^i(\tilde{s}^i) \frac{\dot{\theta}^i_t(\tilde{s}^i)}{\theta^i_t(\tilde{s}^i)} \right) P_{\sigma^i}(\theta^i_t),$$

which is strictly negative on the interior of the simplex from convex monotonicity and the fact that $E_{\sigma^i}(\theta^i)$ is bounded away from 0. Thus P must converge to 0, and so (again using the fact that $E_{\sigma^i}(\theta^i)$ is bounded away from 0) we conclude that $\theta^i(s^i)$ converges to 0 at an exponential rate.

To show that the process continues to iteratively delete the dominated strategies, we now simply paraphrase the analogous argument from the proof of proposition 3.4 (which was actually taken from Hofbauer and Weibull 1996) replacing every dominating pure strategy by the dominating mixture.   ∎

As a final remark on results about iterative deletion, we should note that even the replicator dynamic need not eliminate a strategy that is weakly dominated, since Nash equilibria in weakly dominated strategies can be stable (but not asymptotically stable.) Section 3.9 gives an example of this and has an extended discussion of one response to it.

3.8 Myopic Adjustment Dynamics

Besides the aggregate and convex monotonicity discussed in the previous section, there is another useful generalization of monotonicity, called myopic adjustment. This class includes not only the replicator dynamic but also the best-response dynamic, and it simply requires that utility increase along the adjustment path (holding fixed the play of other players). We consider two applications of this idea. First, we give a complete characterization of myopic adjustment in the case of 2×2 symmetric games with a single population. Second, we consider the set-valued notion of strategic stability, and how it is connected to the property of being an attractor for a myopic adjustment process.

3.8.1 Myopic Compared to Monotone Adjustment

The notion of myopic adjustment is due to Swinkels (1993). This generalization of monotonicity includes as a special case not only the replicator dynamic but also the best-response dynamic.

Swinkels's condition of myopia is that holding other players' play fixed, utility should be nondecreasing along the adjustment path. Formally

Definition 3.4 A system is a *myopic adjustment dynamic* if

$$\sum_{s^i} u_t^i(s^i)\dot{\theta}(s^i) \geq 0.$$

We next reconsider the monotonicity condition, that higher utilities imply weakly higher growth rates. One implication of this is that strategies whose share is expanding must have higher utility than strategies whose shares are contracting. Let $\underline{u}^i$ denote the least utility of any strategy whose share is (weakly) expanding, and let $\bar{u}^i$ denote the greatest utility of any strategy whose share is strictly declining. Monotonicity implies that $\underline{u}^i \geq \bar{u}^i$. Notice that

$$\sum_{s^i} \dot{\theta}(s^i) = 0 \Rightarrow \sum_{s^i|\dot{\theta}(s^i)\geq 0} \dot{\theta}(s^i) = - \sum_{s^i|\dot{\theta}(s^i)<0} \dot{\theta}(s^i).$$

If we calculate the sum defining the time rate of change of utility separately over those strategies that are expanding, and those that are contracting, we find that

$$\sum_{s^i|\dot{\theta}(s^i)\geq 0} u_t^i(s^i)\dot{\theta}(s^i) + \sum_{s^i|\dot{\theta}(s^i)<0} u_t^i(s^i)\dot{\theta}(s^i)$$

$$\geq \underline{u}_t^i \sum_{s^i|\dot{\theta}(s^i)\geq 0} \dot{\theta}(s^i) + \bar{u}_t^i \sum_{s^i|\dot{\theta}(s^i)<0} \dot{\theta}(s^i)$$

$$= \underline{u}_t^i \sum_{s^i|\dot{\theta}(s^i)\geq 0} \dot{\theta}(s^i) + \bar{u}_t^i \left(- \sum_{s^i|\dot{\theta}(s^i)\geq 0} \dot{\theta}(s^i) \right)$$

$$= (\underline{u}_t^i - \bar{u}_t^i) \sum_{s^i|\dot{\theta}(s^i)\geq 0} \dot{\theta}(s^i) \geq 0.$$

This enables us to conclude that

Proposition 3.6 Every monotonic regular system is a myopic adjustment dynamic.

As we mentioned above, the best-response dynamic is also a myopic adjustment dynamic. That is, reinterpreting the state variable as beliefs rather than a population distribution of play, the system

$$\dot{\theta}^i = BR^i(\theta^j) - \theta^i$$

also increases utility holding the opponent's strategy fixed. Indeed, in a certain sense, the best-response dynamic increases utility holding the opponent's strategy fixed as rapidly as possible. Consequently results that apply to all myopic adjustment dynamics are applicable to the best-response dynamic and, by implication, continuous-time fictitious play as well as to the replicator dynamic.[24]

3.8.2   Two-by-Two Symmetric Games

The myopic adjustment dynamic is strong enough to yield results in the special case of a symmetric 2×2 game with a symmetric initial condition (or equivalently, one population). In this case the state variable is one-dimensional, so in continuous-time models the system cannot cycle and must converge to a steady state. Moreover the only possible steady states are Nash equilibria of which, generically, there are at most three. The stability properties of steady states is entirely determined by the direction of the flow at each point; the rate of movement makes no difference.

In a symmetric, one-population 2×2 game, a myopic adjustment dynamic cannot move the system in the direction that corresponds to a decrease in utility holding the opponent's strategy fixed.[25] If we add to the assumption of myopic adjustment the assumptions that (1) movement must be strictly positive in the utility-improving direction (if there is one) and (2) every Nash equilibrium is a steady state, then the direction of flow is pinned down everywhere except at non-Nash pure-strategy profiles. (Note that these two assumptions are satisfied in both the replicator and best-response cases.) Consequently, except for the issue of whether non-Nash profiles are (unstable) steady states (as they are in the replicator

---

24. Remember that the equivalence between the fictitious play and best-response dynamic hold only in continuous time and that the continuous-time model can capture the asymptotic behavior of discrete-time fictitious play but not that of the discrete-time best-response dynamic, for the latter dynamic is time homogenous and does not "slow down" asymptotically.

25. This is true in all games but considerably more useful in the 2×2 symmetric case.

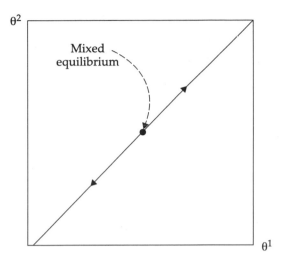

Figure 3.10
Phase portrait for 2 × 2 symmetric case

dynamics but not under best response), the global properties of all myopic dynamical systems are exactly the same. In particular, if there is a unique Nash equilibrium (either in the interior or on the boundary), it is an attractor from all interior initial conditions. The other generic possibility is that there is a mixed equilibrium and two strict pure equilibria, for example, as in coordination games. Here the two pure equilibria are stable, and the mixed equilibrium is unstable, as illustrated in figure 3.10. (If one of the pure equilibria were unstable, then the other strategy would need to be the best response to mixed strategies arbitrarily near the unstable equilibrium, which would contradict the assumption that the first equilibrium is strict.)

3.8.3 Stable Attractors and Strategic Stability

Swinkels (1993) proves a general result about myopic adjustment dynamics: He establishes a connection between stability of the dynamical system, and strategic stability in the game-theoretic sense of Kohlberg and Mertens (1986). A set of mixed-strategy Nash equilibria is hyperstable if (1) for every addition of redundant strategies to the game, and every sufficiently small perturbation to payoffs generated by forcing opponents to tremble, the perturbed game has a Nash equilibrium that is close to the original set, and (2) the set is a minimal set with property 1. Kohlberg and

Mertens show, for example, that every hyperstable set must contain a subgame perfect equilibrium and, indeed, a sequential equilibrium.

Swinkels's result, stated below, restricts attention to asymptotically stable sets that are convex. This effectively rules out limit cycles, focusing attention on sets of steady states and thus on sets of Nash equilibria. Now recall from chapter 1 that every Nash equilibrium is locally isolated for generic strategic-form payoffs. In fact more is true: For generic payoffs every pure Nash equilibrium is strict and hence hyperstable. This of course is not surprising: The main motivation for looking at refinements of Nash equilibria such as hyperstability comes from the consideration of the sort of nongeneric strategic form payoffs that arise when the strategies in the strategic form are complete contingent plans in a nontrivial extensive-form game. In effect Swinkels is following the Kohlberg and Mertens program of adopting a strategic-form approach to a problem that arises from extensive-form games. The second part of the book will discuss learning in extensive-form games using models that explicitly reflect the extensive-form structure.

Proposition 3.7 (Swinkels 1993) If a set is asymptotically stable under a myopic adjustment dynamic for which every Nash equilibrium is a steady state and has a neighborhood contained in the basin of attraction that is homeomorphic to a convex set (and in particular is connected), it contains a hyperstable set. In particular, it also contains a sequential equilibrium.

Although the details of Swinkels's proof are quite complex, the basic idea is not. Consider the special case of strictly myopic dynamics, in which the population's utility holding the opponents' strategy fixed strictly increases except at steady states. In this case, steady states coincide with Nash equilibria. The idea of the proof is that since the set in question is asymptotically stable, it must remain so even when the game is perturbed. In other words, we may find a new myopic dynamic in the perturbed game that is close to the old dynamic. Since the original vector field pointed inward on the boundary of a neighborhood of the set, a small perturbation will not change this. But then the flow maps a set homeomorphic to a convex set to itself, so by the Brower fixed-point theorem, the set contains a fixed point of the flow, that is, a steady state, and by construction, this lies near the original set. Since in the strictly myopic case a steady state is a Nash equilibrium, this completes the proof. Swinkels full proof is considerably more complicated because of the need to remove steady states that are not Nash equilibria in the case of weak

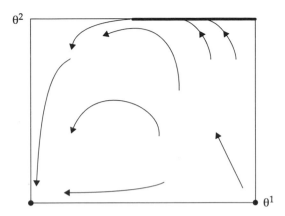

Figure 3.11
A set that is stable but not asymptotically stable

myopia and because the missing step of finding a new myopic dynamic in the perturbed game that is close to the old dynamic requires some work.

We should point out, however, that the property of a set being asymptotically stable is much stronger than that of a point being asymptotically stable. If a steady state fails to be asymptotically stable, then (generically) the set of initial conditions that leads to that steady state in the long run has measure zero: It must be a source or a saddle. However, this need not be true for a set, as figure 3.11 of a set that is not asymptotically stable illustrates. Here the solid line on the top represents a set of steady states. Initial conditions on the right of the line converge to the line; those near on the left come close but do not converge to it. None of the steady states are individually asymptotically stable, since a small perturbation can lead to another nearby steady state. Nor is the set asymptotically stable, since a small perturbation away from the set on the left side of the line does not lead back to the line. However, there is a very large (open set) of initial conditions for which there is convergence to the set.

3.9   Set-Valued Limit Points and Drift

Binmore and Samuelson (1995) expand on the idea that there may be sets of equilibria that are not stable but may nevertheless be good asymptotic descriptions of the long-run behavior of the system. They argue that it is a mistake to take the exact predictions of deterministic learning dynamics too seriously in the neighborhood of a set of steady states, since predictions here can be very sensitive to small perturbations of its flow, and

	Y	N
H	2, 2	2, 2
L	3, 1	0, 0

Figure 3.12
Binmore-Samuelson's ultimatum minigame

we suspect that there may be various unmodeled forces that could generate small amounts of deterministic "drift." Of course the reason that we leave drift out of the model in the first place is that we feel that it is "small," and a sufficiently small amount of drift has only a negligible effect on an isolated and hyperbolic steady state: Although the drift may cause a slight change in the location of the steady state, a small drift is neither strong enough to allow paths that escape from a stable steady state nor strong enough to force convergence to a steady state that is unstable in the absence of drift.

Near a set of equilibria, Binmore and Samuelson argue, the situation is quite different. This is most easily seen in their example of the ultimatum mini-game in figure 3.12. The story of this game is that the first player proposes either to split four dollars equally or to keep three dollars for himself. If an equal split is proposed, it is accepted, but if the first player proposes an unequal split, the second player may choose to either accept the split or reject it, in which case neither player gets anything.

The set of Nash equilibria and the replicator dynamic for this game is sketched in figure 3.13. In this game there is a strict Nash equilibrium at (L, Y) and a component C of Nash equilibria in which player 1 plays H and player 2 gives probability of 1/3 or more to the weakly dominated strategy N. Since the equilibrium at (L, Y) is strict, it is an attractor of the replicator dynamic. The component of equilibria where 1 plays H is unstable: A small fraction of the population playing L causes the player 2's to gradually move toward Y, so eventually more than a third of them are playing Y, and the system then moves off toward (L, Y).

The key point of Binmore and Samuelson is that at points near the unstable component C, the "force" or velocity of the original system is very slow, since the player 2's are near indifference. Suppose that there is drift due to some people in the population occasionally choosing at random (50-50) from their two strategies so that there is a weak tendency, ceteris paribus, to move to the center. Suppose moreover that the player 2's, who have less to lose, are more likely to choose randomly. Then superimposed on the replicator dynamic is a small drift dynamic of the

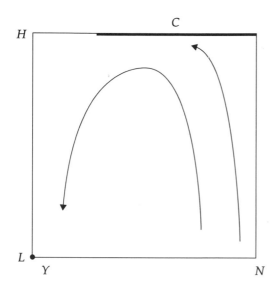

Figure 3.13
Replicator phase portrait for ultimatum minigame

sort illustrated in figure 3.14. When we combine the two dynamics, putting most of the weight on the replicator and very little weight on the drift, the combined dynamic has the appearance shown in figure 3.15. Now the tendency of player 2's to randomize between Y and N overcomes their tendency to move toward L when there is a very low probability of L, and the system has stable steady states near the set of equilibria.

Binmore and Samuelson make several other useful observations. First, they note that whether or not drift is important depends both on the nature of the drift and on the nature of the deterministic dynamic. In particular, if both players drift at the same rate, the flow diagram looks much like that without drift, and in particular, the set of equilibria is unstable. Moreover, fixing the drift as in figure 3.14, and continuing to suppose that player 2 drifts more rapidly than player 1, we can modify the payoffs of the game and thus modify the corresponding deterministic dynamics. For example, we can consider the family of games in figure 3.16. The case $a = 0$ reduces to the game originally studied; as a increases to 1, the range of mixed strategy equilibria is reduced until the probability of Y drops from 2/3 to 1/3 as illustrated in figure 3.17.

Under the proposed model of drift (see figure 3.14) when $a = 1$, the drift does not make any difference, since to the right of player 1 randomizing 50-50 the system is drifting left anyway. The drift only matters

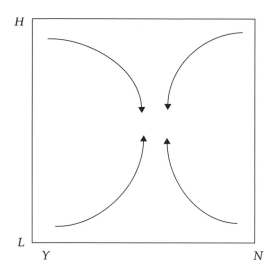

Figure 3.14
Drift

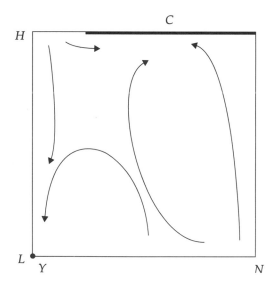

Figure 3.15
Replicator plus drift in ultimatum minigame

	Y	N
H	2, 2	2, 2
L	3(1 + a), 1	0, 0

Figure 3.16
Family of ultimatumlike minigames

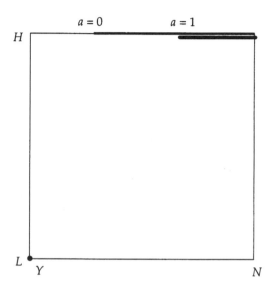

Figure 3.17
Equilibrium sets in ultimatumlike minigames

when $a < 1/3$, so the system drifts to the right near a portion of the equilibrium set; here it begins to stabilize the set of equilibria. Binmore and Samuelson argue that this has important predictive consequences: The bigger is a, the more likely we are to see the strict equilibrium at L, Y. Note, however, that this analysis is based on assuming the drift does not change when the payoffs do, while the argument about player 2 drifting faster than player 1 assumes that the drift is in part determined by players' payoffs. In this particular example the same change in payoff that makes the set of equilibria smaller (bigger a) also makes player 1 relatively less indifferent and so by the argument should decrease the rate at which he drifts, thereby tending to reinforce the stability of the set of equilibria. However, this does not upset the basic conclusion, since once the segment of equilibria lies entirely to the right of $1/2$, regardless of its strength, any drift toward $1/2$ reinforces the instability of the segment.

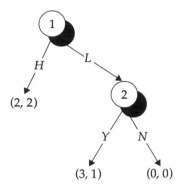

Figure 3.18
Extensive-form ultimatum minigame

This agrees with Binmore and Samuelson's basic conclusion that a shorter segment is less likely to be stable but provides a cautionary note about treating the drift as fixed.

These ideas are important because many of the systems we will examine, including the smooth version of fictitious play, do exhibit drift. However, as remarked above, all steady states are locally isolated for generic strategic-form payoffs, so this observation is not too important in the case of one-shot simultaneous-move games. As with Swinkels's result, Binmore and Samuelson's analysis is most relevant for strategic forms arising from nontrivial extensive forms. For example, the strategic form mini-ultimatum game is derived the extensive-form mini-ultimatum game shown in figure 3.18.

Not only do Binmore and Samuelson have this extensive form in mind, they make the stronger argument that learning together with the kind of drift described above can be a theoretical explanation of the empirical phenomenon found in experimental play of extensive-form ultimatum games, namely that the first mover does not get most of the pie.[26]

There are two potential difficulties with this argument. First, Binmore and Samuelson study the replicator dynamic. As we argued above, the stimulus-response rationale for this model is unconvincing, and the asking-around model clearly does not apply in an experimental setting. Of course the replicator here is used as a convenient way of making things precise; Binmore and Samuelson are motivated by the belief that

---

26. A good discussion of this experimental fact, along with many references can be found in Prasnikar and Roth (1992).

their result would also obtain in related payoff-monotone dynamics that are more readily justified.

More fundamentally, we find it unappealing to attribute the play of N by player 2 to a short-run lack of "knowledge" that player 2 will eventually "learn," since if player 2 understands the rules of the game and her own payoff function, she will understand that playing N *is* a mistake. One might argue that despite the experimental instructions, player 2 does not in fact understand (or believe) that the experiment is being conducted anonymously and so adopts a rule ("do not be taken advantage of") that is optimal in a repeated bargaining setting. However, we find the standard explanation in the experimental literature, namely that the player 2's payoffs depend on other things than the money they receive, to be more convincing.

Note, incidentally, that playing N is weakly dominated in the strategic-form game. One might want to argue that we should consider only rules that put positive weight on strategies that are not weakly dominated, since if players know the rules of the game from the outset, they can deduce which strategies are weakly dominated without any need for "learning." This idea needs to be qualified, since in some extensive-form games it can make sense to play a weakly dominated strategy for the information it reveals about opponents' play, a point we develop further in chapter 7. However, this information-gathering explanation does not apply to a decision at the "end" of the game tree, like strategy N in this game, and we find it hard to see why a player whose only objective is to maximize money income would ever play N.

3.10   Cheap Talk and the Secret Handshake

One interesting set-valued notion of stability closely connected to the best-response dynamic and to the idea of drift is the idea of a "cyclically stable set" introduced by Gilboa and Matsui (1991). A strategy profile is said to be *accessible* from another profile if there is a continuous-time best-response dynamic path to the other profile. (Note that the relative rates of adjustment of the players may differ or vary over time if necessary.) A set is *cyclically stable* if no point outside the set is accessible from inside it and every point inside the set is accessible from every other point inside.

The idea that a set that is cyclically stable is relatively stable seems incontrovertible. More questionable is the notion that a set of equilibria that is not cyclically stable is unstable; that is, merely because there is some best-response path that leads out, what reason do we have to

	L	R
L	2, 2	−100, 0
R	0, −100	1, 1

Figure 3.19
A coordination game

believe that this particular path will be followed in practice? This is where the idea of drift is important. Multiple best-response paths occur when there is indifference, and a small amount of drift will tend to move players from one point of indifference to another anyway. So if there are multiple best-response paths, only one of which leads out of a particular set, we can imagine that random drift will eventually cause that particular path to occur.

One interesting class of games in which cyclically stable sets lead to interesting conclusions is "cheap talk" discussed above in the context of evolutionary stability. Consider the coordination game example in figure 3.19. In addition we allow players a pre-move in which they may send the message L or the message R. We previously saw that an ESS cannot eliminate "babbling" equilibria in which all messages are sent with positive probability.

Instead of an ESS, Matsui (1991) uses the cyclically stable set idea. Matsui shows that when a round of cheap talk is added to any 2×2 game of common interest, there is a unique cyclically stable set[27] and that it has a unique outcome that is the Pareto-efficient outcome.

The intuition behind this idea is closely connected to the idea of drift. Suppose that the outcome in the game above is (R, R). If all players use a strategy that ignores first-stage messages and always plays R in the second stage, it is a best response to say anything. Consequently there is nothing to prevent the system from drifting to a state in which all players are saying (R, R) as well as doing it; that is, there is a path of the continuous-time best-response dynamics that leads from a "babbling state" to a state in which only a single signal is being sent. Now, however, consider a player 1 who says L and then plays L if and only if his opponent says L. Since all player 2's will play R anyway, this strategy is also a best response. Moreover it is also a best response for some of the player 2's to drift onto this strategy when all player 1's play R, and moreover once

---

27. This is a two-population model; it is not assumed that the two players always play the same way.

the process of drift is underway, the new strategy becomes a *strict* best response. On the other hand, Matsui shows that when all agents are playing *L*, the equilibrium does not unravel. It is true that there is no disadvantage to saying *R* and doing *R* if the opponent says *R*, and so the system may drift to this state; once it is reached, no player will ever wish to make use of the opportunity to induce *R* to be played.

We will return to this example in chapter 7, in the context of learning in extensive-form games; for the moment we point out only that the continuous-time best-response dynamic on *strategies* used to define cyclically stable sets implicitly supposes that players observe the entire strategies of their opponents and not just the realized action.

3.11 Discrete-Time Replicator Systems

While much of the literature on the replicator dynamics concerns the continuous-time system, it is also interesting to consider the extent to which, as in our earlier discussion of the Borgers-Sarin stimulus-response model, discrete-time systems give similar or different conclusions. To do so, the first step is of course to define what we mean by the discrete-time replicator system. While several alternatives are possible, perhaps the most obvious discrete-time formulation of the asymmetric-population case (again supposing that each population has the same size) is

$$\phi_{t+1}^i(s) - \phi_t^i(s) = \Delta\phi_t^i(s)u_t(s),$$

where Δ is the length of the time interval[28] and payoffs correspond to the net reproduction rate per unit of time that leads to the population share equation[29]

$$\theta_{t+1}^i(s) - \theta_t^i(s) = \frac{\phi_t^i(s)(1 + \Delta u_t^i(s))}{\sum_{s'} \phi_{t+1}^i(s')} - \theta_t^i(s) = \frac{\Delta\theta_t^i(s)(u_t^i(s) - \bar{u}_t^i)}{1 + \Delta\bar{u}_t^i}.$$

Note that as the period length Δ goes to 0, this equation converges to the continuous-time replicator dynamics; note also that the step size in this system depends on the absolute size of the payoffs, so that, for example, adding 100 to all payoffs shrinks the step size. This is because an additional 1% in absolute growth rate leads to an additional 1% population

---

28. If we take the continuous-time model more literally, we may wish to view Δ as the exponential of the time interval.

29. The alternative system mentioned in note 5 leads to a corresponding discrete-time alternative.

1.00, 1.00	2.35, 0.00	0.00, 2.35
0.00, 2.35	1.00, 1.00	2.35, 0.00
2.35, 0.00	0.00, 2.35	1.00, 1.00

Figure 3.20
Dekel and Scotchmer's nonzero-sum rock-scissors-paper variant

share if the total population is constant, while it becomes insignificant if all strategies have absolute growth rates that are large.

Alternatively, one can interpret the payoff function as giving the reproduction rate per period instead of per unit of time. With this interpretation the parameter Δ disappears from the equation of motion, and the way that one models shorter time periods is by lowering all of the payoffs toward 0: In the limit of infinitesimal periods, the population is almost constant from one period to the next.

As is typically the case, the convergence and stability properties of the discrete-time replicator dynamics can be different from the continuous-time version, with "long" time periods causing more of a change than small ones do. The most striking example of the effect of long time periods is Dekel and Scotchmer (1992), who show that the discrete-time replicator dynamics need not remove all strictly dominated strategies. (We follow Dekel-Scotchmer in discussing the one-population case; recall that this also describes the evolution of the two-population system from a symmetric initial position.)

Dekel and Scotchmer start with the nonzero-sum version of the rock-scissors-paper game shown in figure 3.20. In this game the mixed equilibrium (1/3, 1/3, 1/3) is an ESS. The equilibrium payoff is 3.35/3; the payoff of any of the strategies against itself is 1. Thus we know that the mixed equilibrium is asymptotically stable in the continuous-time replicator dynamic. However, computation reveals that the discrete-time replicator dynamics (with $\Delta = 1$ so that the "large" payoffs here implicitly correspond to a nonnegligible period length) spiral outward toward the boundary.

Dekel and Scotchmer then add a fourth strategy to the game, resulting in the game described in example 3.4, and shown also in figure 3.21. Recall that this fourth strategy is strictly dominated by a mixture of the other three strategies but not by any one of the first three strategies alone, and it does very poorly against itself. However, the fourth strategy is a better-than-average response against states where it and one other strategy are scarce. Since this new strategy is not a best response to the

1.00, 1.00	2.35, 0.00	0.00, 2.35	0.10, 1.10
0.00, 2.35	1.00, 1.00	2.35, 0.00	0.10, 1.10
2.35, 0.00	0.00, 2.35	1.00, 1.00	0.10, 1.10
1.10, 0.10	1.10, 0.10	1.10, 0.10	0.00, 0.00

Figure 3.21
Dekel and Scotchmer's rock-scissors-paper variant with a fourth strategy added

equilibrium $(1/3, 1/3, 1/3, 0)$, that point is an ESS and hence is asymptotically stable in the continuous-time replicator dynamic.[30] Moreover, as we
know from section 3.7, the continuous-time replicator must eliminate the
dominated fourth strategy, starting from any interior point. However, a
proof by contradiction shows that in discrete time, the share of this fourth
strategy does not go to 0: If its share became small, the state would spiral
out toward the boundary of the simplex corresponding to the other three
strategies, and at most points on this boundary, the fourth strategy has a
positive growth rate.

The difference between the asymptotic behaviors of the discrete- and
continuous-time systems raises the question of what can be said about the
general relationship between these behaviors. Standard results on the
structural stability of dynamical systems (e.g., see Hirsch and Smale 1974)
imply the following:

1. If a steady state is hyperbolic and asymptotically stable under the
continuous-time dynamics, then it is asymptotically stable for sufficiently
small time periods.

2. If a steady state is hyperbolic and unstable under the continuous-time
dynamics, then it is unstable for sufficiently small time periods.

Because the steady state $(1/3, 1/3, 1/3, 0)$ is hyperbolic and asymptotically stable in the continuous-time replicator, it is also asymptotically
stable with sufficiently small time periods. Consequently the issue in the
Dekel-Scotchmer example is whether long or short time periods are the
better description of the situation.

More generally, facts 1 and 2 above show that in many situations the
discrepancy between the discrete- and continuous-time dynamics vanishes
in the limit of smaller time periods. A notable exception is the case discussed at the end of section 3.5 where the continuous-time dynamics has
a center. If a steady state is a center in the continuous-time dynamics, it is

---

30. This was first noted by Cabrales and Sobel (1992).

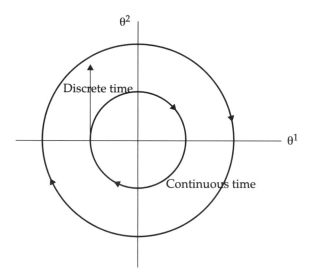

Figure 3.22
Replicator phase portrait in matching pennies

unstable in the discrete-time dynamics even for arbitrarily small period lengths. This is easily seen in figure 3.22 taken from Borgers and Sarin (1995) on the replicator dynamics in the zero-sum game "matching pennies" (see also Akin and Losert 1984). In continuous time the system orbits around the center. To a good approximation, in discrete time, the system moves along tangents to the circle; as can be seen in figure 3.22. As a result the dynamical system moves points on continuous-time orbits to points more distant from the center.

While centers are not structurally stable to general perturbations of the dynamics, they can arise for a "fat" set of payoffs under the replicator dynamics. In particular, as noted in section 3.5 above, centers occur in all 2×2 games with a unique completely mixed-strategy equilibrium in the two-population model. Thus, if one considers the narrow question of the relation between discrete- and continuous-time replicator dynamics, the conclusion is that there are open sets of payoffs for which the two differ even in the limit of period lengths that converge to 0. However, if one allows for other small perturbations of the dynamics, and thus considers the discrete- to continuous-time limit in dynamics "near" the replicator, the answer changes, for such perturbations will (generically) make the centers hyperbolic and either asymptotically stable or unstable, and in either case the asymptotic behavior of the system in the limit of very short discrete-time periods will be the same as the asymptotic behavior in continuous time.

Appendix: Liouville's Theorem

The effect of a flow on volume[31] has important consequences for the long-run dynamics of the system. For example, it is easy to see that in a one-dimensional system, if the volume of sets is reduced over time, then the system must converge to a unique globally stable steady state. More generally, fix an n-dimensional dynamical system and a measurable set A in the interior of the system's domain of definition. The image of A at time t is $A(t) = \{x(t, x_0)|x_0 \in A\}$. Consider what happens to this image under the flow. The change in the volume of such a set is determined entirely by the *trace* of the matrix $Df(x)$. This is known as the *divergence* of the vector field; that is,

$$\text{div}(f) = \text{tr}(Df) = \sum_i \frac{\partial f_i}{\partial x_i}$$

Liouville's theorem says that if the divergence is 0 on an open domain X, the image $A(t)$ has the same euclidean volume as the original set A as long as the system remains in the domain X. If the divergence is negative, the volume of the image strictly decreases over time; if it is positive, the volume of the image strictly increases.

As noted, in a one-dimensional system volume contraction is a strong property, since it guarantees convergence to a unique globally stable steady state. Volume contraction is also significant in dimension two, since it implies that the system cannot have a nontrivial closed orbit or "cycle:" A cycle separates the plane into interior and exterior regions, and so the closed set composed of the cycle and its interior must be invariant. Then, however, the flow would be volume-preserving instead of volume-contracting on this set. Volume contraction is less significant in higher dimensions, but it does imply that the system converges to a manifold at least one dimension smaller than the original system.

The case of 0 divergence is of particular use in studying the replicator dynamic. Since asymptotically stable steady states contract volume, a system with 0 divergence cannot have an asymptotically stable steady state. The standard replicator dynamic does not have divergence 0, but it can be

---

31. By volume here we mean the ordinary euclidean volume.

transformed into such a system by a (smooth) change of variables. One such transformation is given by Hofbauer (1995): First, normalize using the size of the population playing one of the strategies as a numéraire, that is set $\zeta^i(s^i) = \theta^i(s^i)/\theta^i(\tilde{s}^i)$ for some strategies $\tilde{s}^i$. Then set $v^i = \log \zeta^i$. Note that this transformation is valid only on the interior of the strategy simplex. The resulting system is *bipartite*, meaning that the terms governing the evolution of v^i depend only on the state variables corresponding to player $j \neq i$. It follows that the diagonal of the Jacobian matrix Df is zero, and so its trace (the divergence) is 0.

What does the fact that this transformed system has zero divergence reveal about the original system? The paths of the transformed system are transforms of the paths of the original one, so the steady states and their stability properties are unchanged. In particular, in the interior, the original system cannot have any asymptotically stable steady states.[32] However, the transformation does change the divergence of the map, so the fact that the transformed map preserves volume does not mean that the original one did. Indeed, since boundary steady states that are strict are certainly stable, volume must be contracted near such steady states in the original system. Note also that the transformed map may have a different velocity than the old one, and in particular, the sets of points that are reached in finite time need not be preserved under transformations; Weibull (1995) gives an example where a similar transformation of the replicator dynamic results in a system that reached a boundary equilibrium in finite time.

References

Akin, E. and V. Losert. 1984. Evolutionary dynamics of zero-sum games. *Journal of Mathematical Biology* 20: 213–58.

Banerjee, A., and D. Fudenberg. 1995. Word of mouth communication. Mimeo. Harvard University.

Binmore, K., and L. Samuelson. 1992. Evolutionary stability in repeated games played by finite automata. *Journal of Economic Theory* 57: 278–305.

Binmore, K., and L. Samuelson. 1997. Muddling through: Noisy equilibrium selection. *Journal of Economic Theory* 74: 235–65.

Binmore, K., and L. Samuelson. 1995. Evolutionary drift and equilibrium selection. Mimeo. University College London.

---

32. This conclusion cannot be extended to the entire system, since (1) Liouville's theorem only holds on open domains and (2) the transformation we used is badly behaved at the boundaries of the simplex.

Bjornerstedt, J. 1995. Experimentation, imitation, and evolutionary dynamics. Mimeo. Stockholm University.

Bjornerstedt, J., and J. Weibull. 1995. Nash equilibrium and evolution by imitation. In *The Rational Foundations of Economic Behavior*, ed. by K. Arrow et al. London: Macmillan.

Blume, A., Y. G. Kim, and J. Sobel. 1993. Evolutionary stability in games of communication. *Games and Economic Behavior* 5: 547–75.

Bomze, I. 1986. Noncooperative two-person games in biology: A classification. *International Journal of Game Theory* 15: 31–57.

Borgers, T., and R. Sarin. 1995. Learning through reinforcement and replicator dynamics. Mimeo. University College London.

Borgers, T., and R. Sarin. 1996. Naïve reinforcement learning with endogenous aspirations. Mimeo. University College London.

Boylan, R. 1994. Evolutionary equilibria resistant to mutation. *Games and Economic Behavior* 7: 10–34.

Bush, R., and R. Mosteller. 1955. *Stochastic Models of Learning*. New York: Wiley.

Cabrales, A., and J. Sobel. 1992. On the limit points of discrete selection dynamics. *Journal of Economic Theory* 57: 473–504.

Crawford, V., and J. Sobel. 1982. Strategic information transmission. *Econometrica* 50: 1431–52.

Dekel, E., and S. Scotchmer. 1992. On the evolution of optimizing behavior. *Journal of Economic Theory* 57: 392–406.

Ellison, G., and D. Fudenberg. 1993. Rules of thumb for social learning. *Journal of Political Economy* 101: 612–43.

Er'ev, I., and A. Roth. 1996. On the need for low rationality cognitive game theory: Reinforcement learning in experimental games with unique mixed strategy equilibria. Mimeo. University of Pittsburgh.

Eshel, I., and E. Akin. 1983. Coevolutionary instability of mixed Nash solutions. *Journal of Mathematical Biology* 18: 123–233.

Farrell, J. 1986. Meaning and credibility in cheap talk games. Mimeo. University of California at Berkeley.

Friedman, D. 1991. Evolutionary games in economics. *Econometrica* 59: 637–66.

Fudenberg, D., and E. Maskin. 1990. Evolution and cooperation in noisy repeated games. *American Economic Review* 80: 274–79.

Gaunersdorfer, A., and J. Hofbauer. 1995. Fictitious play, Shapley polygons and the replicator equation. *Games and Economic Behavior* 11: 279–303.

Gilboa, I., and A. Matsui. 1991. Social stability and equilibrium. *Econometrica* 58: 859–67.

Hirsch, M., and S. Smale. 1974. *Differential Equations, Dynamical Systems, and Linear Algebra*. New York: Academic Press.

Hofbauer, J. 1996. Evolutionary dynamics for bimatrix games: A hamiltonian system? *Journal of Mathematical Biology* 34: 675–688.

Hofbauer, J., and J. Weibull. 1996. Evolutionary selection against dominated strategies. *Journal of Economic Theory* 71: 558–73.

Hofbauer, J., and K. Sigmund. 1988. *The Theory of Evolution and Dynamical Systems.* Cambridge: Cambridge University Press.

Hofbauer, J., P. Schuster, K. Sigmund, and K. Sigmund. 1979. A note on evolutionary stable strategies and game dynamics. *Journal of Theoretical Biology*, 81: 609–12.

Kim, Y. G., and J. Sobel. 1991. An evolutionary approach to preplay communication. Mimeo. University of California at San Diego.

Kohlberg, E., and J.-F. Mertens. 1986. On the strategic stability of equilibria. *Econometrica* 54: 1003–38.

Kreps, D., and B. Wilson. 1982. Sequential equilibria. *Econometrica* 50: 863–94.

Matsui, A. 1991. Cheap-talk and cooperation in a society. *Journal of Economic Theory* 54: 245–58.

Maynard Smith, J. 1974. The theory of games and evolution of animal conflicts. *Journal of Theoretical Biology* 47: 209.

Milgrom, P., and J. Roberts. 1990. Rationalizability, learning, and equilibrium in games with strategic complements. Mimeo. Stanford University.

Nachbar, J. 1990. "Evolutionary" selection dynamics in games: Convergence and limit properties. *International Journal of Game Theory* 19: 59–89.

Norman, M. F. 1972. *Markov Processes and Learning Models.* New York: Academic Press.

Prasnikar, V., and A. Roth. 1992. Considerations of fairness and strategy: Experimental data from sequential games. *Quarterly Journal of Economics* 107: 865–88.

Rabin, M. 1990. Communication between rational agents. *Journal of Economic Theory* 51: 144–70.

Ritzberger, K., and J. Weibull. 1995. Evolutionary selection in normal-form games. *Econometrica* 63: 1371–99.

Robson, A. J. 1990. Efficiency in evolutionary games: Darwin, Nash and the secret handshake. *Journal of Theoretical Biology* 144: 379–96.

Samuelson, L., and J. Zhang. 1992. Evolutionary stability in asymmetric games. *Journal of Economic Theory* 57: 363–91.

Schlag, K. 1993. Cheap talk and evolutionary dynamics. Mimeo. Universität Bonn.

Schlag, K. 1994. Why imitate, and if so, how? Exploring a model of social evolution. Mimeo, D.P. B-296. Universität Bonn.

Schuster, K. P., and K. Sigmund. 1981. Coyness, philandering and stable strategies. *Animal Behavior* 29: 186–92.

Swinkels, J. 1993. Adjustment dynamics and rational play in games. *Games and Economic Behavior* 5: 455–84.

Taylor, P., and L. Jonker. 1978. Evolutionarily stable strategies and game dynamics. *Mathematical Biosciences* 16: 76–83.

van Damme, E. 1987. *Stability and Perfection of Equilibria*. Berlin: Springer.

Warneryd, K. 1991. Evolutionary stability in unanimity games with cheap talk. *Economic Letters* 36: 375–78.

Weibull, J. 1995. *Evolutionary Game Theory*. Cambridge: MIT Press.

Zeeman, E. 1980. Population dynamics from game theory. In *Global Theory of Dynamical Systems*. Lecture Notes in Mathematics, 819: 472–97. Berlin: Springer.

4   Stochastic Fictitious Play and Mixed-Strategy Equilibria

4.1   Introduction

This chapter examines stochastic models in the spirit of fictitious play, in which players randomize when they are nearly indifferent between several choices. One motivation for the material in this chapter is to provide a more satisfactory explanation for convergence to mixed-strategy equilibria in fictitious playlike models. Another motivation for looking at stochastic models is to avoid the discontinuity inherent in standard fictitious play, where a small change in the data can lead to an abrupt change in behavior. Such discontinuous responses may not be descriptively realistic in many situations, as psychological experiments show, since choices between alternatives that are perceived as similar tend to be relatively random. Moreover a discontinuous response creates the possibility that the infrequent switching condition described in chapter 2 is violated, which opens the player to the sorts of "mistakes" described there, where she persistently makes less than her reservation value. In contrast, players can ensure that they will obtain at least their reservation value in time average by using the sorts of stochastic rules we develop in this chapter.

The traditional process of fictitious play is deterministic, except possibly when the historical average is such that the player is indifferent between several actions. Of course, for generic strategic-form payoffs and a generic prior, there is no sample that makes any player exactly indifferent, so typically players will use pure strategies in every period. The variations on fictitious play we discussed at the end of chapter 2 do permit players to randomize. Recall, in particular, the notion of asymptotically empirical beliefs, which requires that beliefs in the limit converge to the frequencies generated by fictitious play while allowing beliefs at any finite time t to be arbitrary. As we will see, such procedures permit players to randomize in every period, so potentially such a procedure could converge to a mixed-strategy equilibrium. However, the reason that players randomize in this setup is not very satisfactory.

As we mentioned earlier, another motivation for looking at stochastic models is to avoid the discontinuity inherent in standard fictitious play, which is troubling descriptively and can lead to poor long-run performance. These considerations lead us to consider variations on fictitious play in which players randomize when they are nearly indifferent. In studying these stochastic fictitious playlike procedures in discrete time, we will argue that the asymptotic properties of these systems can be understood by reference to a limiting continuous-time deterministic dynamical system. Roughly speaking, in fictitious playlike procedures, the averaging of observations over time causes the noise in the system to decrease relative to the speed with which the system moves. If the noise remains large relative to the deterministic movement of the system, then the continuous-time limit is less useful, a situation considered in the next chapter.

4.2   Notions of Convergence

Our discussion of fictitious play in the chapter 2 followed the standard practice of saying that play converged if the empirical frequencies of each player's actions converged. As we noted there, this notion of convergence is very weak: Since it requires convergence only of the marginal distribution of individual players' play, it allows the possibility that the joint distribution of play is correlated, and this can lead to payoffs that are very different from Nash equilibrium payoffs, as in the example of the coordination game where players always fail to coordinate. If we strengthen the notion of convergence to require convergence of the joint distribution of play, then from a frequency point of view, play in the game does resemble a Nash equilibrium. However, this response is not completely satisfactory because it allows persistent cycles. For example, in a game of matching pennies, deterministic alternation between (H, H), (H, T), (T, H), (T, T) would be viewed as a sequence that "converges" to a Nash equilibrium.

In this chapter we will follow the approach adopted by Fudenberg and Kreps (1993) and define convergence of the learning process to mean that the players' intended play converges. Note that it is not immediately obvious that this is a stronger condition than convergence of either the marginal distribution of the players' play or the joint distribution of their play. However, Fudenberg and Kreps use a variation on the strong law of large numbers that leads to the conclusion[1] that when the intended play converges, the realized joint empirical distribution over profiles converges almost surely to the product of the intended marginals.

Following Fudenberg and Kreps (1993), we say that a strategy profile is *locally stochastically stable* if for every $\varepsilon < 0$ there is some history of play such that the subsequent probability that intended play converges to that profile is at least $1 - \varepsilon$. This stochastic version of local stability does not require that behavior converge almost surely, since when behavior is stochastic there is always a small probability of unrepresentative outcomes that would lead players away from the target strategy. It also uses a very weak notion of "local," for it suffices that there be *some* history for which the convergence has high probability, as opposed to requiring that convergence occur for every history in some (suitably defined) neighborhood of the target profile.

4.3 Asymptotic Myopia and Asymptotic Empiricism

We next investigate the extent to which procedures that are asymptotically like fictitious play are locally stable. Since we have now defined convergence to mean the convergence of intended play, behavior that follows a deterministic cycle does not converge and, in particular, cannot converge to a Nash equilibrium even if the empirical marginal frequencies converge to a Nash equilibrium strategy profile. Rather, the only way that play can converge to a mixed equilibrium is if the distribution of play in each period is mixed. This in turn is possible only if players use some type of explicit randomization, which leads to the question of why the distribution of intended actions at a given date should be random in the first place.

This question is familiar as a critique of mixed-strategy equilibrium, so it is not surprising that it reemerges here. One trivial defense is that players are willing to play a mixed strategy so long as every action in the strategy's support yields the same expected payoff. This is true by definition in a mixed-strategy equilibrium. To turn this into an ad hoc and unsatisfactory "learning" story, one could suppose that players start off with the assessment that their opponent's play exactly corresponds to the mixed equilibrium and that players maintain this assessment unless they

---

1. Although they show only that convergence of intended play implies the convergence of marginal distributions of play to the intended play, the same argument easily gives the stronger result mentioned here.

get "overwhelming" statistical evidence against it.[2] Suppose moreover that so long as a player does maintain this belief, he chooses his own actions according to his part of the mixed equilibrium. If each player follows this rule, then, by the law of large numbers, neither player will reject the hypothesis that his opponent is following the mixed equilibrium, and play will indeed converge to the mixed equilibrium we specified. Of course this "explanation" of the persistent mixing in a mixed-strategy equilibrium has the defect of building a weak preference for the mixed equilibrium directly into the players' behavior. But then the story is based on an explanation of equilibrium learning that has the same defect: Players are supposed to follow the mixed equilibrium for no positive reason at all.

More generally, we can consider the stability properties of procedures that are asymptotically similar to fictitious play. A behavior rule ρ_t^i for player i specifies a mixed strategy based on the history of play. An *assessment for player i* is a map from histories to distributions over the space Σ^{-i} of the opponent's mixed strategies. As in chapter 2, assessments are *asymptotically empirical* if they converge to the empirical average along every sequence of observations, and a behavior rule is *asymptotically myopic* if the loss from player i's choice of action at every history given his assessment goes to zero as the history grows longer.[3] A profile is *unstable* if for every positive ε, players' behavior is almost surely more than ε away from the profile infinitely often.

Proposition 4.1 (Fudenberg and Kreps 1993)   If σ is not a Nash equilibrium, then it is unstable with respect to any behavior rules that are asymptotically myopic with respect to asymptotically empirical assessments.

---

2. To be somewhat more precise, fix a mixed-strategy equilibrium σ_* of a two-player game, and let player i's date-t assessment be that $\mu_t^i = \sigma_*^{-i}$ so long as $\|\sigma_*^{-i} - d_t^{-i}\| < 1/n(t)$, with $\mu_t^i = d_t^{-i}$ if the inequality is violated. By the strong law of large numbers, the sequence $n(t)$ may be chosen to converge to infinity slowly enough that there is probability 1 that the above inequality is always satisfied so long as player $-i$ follows σ_*^{-i}. Then the assessments are asymptotically empirical (since $n(t) \to \infty$), and if both players use this assessment rule and play their part of the mixed strategy when indifferent, there is probability 1 that they play according to σ_* in every period.

3. Formally behavior rule ρ_t^i is asymptotically myopic with respect to an assessment rule γ_t^i if for some sequence of positive numbers $\varepsilon_t \to 0$, $u^i(\rho_t^i, \gamma_t^i) + \varepsilon_t \geq \max_{s^i} u^i(s^i, \gamma_t^i)$. Note that this definition is in terms of player i's expected utility, where the expectation is taken over any randomness in the play of any player. In particular, a strategy that incurs a large loss with a low probability regardless of the opponents' play is treated as having a small loss. Thus this definition of asymptotic myopia is less restrictive than one that requires that player i only assign positive probability to pure strategies that come close to maximizing his expected payoff. Moreover a strategy that is weakly dominated can still be a best response provided that the player's beliefs assign a sufficiently small probability (converging to 0) to opponents' strategies under which the dominated strategy incurs a loss.

The intuition for this is the same as for the corresponding result in chapter 2: If play converged to σ, players assessment would converge to σ as well, but then since σ is not a Nash equilibrium, some player would choose to deviate.

Conversely, Fudenberg and Kreps show that any Nash equilibrium is locally stochastically stable for some behavior rules that are asymptotically myopic with respect to asymptotically empirical assessments. However, the proof of this relies on the construction, sketched above, in which players start out with a strong prior belief in the particular equilibrium and maintain that belief unless they receive overwhelming evidence to the contrary. Consequently the stability result just cited does not do a great deal to lend credence to the idea that mixed distributions actually will arise as the result of learning.[4]

4.4 Randomly Perturbed Payoffs and Smoothed Best Responses

To develop a sensible model of learning to play mixed strategies, one should start with a sensible explanation for mixing in the equilibrium context. One such explanation is Harsanyi's (1973) purification theorem, which explains a mixed distribution over actions as the result of unobserved payoff perturbations that sometimes lead players to have a strict preference for one action, and sometimes a strict preference for another.[5] Fudenberg and Kreps (1993) develop a model of fictitious play along these lines. Before considering the application to fictitious play, it is useful to see how in the static case random preferences can provide a positive story of mixed-strategy equilibrium.

Ordinarily the payoff to player i to the strategy profile s would be $u^i(s)$. Now, however, we assume that the payoff to player i is $u^i(s) + \eta^i(s^i)$, where η^i is a random vector absolutely continuous with respect to Lesbesgue measure on a finite interval. This simplifies Harsanyi's general formulation in that the realized shock to player i's payoff depends on the action he chose but not on the actions of the other players. The basic

---

4. Fudenberg and Kreps (1993) provide a parallel, and no more satisfying, result showing that any Nash equilibrium is locally stochastically stable for behavior that is asymptotically myopic with respect to the exactly empirical assessment rule. Here the players choose to use precisely the equilibrium mixed strategy so long as their perceived loss from doing so is small.

5. See, for example, Fudenberg and Tirole (1991, ch. 6) or Myerson (1991) for a discussion of the Harsanyi purification theorem and an explanation of the sorts of payoff perturbations it uses.

assumption is that the random payoff shock η^i to each player is private information to that player. Consequently the game is a Bayesian game of incomplete information, where each player chooses a rule mapping his type to a strategy.

Since each player's type only influences his own payoff, the equilibria of this game can be described in terms of the marginal distributions σ^i over each player's strategies. For each distribution σ^{-i} over the actions of i's opponents, let player i's *best-response distribution* $\overline{BR}^i(\sigma^{-i})$ be given by $\overline{BR}^i(\sigma^{-i})(s^i) = \text{Prob}[\eta^i \text{ s.t. } s^i$ is a best response to $\sigma^{-i}]$. Since η^i is assumed to have a distribution that is absolutely continuous with respect to Lesbesgue measure, there is a unique best response for almost every type. Consequently, unlike the usual best-response correspondence, the best-response distribution is actually a function. More strongly, the absolute continuity assumption implies that the best-response distribution is a continuous function.[6] Looking ahead to the learning model, this means that if the player's assessment converges, his behavior will too, which is not the case with standard fictitious play.

The notion of a Nash equilibrium in games with randomly perturbed payoffs can now be defined in terms of the best-response distribution.

Definition 4.1   The profile σ is a *Nash distribution* if $\overline{BR}^i(\sigma^{-i}) = \sigma^i$ for all i.

This distribution may be very different from any Nash equilibria of the original game if the payoff perturbations are large. However, Harsanyi's purification theorem shows that for generic payoffs in the original strategic form, the Nash distributions of the perturbed game approach the Nash equilibria of the original game as the support of the payoff perturbations becomes concentrated about 0. Consequently, for small supports, we can identify a Nash distribution of the perturbed game with the corresponding, possibly mixed, equilibrium of the original game.

The key feature here is that the function $\overline{BR}^i$ is both continuous and close to the actual best-response function. For example, in the game of matching pennies, where player 1 wins if he matches his opponent the best-response correspondence BR^1 and the smooth counterpart $\overline{BR}^i$ are drawn in figure 4.1. Notice that generally even if the opposing player is playing a pure strategy, the smoothed best response $\overline{BR}^i$ will still be random, as illustrated in the figure.

---

6. This is lemma 7.2 in Fudenberg and Kreps (1993).

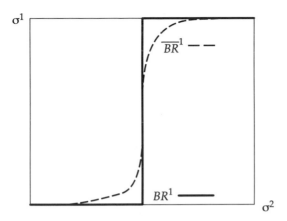

Figure 4.1
Best response and smoothed best response

At this point we can note that there are other reasons why players may use a smooth best-response function such as $\overline{BR}^i$. Here are two of them:

• Random behavior can prevent the player from being "manipulated" by a clever opponent. Thinking of the game of matching pennies, if a player plays a deterministic rule, no matter how complex, an opponent clever enough to deduce what the deterministic rule is can win all the time despite the fact that the player can win half the time (on average) using a simple 50-50 randomization. By explicitly randomizing when nearly indifferent, it is possible to prevent this type of manipulation. We will examine the performance of randomized rules in greater depth later in this chapter, and also in chapter 8.

• As mentioned in the discussion of the rote learning model in chapter 3, research in psychology on threshold perception shows that when asked to discriminate between two alternatives, behavior is random, becoming more reliable (i.e., deterministic) as the alternatives become more distinct. In choosing between two different strategies, one measure of the distinctness of the strategies is the difference in utility between the strategies. With this interpretation, Thurstone's (1927) law of comparative judgment becomes similar to the random utility model described above. Indeed, the picture of the smooth best-response curve drawn above is very similar to behavior curves that have been derived empirically in psychological experiments (including the fact that behavior remains slightly random even far from indifference). A good discussion of psychological models,

	A	B
A	2, 2	0, 0
B	0, 0	1, 1

Figure 4.2
A coordination game

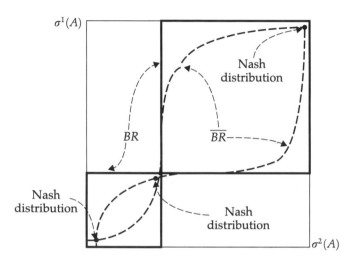

Figure 4.3
Best response and smoothed best response for figure 4.2

together with many references and some experimental results, can be found in Massaro and Friedman (1990).[7]

The connection between a Nash distribution and Nash equilibrium may perhaps be best seen in an example. Consider the coordination game in figure 4.2. The best responses and smooth best responses are shown in figure 4.3.

Five points deserve note here. First, there are three Nash distributions corresponding to the three Nash equilibria. Second, none of these three

---

7. Note, though, that the link between threshold perception and utility maximization is not immediate because strategies may be perceptibly different even if the utility difference is quite small: We would not expect subjects in a decision problem to randomize when faced with a clear choice between $9.99 and $10.00. On the other hand, there is evidence that some subject do play strictly dominated strategies in games, at least in the early rounds of experiments; we are uncertain how to explain this behavior. In any event, it seems that some choices between strategies yielding nearly the same utility are relatively ambiguous, while others are not.

distributions exactly coincides with the corresponding Nash equilibrium of the unperturbed game. The Nash distribution corresponding to the mixed equilibrium lies to the left of it and below, meaning that A is slightly less likely to be played than at the mixed equilibrium. Also the Nash distributions corresponding to the pure equilibria (A, A) (upper right corner) and (B, B) (lower left corner) both involve some randomization. This is typical: If the best responses involve randomization because, for example, some utility draws make A as a best response no matter what the other player does, then there cannot be any "pure" (i.e., degenerate) Nash distributions. The third point is that the Nash distribution corresponding to the mixed equilibrium lies to the left and below the actual mixed equilibrium, meaning that A is slightly less likely to be played than at the mixed equilibrium. If the utility shocks are symmetric around zero, this is necessarily the case for this payoff matrix. The reason is easy to see: At the mixed equilibrium players are indifferent between A and B. Symmetric utility shocks imply in this case that both players have an equal chance of playing A or B. In order to reduce the chance of playing A to approximately 1/3 as it is in the mixed equilibrium, the probabilities must be adjusted to lower the payoff from playing A. This will be the case only if the actual chance of playing A in the Nash distribution is smaller than 1/3.

Fourth, from Harsanyi's purification theorem we know that the distance between the Nash distributions of the perturbed game and the corresponding Nash equilibria of the original game goes to 0 with the magnitude of the payoff shocks. (Think of multiplying the original payoff shocks $\eta_i(s_i)$ by some positive ε and then sending that ε to 0.)

Finally, note that the above diagram would apply to any situation where the player's behavior is described by the smooth best-response distributions pictured, whether or not those distributions arose from unobserved payoff distributions. When these distributions are treated as exogenous and arbitrary functions, there is no obvious reason for their intersection to be called a "Nash distribution," but since doing so will not lead to ambiguity, we will use that name anyway.

Corresponding to the static notion of a Nash distribution is the dynamic variation on fictitious play in which, in place of best responses, players respond to an assessment γ_{t-1}^i with a smooth approximation $\overline{BR}^i(\gamma_{t-1}^i)$ to the best response. We refer to such a learning rule as *smooth fictitious play*.

4.5   Smooth Fictitious Play and Stochastic Approximation

As we just mentioned, the basic idea of smooth fictitious play is that instead of using the exact best-response map BR^i as in fictitious play, players take an independent draw from $\overline{BR}^i$ at each date. For a fixed and smooth function $\overline{BR}^i$, we denote the associated smooth fictitious play by $\overline{BR}^i(\gamma_t^i)$, where γ_t^i is a sequence of assessment rules of the kind used in standard fictitious play. One rationale for this type of smooth fictitious play is the random utility model in which players get an independent draw of η^i every period. A second rationale is that players might explicitly choose to randomize. We examine that explanation in section 4.7.

The first analysis of smooth fictitious play was done by Fudenberg and Kreps (1993), who showed that the Nash distribution corresponding to the mixed equilibrium is globally stable in 2×2 games with a unique equilibrium that is mixed, provided that the degree of smoothing is sufficiently small. This result shows that smooth fictitious play provides an explanation of how learning can lead agents' play *in each period* to correspond to a mixed-strategy equilibrium.[8]

To prove global convergence, Fudenberg and Kreps used the techniques of the theory of stochastic approximation. This is based on the idea that the long-run behavior of discrete-time time-averaging stochastic systems can be determined by analyzing a related deterministic system in continuous time. Benaim and Hirsch (1996b) and Kaniovski and Young (1995) use similar techniques to complete the study of smooth fictitious play in 2×2 games. Specifically, if the 2×2 game has a unique equilibrium that is strict, the unique intersection of smoothed best-response functions is a global attractor for smooth fictitious play. In games with two strict equilibria and one mixed equilibrium, with probability one the system converges to one of the strict equilibria, with the relative probabilities depending on the initial conditions.[9]

However, smooth fictitious play does not eliminate the possibility of cycling, even in games with a unique Nash equilibrium. Benaim and Hirsch (1996b) show that smooth fictitious play converges to a cycle in Jordan's (1993) three-player matching pennies game.

---

8. Their result is only for the random-utility version of smooth fictitious play, but it extends to other interpretations of the model.

9. Kaniovski and Young (1995) also show that these conclusions extend to the case where players forecast opponents' play by a randomly drawn finite-sized sample from the overall history of play, as in Young (1993).

Before giving a formal statement of the relevant theory of stochastic approximation, let us first develop a rough intuition. In the case of exact fictitious play, we saw in chapter 2 that along paths where there is infrequent switching, asymptotically the dynamics resemble those of the continuous-time best-response dynamics after a rescaling of the measure of time. While smooth fictitious play is random, the time average of many independent random variables has very little randomness, and as a result a similar result obtains: Asymptotically the dynamics resembles that of the continuous-time "near-best-response" dynamics[10]

$$\dot{\theta}^i = \overline{BR}^i(\theta) - \theta^i.$$

Consequently, if the stochastic system eventually converges to a point or a cycle, the point or cycle should be a closed orbit of the continuous-time dynamics. Moreover, if a point or cycle is an unstable orbit of the continuous time dynamics, then we might expect that the noise would eventually "kick" the system off of the corresponding "knife edge" so that the stochastic system can only converge to stable orbits of the continuous-time system.

In the case of 2×2 games, it is easy to see that the mixed equilibrium is unstable under the smooth best-response dynamics in games with two strict equilibria; it is only slightly more complicated to show that the mixed equilibrium is globally stable in this dynamic in games like matching pennies with a unique mixed-strategy equilibrium. This explains the basis of the results mentioned above.

Conditions that allow the asymptotic limit points of stochastic discrete-time systems to be inferred from the stability of the steady states of a corresponding deterministic system in continuous time have been developed by Kushner and Clark (1978), Ljung and Soderstrom (1983), Arthur, Ermol'ev, and Kaniovski (1983), Pemantle (1990), and Benaim and Hirsch (1996a), among others.

Benaim and Hirsch (1996a) also show that similar results can be obtained for convergence to closed orbits. We present the basic results without proof and show how to use them to characterize the behavior of smooth fictitious play in 2×2 games. The appendix illustrates the techniques involved by giving a proof of a very simple stochastic approximation result.

---

10. To be somewhat more precise, since the noise has a zero mean, its influence is through its variance, which is of order $1/t^2$, while the deterministic drift corresponding to BR^i is of order $1/t$.

Consider a discrete-time stochastic process defined on a compact set in $\Re^n$ by

$$\theta_{t+1} - \theta_t = \frac{F(\theta_t) + \eta_{t+1}}{t+1},$$

where the function F is smooth (C^2), and the η_t are noise terms satisfying $E[\eta_{t+1}|\theta_t, \ldots, \theta_1] = 0$.[11] In the applications to smooth fictitious play, the state space is the empirical distribution of play and the map F is $\overline{BR}(\theta) - \theta$. The noise terms are then the differences between the expected value of $\overline{BR}(\theta_t)$ and its realized value, so the noise terms have a conditional expectation of zero but are not in general i.i.d. or even exchangeable. The assumption that $\overline{BR}$ is C^2 is satisfied in the random utility case if the distribution of payoffs is absolutely continuous with respect to the appropriate Lesbesgue measure.[12]

The idea of this literature is to find conditions under which asymptotic limit points of the sample paths of the $\{\theta_t\}$ are the stable ω-limits of the continuous-time process

$$\dot{\theta} = F(\theta).$$

A first step is to show that almost surely the sample path lies in some invariant set of the continuous-time process.

Proposition 4.2 (Benaim and Hirsch 1996a)   With probability one, the ω-limit set of any realization of the discrete-time process is an invariant set of the continuous-time process; this set is compact, connected, and contains no proper subsets that are attractors for the continuous-time process.

With this result in hand, we can characterize the long-run behavior of smooth fictitious play in 2×2 games with a unique equilibrium in mixed strategies. If the smooth fictitious play arises from utility perturbations, and the distribution of the perturbations is absolutely continuous with respect to the appropriate Lebesgue measure, then the perturbed game has a unique Nash distribution.[13] Proposition 4.2 shows that smooth fictitious play converges to the Nash distribution in any game where the

---

11. Here the step size at date t is $1/t$, as in fictitious play with no initial weights; the extension to positive and unequal prior weights for different players is immediate but complicates the notation. The important thing is that the step sizes ω_t be a decreasing series of positive numbers satisfying $\sum_t \omega_t = +\infty, \sum_t (\omega_t)^2 < \infty$.
12. In the case of explicit randomization considered below, $\overline{BR}$ is C^2 if the v^i are C^3.
13. Fudenberg and Kreps (1993).

Nash distribution is a global attractor for the continuous-time dynamics. One way to show this latter fact is by constructing a strict Lyapunov function, and indeed Fudenberg and Kreps construct such a function in the course of providing a direct proof of global convergence.

Benaim and Hirsch (1996) use an alternative and shorter argument: They note first that since the continuous-time smooth best-response process has the form $\dot{\theta}_t^i = \overline{BR}^i(\theta_t^{-i}) - \theta_t^i$, all of the diagonal entries of its Jacobian are -1, so the process is volume contracting, and second that a volume-contracting process on $\Re^2$ cannot have a limit cycle and so must converge to a steady state.[14]

Returning to the general stochastic approximation case, the next order of business is to determine which of the ω-limit sets will be selected when there is more than one of them. Say that a steady state is *linearly unstable* if at least one of its associated eigenvalues has positive real part. The next result says that discrete-time system has probability 0 of converging to a steady state that is linearly unstable provided that there is a nonnegligible amount of noise in the evolution of every component of the state.

Proposition 4.3 (Pemantle 1990)[15]   Suppose that the distribution of the noise term η_t is such that for every unit vector e_i, $E(\max(0, e_i \circ \eta_t)) > c > 0$. Then, if θ^* is linearly unstable for the continuous time process, $P\{\lim_{t \to \infty} \theta_t = \theta^*\} = 0$.

This result is almost enough to show that Nash distributions approximating the mixed equilibrium will not occur in 2×2 games like battle of the sexes, with two strict equilibria and one mixed one, since in these game the mixed equilibria is unstable under the exact best-response correspondence. Of course large perturbations of the best-response correspondence can introduce interior Nash distributions that are stable, but we expect that this cannot occur when the smoothed best responses are sufficiently close to the original ones. Benaim and Hirsch show that this is indeed true for smooth fictitious play that arises from sufficiently small payoff perturbations.

To complete the analysis of these 2×2 games with three equilibria, we want to verify that the process will end up at a Nash distribution approximating one of the pure equilibria. That verification has three parts: first,

---

14. As we noted in the appendix to chapter 3, the closed orbit plus its interior must be invariant, which would contradict the flow being volume contracting.

15. There are many earlier and similar results; see the references cited at the beginning of this subsection.

as noted above, smooth fictitious play must converge to a steady state in 2×2 games. Second, if the payoff perturbations are small, then there are asymptotically stable Nash distributions in the neighborhood of each pure equilibrium, and these are the only asymptotically stable steady states. Finally, every asymptotically stable steady state has positive probability of being the long-run outcome, again provided that there is "enough noise" in the system. This is a fairly general observation and not limited to smooth fictitious play, but to keep things simple, we will state the version that applies to fictitious play.

Proposition 4.4 (Benaim and Hirsch 1996b) Consider a two-player smooth fictitious play in which every strategy profile has positive probability at any state θ. If θ^* is an asymptotically stable equilibrium of the continuous-time process, then regardless of the initial conditions $P[\theta_t \rightarrow \theta_*] > 0$.

4.6 Partial Sampling

Fictitious play requires players to track the entire past history. A variant on fictitious play has them randomly sample independently (of one another) from their "recollection" of past observations. There are two models, depending on whether players' recollections go back to the beginning of the game or only a finite length of time.

The model where observations are draw from the entire past is very much like a smooth fictitious play; it has been studied by Kaniovski and Young (1995). Here every past period has an equal probability of being sampled. Since all past observations get equal weight, the effect of each successive period on subsequent play diminishes at rate $1/t$, just as in fictitious play, and once again the long-run behavior of the system can be determined by stochastic approximation techniques, as noted above. Moreover the limit is exactly the same type of smooth near-best-response dynamic discussed above.

When players not only sample randomly but also have finite memory, a situation examined by Canning (1991) and Young (1993), the result is different, since even at large dates t there is only a fixed amount of data available, so each period's observation has a nonnegligible impact on the state. This means that the effects of the noise terms need not vanish asymptotically and that the system does not tend to a continuous-time system in the limit. In these papers each player plays an exact best response to a randomly chosen sample of k observations drawn without replacement from the outcomes in the $m \geq k$ previous periods. In the case $m - k$, we can interpret the bounded memory as the result of players leaving the game and being replaced; $k < m$ corresponds to a situation where each period new individuals replace the old ones, and the new ones conduct a random poll of recent players.

With this dynamic, strict Nash equilibria are absorbing in the following sense: If a strict equilibrium s^* is played for m periods in a row, it is played forever afterward, since the only outcome anyone can remember is s^*. Moreover play cannot converge to a non-Nash equilibrium.

Young (1993) considers the class of *weakly acyclic games*. This means that beginning at any pure-strategy profile, the alternating-move or Cournot best-response dynamic (considering pure best responses only) converges in a finite number of steps L to a strict Nash equilibrium. Young shows that if the sample size k is less than or equal to $m/(L + 2)$, and the draws are without replacement, then in this class of games the dynamics converge almost surely to a strict equilibrium. The method of proof has little to do with stochastic approximation and instead uses the sort of Markov chain methods discussed in the next chapter.

Rather than give a proof, we will use an example from Young's paper shown in figure 4.4 to illustrate this result. If the initial weights in the assessment are (1, 1) for both players, then fictitious play cycles between the outcomes (A, A) and (B, B) as in the Fudenberg-Kreps example we examined above.

In this example the path length $L = 1$, so Young's result shows that if $k \leq m/3$, play eventually stops cycling and is absorbed at one of the strict equilibria. For simplicity, suppose that $k = 1$ and $m = 3$. Then at any date t there is probability 1/81 that both players sample the date-t outcomes at dates $t + 1$ and $t + 2$. This implies that every time that play at any date t is either (A, B) or (B, A), there is probability 1/81 that play remains at that profile at all subsequent dates. Thus to prove that there is probability 1 that play converges to a Nash equilibrium, it suffices to show that there will almost surely be infinitely many periods in which either (A, B) or (B, A) is played. But no path can have a run of three or more occurrences

	A	B
A	0, 0	1, $\sqrt{2}$
B	$\sqrt{2}$, 1	0, 0

Figure 4.4
Young's example

of (A, A) or of three or more occurrences of (B, B), and at any date t where both (A, A) and (B, B) have been played in the last three periods, there is a nonnegligible probability that one player will sample (A, A) and the other will sample (B, B), so there is a nonnegligible probability that the outcome in period $t + 1$ will be (A, B).

This example is special in that the length L of the Cournot adjustment process is 1; in the general case Young shows that each step of the Cournot path has positive probability at every date. As in the example, the intuition is that the noise in the sampling breaks up the "miscoordination" in the cycles. Of course all of this relies on the restriction to weakly acyclic games, so the best-response process itself does not cycle.

Hurkens (1994) and Sanchirico (1996) use closely related models[16] to study convergence to CURB (closed under best reply) sets in general games. (CURB sets are sets of strategies E^i for each player such that for each player i, every best response to probability distributions on $E^{-i} \equiv \times_{j \neq i} E^j$ is in E^i.) As in Young's paper, agents in the systems studied by Hurkens and Sanchirico ignore all observations form the sufficiently distant past.[17] Thus, if every "recent" observation has belonged to a particular CURB set, the current period's play will lie in that CURB set as well; that is, CURB sets are absorbing. On its own this result is not very interesting, since the whole strategy space is always a CURB set, but it does help to give a hint of the behavior of these "partially stochastic" systems.

The more interesting result of both Hurkens and Sanchirico gives conditions for the system to be absorbed in a minimal CURB set, that is, one that has no strict subset that is also a CURB set. (Pure-strategy strict Nash equilibria are always singleton and hence minimal CURB sets[18]; in Young's weakly acyclic games these are the only minimal CURB sets.) This latter conclusion requires two additional assumptions. First of all, since an action might only be a best response if the opponents assign positive probability to all of their actions, the agents must have a long enough memory that the history can generate an assessment that has this

---

16. Hurkens considers the case where the players' samples from the recent history are drawn with replacement, while Young considers sampling without replacement. If k is large, this should not be an important difference. Sanchirico's model is similar but more general in many respects.

17. Sanchirico allows for positive but negligible weight even on observations from the distant past; the weight is required to decline to 0 sufficiently quickly.

18. With Nash equilibria that are not strict, it may be necessary to include non-Nash best responses to get a minimal CURB set: Recall that CURB requires all best responses to be included in the set.

full-support property. Second, as in Young's model, there must be a source of randomness. Sanchirico arranges both this and the "long enough memory" condition by requiring that there is a positive probability of the agent playing every strategy that is a best response to any distribution of opponents' play whose support is concentrated on strategies played in the last k periods, where k is the number of strategy profiles. An example of a rule with this property would be for each player first to construct an assessment over an opponent's play by sampling with replacement from the last k periods and then either to play a best response to that assessment or continue playing the strategy he used in the previous period.

4.7   Universal Consistency and Smooth Fictitious Play

In this section we argue that there is a another explanation for smooth fictitious play besides the random utility model, namely that players may choose to randomize even when not indifferent as a sort of protection from mistakes in their model of opponents' play. This randomization in a sense provides a "security level"; it is closely related to the use of randomized maximin strategies in the theory of two-player zero-sum games.

In our study of deterministic fictitious play, we saw that fictitious play was approximately consistent for histories that satisfy the infrequent switching condition but that in the Fudenberg-Kreps example in which infrequent switching was not satisfied, both players got considerably less than the amount they could have guaranteed themselves by randomizing 50-50 in every period. These observations lead to the two *desiderata* for a learning rule studied in Fudenberg and Levine (1995a). The first is *safety*, meaning that the player's realized average utility is almost surely at least his minmax payoff regardless of an opponent's play. The second is *universal consistency*, which requires, again regardless of their opponents' play, that players almost surely get at least as much utility as they could have gotten had they known the frequency but not the order of observations in advance. Since the utility of a best response to the actual frequency distribution must be at least the minmax payoff, it follows that universal consistency implies safety, so we focus on the latter criterion.

Definition 4.2   A rule ρ^i is ε-*universally consistent* if for any ρ^{-i}

$$\lim_{T \to \infty} \sup \max_{\sigma^i} u^i(\sigma^i, \gamma_t^i) - \frac{1}{T} \sum_t u^i(\rho_t^i(h_{t-1})) \le \varepsilon$$

almost surely under the distribution generated by (ρ^i, ρ^{-i}).

Notice that specifying universal consistency as an objective differs from the Bayesian approach of specifying prior beliefs about strategies used by opponents and playing a learning rule that is a best response to those beliefs. However, any Bayesian expects almost surely to be both safe and consistent. These criteria ask for the procedure to be safe and consistent against all alternatives and not only for those that are regarded a priori as having probability one.

It is obvious that no deterministic decision procedure can be safe or, by implication, universally consistent. In the game of matching pennies in which a win counts 1 and a loss -1, any deterministic decision rule can be perfectly defeated by an opponent who knows the rule, resulting in a payoff of -1 for sure. However, by randomizing with equal weights, the minmax payoff of 0 can be guaranteed almost surely. The issue is whether through an explicitly randomized fictitious play procedure, it is possible to (nearly) attain universal consistency.

The affirmative answer was originally given by Hannan (1957), and by Blackwell (1956a) who derived the result from his vector minmax theorem in Blackwell (1956b). A good exposition of these early results can be found in the appendix of Luce and Raiffa (1957). The result has been lost and rediscovered several times since then by many authors, including Banos (1968), Megiddo (1980), Auer et al. (1995), Foster and Vohra (1995), and Fudenberg and Levine (1995a). In the computer science literature the basic problem is referred to as the "on-line decision problem," and the result has many applications, including the problem of data compression. Our exposition is based on Fudenberg and Levine (1995b) who, using an argument from Foster and Vohra (1995), show that universal consistency can be accomplished by a smooth fictitious play procedure in which $\overline{BR}^i$ is derived from maximizing a function of the form $u^i(\sigma) + \lambda v^i(\sigma^i)$. Formally,

Proposition 4.5 Suppose that v^i is a smooth, strictly differentiably concave function satisfying the boundary condition that as σ^i approaches the boundary of the simplex the slope of v^i becomes infinite. Then for every $\varepsilon > 0$ there exists a λ such that the smooth fictitious play procedure is ε-universally consistent.

Before proving this result, it is important to note that the function v^i is assumed to be not just continuous but smooth and that it satisfies assumptions guaranteeing a unique $\overline{BR}^i$. Moreover the boundary condition implies strict interiority of the solution to the maximization problem so that every strategy is played with strictly positive probability regardless of the frequency of opponents' play.

It may also be useful to have an explicit example of a function that satisfies these assumptions. If we take $v^i(\sigma^i) = \sum_{s^i} -\sigma(s^i) \log \sigma^i(s^i)$, we can explicitly solve for $\overline{BR}^i$:

$$\overline{BR}^i(\sigma^{-i})[s^i] \equiv \frac{\exp((1/\lambda)u^i(s^i, \sigma^{-i}))}{\sum_{r^i} \exp((1/\lambda)u^i(r^i, \sigma^{-i}))}.$$

This is a special case referred to as logistic fictitious play, since each strategy is played in proportion to an exponential function of the utility it has historically yielded. Logistic fictitious play corresponds to the logit decision model that has been extensively used in empirical work. Notice that as $\lambda \to 0$ the probability that any strategy that is not a best response is played goes to zero. Note also that this function has the property of convex monotonicity which we discussed in chapter 3 . Finally, before proving the theorem, it is useful to define $\vec{u}^i(\sigma^{-i})$ to be the vector of utilities that accrue to different actions for player i when opposing players play σ^{-i}. Letting $\vec{u}^i_t = \vec{u}^i(\gamma^i_t)$, the objective function that $\overline{BR}^i$ maximizes may then be written as

$$u^i(\sigma) + \lambda v^i(\sigma^i) = \sigma^i \cdot \vec{u}^i_t + \lambda v^i(\sigma^i).$$

This is important because it makes clear that to implement a cautious fictitious play, a player need not base his decision on the historical frequencies γ^i_t but may base his decision solely on the historical utilities $\vec{u}^i_t$ that would have been achieved by different actions.[19]

Proof of Proposition 4.5 We set $V^i(\vec{u}^i_t) = \max_{\sigma^i} \sigma^i \cdot \vec{u}^i_t + \lambda v^i(\sigma^i)$ to be the maximized value of the objective function and denote realized utility by $u^i_t = \sum_{\tau \le t} u^i(s_\tau)$. We then define the cost to be the difference $c^i_t = tV^i(\vec{u}^i_t) - u^i_t$ between the utility that could have been received (according to the approximate function V^i) and the utility actually received. Notice that the loss $\max_{\sigma^i} \sigma^i \cdot \vec{u}^i_T - (1/T) \sum_{t=1}^T u^i(\overline{BR}(\vec{u}^i_t), \rho^{-i}_t(h_{t-1}))$ defining ε-universal consistency is just the expected value of $c^i_t/t - \lambda v^i(\overline{BR}^i(\vec{u}^i_t))$.

---

19. Suppose that instead of having the same utility function in each period, player i has a sequence of time-varying utility functions $u^i_t(s^i, s^{-i})$ that is uniformly bounded. Define $\vec{u}^i_t(s^i) = (1/t) \sum_{\tau=1}^t u^i_\tau(s^i, s^i_\tau)$, replace $u^i(\sigma^i, \gamma^i_t)$ in the definition of universal consistency with $\sigma^i \cdot \vec{u}^i_t$, and define smooth fictitious play as the solution to maximizing $\sigma^i \cdot \vec{u}^i_t + \lambda v^i(\sigma^i)$. Then proposition 4.5 still holds, and the proof requires only the obvious notational change of subscripting period-t utility. This nonstationary version of the proposition will be used in chapter 8 when we study the choice of experts.

Consequently, to demonstrate ε-universal consistency, we can show that for small λ the cost is small.

The increment added to the cost in period t if the period-t outcome is s is

$$g_t^i(s) = tV^i\left(\frac{(t-1)\bar{u}_{t-1}^i + \vec{u}^i(s^{-i})}{t}\right) - u^i(s) - (t-1)V^i(\bar{u}_{t-1}^i).$$

In other words, $c_t^i - c_{t-1}^i = g_t^i(s_t)$. The first step of the proof is to show that if, for all σ^{-i} and h_{t-1}, and all sufficiently large t, $g_t^i(\rho^i(h_{t-1}), \sigma^{-i}) \leq \varepsilon'$, then ρ' is $\varepsilon' + \lambda\|v^i\|$ universally consistent. This is shown by a relatively routine application of the strong law of large numbers: The idea is that the realized increment to the costs g_t^i are, given the history, independent random variables, so their average value must remain close to the average of the conditional expectations $g_t^i(\rho^i(h_{t-1}), \rho^{-i}(h_{t-1}))$. This then implies that the average value of the cost c_t^i is almost surely asymptotically bounded by ε'.

The second step of the proof is to show for any σ^{-i} that $g_t^i(\overline{BR}^i(\bar{u}_{t-1}^i), \sigma^{-i}) \leq \lambda\|v^i\| + \lambda^{-1}B/t$, where B is a constant that depends only on v^i. The first term in the right-hand side of this inequality is the error introduced because $\overline{BR}^i$ maximizes V^i instead of u^i; the second term is the approximation error from replacing the change in V^i with its first derivative times the change in player i's assessment, which is proportional to $1/t$. This upper bound yields the conclusion of the theorem: We choose λ so that $2\lambda\|v^i\| \leq \varepsilon/2$, and we observe that for sufficiently large t, $\lambda^{-1}B/t \leq \varepsilon/2$ as well.

We now derive this upper bound. Let $\hat{\sigma}_{t-1}^i = \overline{BR}(\bar{u}_{t-1}^i)$ be the mixed strategy that player i will choose at date t given assessment y_{t-1}^i. From the definition of g_t^i, we find that its value at date t when i's opponent plays an arbitrary σ^{-i} is

$$g_t^i(\hat{\sigma}_{t-1}^i, \sigma^{-i}) = \sum_{s^{-i}} tV^i\left(\frac{(t-1)\bar{u}_{t-1}^i + \vec{u}^i(s^{-i})}{t}\right)\sigma^{-i}(s^{-i})$$

$$- u^i(\hat{\sigma}_{t-1}^i, \sigma^{-i}) - (t-1)V^i(\bar{u}_{t-1}^i)$$

$$= \sum_{s^{-i}} t\left[V^i\left(\frac{(t-1)\bar{u}_{t-1}^i + \vec{u}^i(s^{-i})}{t}\right) - V^i(\bar{u}_{t-1}^i)\right]\sigma^{-i}(s^{-i})$$

$$- u^i(\hat{\sigma}_{t-1}^i, \sigma^{-i}) + V^i(\bar{u}_{t-1}^i).$$

The term in square brackets is the difference between the maximized payoff given the assessments at dates t and $t-1$, respectively. Since we constructed V^i to be smooth, with second derivative proportional to λ^{-1}, we can replace this discrete difference with its linear approximation and introduce an error of order no more than $\lambda^{-1}(1/l)^2$.[20] Using the envelope theorem to replace the derivative of V^i with realized utility at the optimum, and noting that the change in player i's assessment from $t-1$ to t is of order $1/t$, we find, for some B that depends only on v^i, that

$$g_t^i(\hat{\sigma}_{t-1}^i, \sigma^{-i}) \leq \sum_{s^{-i}} [\hat{\sigma}_{t-1}^i \cdot (\vec{u}^i(s^{-i}) - \vec{u}_{t-1}^i)] \sigma^{-i}(s^{-i})$$

$$- u^i(\hat{\sigma}_{t-1}^i, \sigma^{-i}) + V^i(\vec{u}_{t-1}^i) + \frac{\lambda^{-1}B}{t}$$

$$= -\hat{\sigma}_{t-1}^i \cdot \vec{u}_{t-1}^i + V^i(\vec{u}_{t-1}^i) + \frac{\lambda^{-1}B}{t},$$

where the second step follows from

$$u^i(\hat{\sigma}_{t-1}^i, \sigma^{-i}) = \hat{\sigma}_{t-1}^i \cdot \vec{u}^i(\sigma^{-i}) = \sum_{s^{-i}} \hat{\sigma}_{t-1}^i \cdot \vec{u}^i(s^{-i}) \sigma^{-i}(s^{-i}).$$

Moreover in the problem $\max_{\sigma^i} \sigma^i \cdot \vec{u}_{t-1}^i + \lambda v^i(\sigma^i)$, $\hat{\sigma}_{t-1}^i$ is the argmax and $V^i(\vec{u}_{t-1}^i)$ is the maximized value. It follows that

$$g_t^i(\hat{\sigma}_{t-1}^i, \sigma^i) \leq \lambda\|v^i\| + \frac{\lambda^{-1}B}{t}. \qquad \blacksquare$$

Notice that there is a tension here between the extent to which V^i approximates u^i and the extent to which it is smooth. The smaller is λ, the better the approximation V^i to u^i, and the smaller the approximation error $2\lambda\|v^i\|$ in the proof. However, smaller λ also increases the second derivative of V^i near point at which player i will switch strategies by a factor of λ^{-1}, increasing the loss due to "switching" $\lambda^{-1}B/t$. Consequently a smaller λ implies that player i will have to wait longer before "consistency" becomes relevant.

4.8   Stimulus-Response and Fictitious Play as Learning Models

Fictitious play or smooth fictitious play is one type of learning model, giving rise through stochastic approximation theory to dynamics that resemble the continuous-time best-response dynamic. One interesting

---

20. This is the only step of the proof that uses the fact that V^i is smooth. If $v^i \equiv 0$, the case of ordinary fictitious play, V^i is linear except at points where i switches from one strategy to another; consequently this derivation remains valid except at switch points, which is why ordinary fictitious play is consistent when the no-switching condition is satisfied.

class of alternative learning models is based on the idea of "stimulus-response" or "reinforcement" learning. We discussed one such model in chapter 3, the model of Borgers and Sarin (1995) and we saw that it converged to the same limit as the discrete-time replicator dynamic in the limit of smaller and smaller time periods. This section presents some related models that are intended to better match the way human agents are thought to behave, and it compares the models' descriptive performance with that of models in the spirit of fictitious play.

4.8.1 Stimulus-Response with Negative Reinforcement

Recall the basic Borgers-Sarin (1995) model: Agents at each date use a mixed strategy, and the state of the system at date t, denoted (θ_t^1, θ_t^2) is the vector of mixed actions played at time t by the two players. Payoffs are normalized to lie between zero and one so that they have the same scale as probabilities. The state evolves in the following way: If player i plays s_t^i at date t, and the resulting payoff is $\tilde{u}_t^i(s_t^i)$, then

$$\theta_{t+1}^i(s^i) = (1 - \gamma\tilde{u}_t^i(s_t^i))\theta_t^i(s^i) + E(s_t^i, s^i)\gamma\tilde{u}_t^i(s_t^i),$$

$$E(s_t^i, s_t^i) = 1,$$

$$E(s_t^i, s^i) = 0, \qquad s^i \neq s_t^i.$$

A striking and seemingly unrealistic aspect of this model is that if an action is played, it is more likely to be used again in the future than if it had not been played, even if the action resulted in the lowest possible payoff.

In response, Borgers and Sarin (1996) consider a more general stimulus-response model in which reinforcements can be either positive or negative, depending on whether the realized payoff is greater or less than the agent's "aspiration level." Formally the agent's *aspiration* level in period t is denoted ρ_t^i, and we set $r_t^i(s^i) = \tilde{u}_t^i(s^i) - \rho_t^i$ to be the difference between realized utility in period t and the aspiration level. Restricting attention to the case of two actions, the system evolves according to

$$\theta_{t+1}^i(s^i) = (1 - |r_t^i(s^i)|)\,\theta_t^i(s^i) + E(s_t^i, s^i)\max(r_t^i(s^i), 0)$$
$$- (1 - E(s_t^i, s^i))\min(r_t^i(s^i), 0),$$

where, as above, $E(s_t^i, s^i)$ is the indicator function, that is, 1 if $s_t^i = s^i$. Thus, when the agent is "pleased" with the outcome $(r_t^i(s^i) > 0)$, the probability of the corresponding action is increased, while the probability is decreased when the agent is "dissatisfied."

Note that this model reduces to the previous one (with $\gamma = 1$) in the case $\rho_t^i \equiv 0$. Much of Borgers-Sarin (1996) concerns the implications of the way that the aspiration level might vary with the agent's observations, but the simple case of a constant but nonzero aspiration level is very interesting. Obviously, if the aspiration level is greater than 1 so that all outcomes are disappointing, then the agent can never lock on to a pure action. Less obviously, if there are only two strategies H and T, all payoff realizations are either 0 or 1, the probability that H yields 1 is p, the probability that T yields 1 is $1 - p$ (as if the agent is playing against an i.i.d. strategy in the game matching pennies), and the aspiration level is constant at $1/2$, then $\theta_t^i(s^i)$ converges to p.

This strategy of randomizing with probability equal to the probability of success is known as "probability matching." Although such a strategy is not optimal, at one time psychologists believed it was characteristic of human behavior However, subsequent research has shown that behavior moves away from probability matching in the direction of optimality if subjects are given enough repetitions of the choice (Edwards 1961) or offered monetary rewards[21] (Siegel and Goldstein 1959) and so the claim that probability matching is prevalent has in our view been discredited. (See the review of this literature in Lee 1971.) Thus the inability to lock on to the optimal strategy for constant intermediate aspiration levels, even with an arbitrarily long horizon, is a drawback of the stimulus-response model.

Er'ev and Roth (1996) develop a closely related variation on the stimulus-response model and use it to study experimental data. The equation of motion they study is

$$\theta_{t+1}^i(s) = \frac{\max\{v, (1 - \gamma)\theta_t^i(s) + E[s^t, s]r_t^i(s^i)\}}{\sum_{s'} \max\{v, (1 - \gamma)\theta_t^i(s') + E[s^t, s']r_t^i(s^i)\}}.$$

They assume that the aspiration level follows the dynamic equation

$$\rho_{t+1}^i = \begin{cases} (1 - w^+)\rho_t^i + w^+\tilde{u}_t^i(s^t) & \text{if } \tilde{u}_t^i > \rho_t^i \\ (1 - w^-)\rho_t^i + w^-\tilde{u}_t^i(s^t) & \text{if } \tilde{u}_t^i \leqslant \rho_t^i \end{cases}$$

This specification is designed to move the system away from probability

---

21. The use of monetary rewards is much less common in psychology experiments than in those run by economists.

matching in the long run; the parameter v is designed to keep the probability of strategies bounded away from zero. If we set $v = 0$, this reduces to

$$\theta_{t+1}^i(s) = \frac{(1-\gamma)\theta_t^i(s) + E[s^t, s]r_t^i(s^i)}{\sum_{s'}(1-\gamma)\theta_t^i(s') + E[s^t, s']r_t^i(s^i)}$$

which like the Borgers-Sarin (1996) model increases the probability of an action when it is positively reinforced and decreases the probability when it is negatively reinforced.

4.8.2   Experimental Evidence

The stimulus-response model was developed largely in response to observations by psychologists about human behavior and animal behavior. One such observation is the randomness and the smoothness of responses; this is of course also true of smooth fictitious play. There is not a great deal of evidence that enables us to distinguish between the two types of models on empirical grounds: Er'ev and Roth (1996) argue that their variation on the stimulus-response model fits the data better than a simple fictitious play. In our view this is largely because they have many free parameters, and most learning models with enough flexibility in functional form are going to fit these data relatively well because of its high degree of autocorrelation. Er'ev and Roth do show that their model does considerably better than either the best-response dynamic or fictitious play in the two experiments in which they examined individual play. However, the very naïve model of "always at the mixed Nash equilibrium" does marginally better than the Er'ev-Roth model in one experiment, and marginally worse in the other, which suggests that any learning model that converges to Nash equilibrium relatively quickly will do about as well as their model does.

Er'ev and Roth's work does, however, point out an important difficulty with the standard fictitious play model. When agents use the exact best-response function, the model predicts a deterministic course of play with abrupt switching from one action to another. This counterfactual prediction is not, however, shared by smooth fictitious play. In addition the version of fictitious play studied by Er'ev and Roth has zero prior weights and so implies that the players will be very responsive to their first few observations, while actual behavior is known to be more "sluggish" than that. The type of exponential weighting of past observations discussed above also seems likely to improve the extent to which fictitious playlike models fit the data while not increasing the number of parameters beyond those used by the Er'ev and Roth model. Cheung and Friedman (1994) have had some success in fitting modified fictitious play models to experimental data, and they report that it does better than stimulus-response type models. It is true that Majure (1994) finds that replicator dynamics fit better than fictitious play, but he uses a less satisfactory method of introducing randomness and does not consider exponentially decreasing weights on past observations.

Finally Van Huyck, Battalio, and Rankin (1996) explicitly consider logistic fictitious play as a learning model and compare it to the replicator and other stimulus-response models. They report on an experimental study based on a simple 2 × 2 coordination game in which players receive nothing if they choose the same action and receive a unit payoff if they choose opposite actions. Four experimental designs are considered: There can be either a single population (i.e., the homogenous-population case) or two of them, and players may or may not have access to a publicly observed coordinating device, namely an assignment of the labels "player 1" and "player 2." In the two-population case, these labels are chosen once and for all at the start of the experiment; in the one-population case, labels are randomly assigned each period.

Without the labels, the situation corresponds to the simple 2 × 2 game shown in figure 4.5. As we discussed in chapter 3, the mixed-strategy Nash equilibrium (1/2, 1/2) is globally stable under the replicator dynamic in the homogeneous population treatment of game 1, while with asymmetric populations it is unstable. With one population and labels, the two stable points of the replicator dynamic are the efficient equilibria "A if labeled 1 and B if labeled 2" and "B if labeled 1 and A if labeled 2;" while the inefficient equilibrium where players ignore their labels is not stable.

In the experiments, the subjects played between 30 and 75 times. The replicator dynamic explains the basic qualitative features of the data, but in cases in which the symmetric equilibrium is unstable due to labeling, play often remained near the symmetric equilibrium much more than is

	A	B
A	0, 0	1, 1
B	1, 1	0, 0

Figure 4.5
Simple coordination game

predicted by the replicator. (This raises the question of what would have happened over a somewhat longer horizon.)

Van Huyck, Battalio, and Rankin examine several models of individual learning behavior. They report that they can reject the hypothesis that players are using historical performance of strategies (as they would in stimulus-response type models) in favor of the hypothesis that they are using forecast performance of strategies (as they would in smooth fictitious playlike models). Indeed, in their data the model of logistic fictitious play fits the data quite well in all but one of twelve sessions.[22]

4.8.3   Learning Effectiveness

Given the difficulty in distinguishing different learning models from experimental data, and given our prior belief that people are often reasonably good at the sort of learning that is at issue in this book, we think it makes sense to ask which learning models do a reasonably good job of learning.[23] For example, in the case of smooth fictitious play, we showed that regardless of opponents' strategies, players do about as well in the time average sense as if they had known the frequencies of opponents play in advance.

The stimulus-response model also is known to have some desirable properties as a learning model. The equations

$$\theta^i_{t+1}(s^i) = (1 - \gamma \tilde{u}^i_t(s^i_t))\theta^i_t(s^i) + E(s^i_t, s^i)\gamma \tilde{u}^i_t(s^i_t),$$

$$E(s^i_t, s^i_t) = 1,$$

$$E(s^i_t, s^i) = 0, \qquad s^i \neq s^i_t,$$

of the simplest version of the positive reinforcement model studied by Borgers-Sarin correspond to what is called a *learning automaton* in the computer science literature. Narendra and Thatcher (1974) showed that against an i.i.d. opponent, as the reinforcement parameter γ goes to zero, the time average utility converges to the maximum that could be obtained against the distribution of opponents' play. However, this rela-

---

22. In the anomalous session two populations with labels played each other. In a smooth fictitious play, if there is little smoothing (so that play is nearly like ordinary fictitious play), then when the system converges it should converge (approximately to) a Nash equilibrium. In this particular trial, there is little randomness observed in play, yet convergence is to a point some distance away from the Nash equilibrium. We suspect that the poor fit results from the fact that the lack of randomness in observed play is not consistent with convergence to a point some distance from any Nash equilibrium.
23. We realize that this belief is controversial among experimentalists.

tively weak property is satisfied by many learning rules that are not universally consistent, including "pure" fictitious play, and on its own, it does not seem strong enough to indicate that a rule is reasonable. By contrast, smooth fictitious play retains its consistency property regardless of how opponents play.

Indeed, while the "learning automaton" does well in the long run against an i.i.d. opponent, it may do very poorly even if in the long run opponents are approximately i.i.d., as would be the case if the system is converging to an equilibrium. The reason for this is that against an i.i.d. opponent the "learning automaton" eventually gets absorbed by a pure strategy. Consequently, if the distribution of opponent's play is for a long time very different from what it will be asymptotically, the system may be absorbed at the "wrong" pure strategy before the opponent's play shifts to its long-run frequency; the probability of this depends on the reinforcement parameter and the length of time before the opponent's play shifts.

To avoid the prediction that play eventually locks onto a pure strategy, the stimulus-response model can be modified so that the probability of each action remains bounded away from zero, as in Er'ev and Roth (1996). In this case Friedman and Shenker (1995) show that if the opponents' play is such that eventually one strategy remains optimal for all time, then the "responsive learning automaton" will in the long run converge to playing the correct strategy with high probability. This covers the case of a system that is converging to equilibrium but still falls considerably short of universal consistency.

4.8.4 Fictitious Play as a Stimulus-Response Model

One important property of the stimulus-response model is that it only uses information about the learner's realized payoffs in making choices. This may be regarded as a disadvantage or advantage: On the one hand, unlike fictitious play, opponent's play need not actually be observed. On the other hand, if this information is available (as it typically is in experimental settings), it ought not to be ignored.

It should be noted that there is a variation on smooth fictitious play that does use only own payoff information. Consider, in particular, the logistic fictitious play

$$\overline{BR}^i(\sigma^{-i})[s^i] \equiv \frac{\exp((1/\lambda)u^i(s^i, \sigma^{-i}))}{\sum_{r^i} \exp((1/\lambda)u^i(r^i, \sigma^{-i}))}.$$

Notice that to compute the probability of playing a strategy, it is necessary only to have an estimate of the utility of each action $u^i(r^i, \sigma^{-i})$. Indeed, we can view these utilities as "propensities" to play strategies, much as in the stimulus response model except that these propensities are computed and used in a different way. This suggests that players keep track of the historic utility of each action; that is, they compute an estimate

$$\bar{u}_t^i(s^i) = \frac{1}{\kappa_{t-1}(s^i)} E(s_t^i, s^i)[\tilde{u}_t^i(s^i) - \bar{u}_{t-1}^i] + \bar{u}_{t-1}^i,$$

where $\kappa_t(s^i)$ is the number of times player i has played s^i up to time t. We then set the probabilities of playing strategies to

$$\theta_t^i[s^i] \equiv \frac{\exp((1/\lambda)\bar{u}_t^i(s^i))}{\sum_{r^i} \exp((1/\lambda)\bar{u}_t^i(r^i))}.$$

If opponents' play is not converging, this variation on logistic fictitious play is not asymptotically the same as fictitious play. This is because strategies with low probabilities are updated less frequently than those with high probabilities, while in actual logistic fictitious play both are updated equally frequently (since data on opponents' play are used). However, if we use the alternative weighting rule

$$\bar{u}_t^i(s^i) = \frac{1}{\theta_t^i(s^i)\kappa_{t-1}(s^i)} E(s_t^i, s^i)[\tilde{u}_t^i(s^i) - \bar{u}_{t-1}^i] + \bar{u}_{t-1}^i,$$

then in a large sample, this behavior rule gives essentially the same result as ordinary logistic fictitious play, so it is also universally consistent. Notice that this rule can be interpreted as a kind of stimulus-response model: Here an action receives positive reinforcement if it does better than expected, and negative reinforcement if it does worse than expected, where the "aspiration level" is simply average utility to date. By making the probabilities a simple function of the "aspiration level," this rule avoids the need to directly combine probabilities and utilities as in traditional stimulus-response models. This "logistic fictitious play" rule strikes us as being at least as intuitive as the way that aspiration levels have been introduced into traditional stimulus-response models.

4.9   Learning about Strategy Spaces

The examples we have considered all involve relatively small strategy spaces. However, in many practical applications, especially those involving repeated play (even in an experimental setting), the space of strategies can be quite large. Both the stimulus-response models and the aspiration level variation on smooth fictitious play we just discussed require a player to track the actual or potential performance of every strategy. This is impractical when the strategy spaces are very large, even in a one-person game, so it is natural to ask whether there are methods that involve tracking a smaller subset of strategies. An example of such a method is John Holland's (1975) *genetic algorithm*, a good discussion of which can be found in Goldberg (1989).

A genetic algorithm is somewhat similar to a stimulus-response method, or the aspiration level variation of smooth fictitious play. There are two significant differences. First, only the performance of a small subset of strategies is tracked at any given moment of time, with randomization between these strategies based on their relative performance. Second, there are two methods by which strategies are added to or removed from the subset of strategies actively under consideration. Both of these methods are based on coding strategies as binary strings; that is, each strategy in the strategy space is assigned a unique binary string to identify it. One method of introducing new strategies is through random mutation: Existing digits in existing strings are randomly changed to yield new strategies. Since this guarantees that eventually all strategies will be considered, appropriately calibrated it guarantees consistency in a stationary problem. A second method of introducing new strategies is through "crossover," which means randomly splitting two existing strings and mating the first half of one string with the second half of the other to create two new strings. The theoretical properties of this procedure are poorly understood; they depend in large part on the way the strategies are "coded," but it is known through practical application that for some methods of coding strategies, crossover results in rapid convergence in relatively difficult problems.

There are two problems with standard genetic algorithms as a model of learning in games. The first problem concerns the long-run performance of the algorithm. The issue here is that genetic algorithms use historical performance to rate strategies. This is unobjectionable if the decision environment corresponds to i.i.d. draws from a fixed distribution, and in such environments genetic algorithms do well. But each agent's decision problem will not be typically be stationary in the context of learning in games, so our analysis of smooth fictitious play suggests that better long-run performance (i.e., universal consistency) can be obtained by replacing the average payoffs of the strategies with a weighted average of past performance, with weights proportional to the inverse of the frequency with which strategies have been used. We are not aware of attempts to incorporate this sort of weighting into genetic algorithms, but it does not seem hard to do.

The second problem lies not with the algorithms in themselves but rather in how they have been used in economic models. These applications, which have primarily been in the context of macroeconomic price-clearing models, have tended to assume that an entire population of players jointly implements a genetic algorithm (as in Bullard and Duffy 1994), rather than each individual player implementing a genetic algorithm. This poses several problems of interpretation and motivation, particularly with respect to the information required for implementing the "crossover" strategies. However, recent work by Price (1997) shows that many of the stability results established in this literature continue to hold when individual players use genetic algorithms rather than entire populations.

Appendix: Stochastic Approximation Theory

In this appendix we illustrate the methods of stochastic approximation by examining when a given discrete-time system $\theta_{t+1} - \theta_t = (F(\theta_t) + \eta_{t+1})/(t+1)$ converges almost surely to a particular state θ^*. Sufficient conditions are obtained by the study of the continuous-time system $\dot{\theta} = F(\theta)$. One case where global convergence obtains is when F admits a "quasi-strict" Lyapunov function V. This is a function that is strictly decreasing along all nonstationary trajectories of F. If moreover the minimum of this Lyapunov function is an isolated steady state, then Benaim and Hirsch show that the system converges with probability one to that steady state.

To provide some intuition for the result, we give here a proof for the case of a one-dimensional state space $[-1, 1]$, with $F(0) = 0$, $\theta F(\theta) < 0$ for all $\theta \neq 0$. Note that the point 0 is globally stable in the continuous-time dynamics. Thus in this setting the general theorem linking the long-term behavior of the discrete-time and continuous-time systems reduces to the conclusion that the discrete-time system converges to 0 with probability 1. This conclusion is virtually immediate if we further specialize to $F(\theta) = -\theta$, for then we have

$$\theta_{t+1} - \theta_t = \frac{-\theta_t + \eta_t}{t+1},$$

or

$$(t + 1)\theta_{t+1} - t\theta_t = \frac{t + 1}{t + 1}(-\theta_t + \eta_t) + \theta_t = \eta_t.$$

Thus $\theta_{t+1} = \sum_{s=1}^{t} \eta_s/(t + 1)$, and the convergence result reduces to the strong law of large numbers.

For general functions F we can use the Lyapunov function $V(\theta) = \theta^2$ to show that the discrete-time system almost surely converges to 0. There are several ways of doing this.

Because the point $\theta = 0$ is a steady state in the continuous-time deterministic dynamics and the Lyapunov function V is positive and strictly decreasing at all other points, it is tempting to think that V should be a supermartingale in the stochastic dynamics. Consideration of the point $\theta = 0$ shows that this is not quite the case, since at this point $E[V(\theta_{t+1})|\theta_t] > V(\theta_t) = 0$. Nevertheless, this intuition is "essentially" correct in that outside of any fixed neighborhood of 0 we eventually have $E[V(\theta_{t+1})|\theta_t] < V(\theta_t)$ for t sufficiently large. Intuitively, the "deterministic drift" of the system tends to reduce V, but since V is convex, the stochastic jumps tend to increase it. However, the size of these jumps diminishes at rate $1/t$, so the drift term eventually dominates in any region where it is bounded away from zero. For example, in the special case where $F(\theta) = -\theta$ and the η_t are generated by a binomial distribution on $\{-1, 1\}$ with parameter $p = 1/2$, we can take $V(\theta) = \theta^2$ and find that

$$E[V(\theta_{t+1})|\theta_t] - V(\theta_t) = \frac{\left(\frac{t\theta_t + 1}{t + 1}\right)^2 + \left(\frac{t\theta_t - 1}{t + 1}\right)^2 - 2\theta_t^2}{2} = \frac{-(2t + 1)\theta_t^2 + 1}{(t + 1)^2},$$

which is negative outside of the interval $[-a, a]$ for all $t > (1/2a^2) - 1/2$. This can be used to show that $\{\theta_t\}$ cannot converge to a limit other than 0.

Instead of pursuing that line, we will offer a direct proof that V (and hence θ) converge to 0. Define $M(\theta_t) = E[V(\theta_{t+1}) - V(\theta_t)|\theta_t]$ to be the expected change in the Lyapunov function, which may be either positive or negative, and let $M^+(\theta_t) = \max\{M(\theta_t), 0\}$. Also define

$$V^*(\theta_t) = V(\theta_t) - \sum_{s=1}^{t-1} M^+(\theta_s)$$

so that

$$V^*(\theta_{t+1}) - V^*(\theta_t) = V(\theta_{t+1}) - V(\theta_t) - \max\{M(\theta_t), 0\}.$$

By construction, this is a supermartingale:

$$E(V^*(\theta_{t+1})|\theta_t) - V^*(\theta_t) = E(V(\theta_{t+1})|\theta_t) - V(\theta_t) - \max\{M(\theta_t), 0\}$$
$$= M(\theta_t) - \max\{M(\theta_t), 0\}$$
$$= \min\{0, M(\theta_t)\} \leq 0.$$

The next step is to check that the supermartingale V^* is bounded below so that we can conclude it converges almost surely. To do this, substitute $V(\theta) = \theta^2$, and compute

$$M(\theta_t) = E\left[\left(\frac{(t+1)\theta_t + F(\theta_t) + \eta_{t+1}}{t+1}\right)^2 - \theta_t^2 | \theta_t\right]$$
$$= \frac{2\theta_t F(\theta_t)}{t+1} + \frac{F(\theta_t)^2 + E\eta_{t+1}^2}{(t+1)^2}$$

so that

$$M^+(\theta_t) \leq \frac{F(\theta_t)^2 + E\eta_{t+1}^2}{(t+1)^2}.$$

In the right-hand side of the equation for M, the first term, which corresponds to the deterministic drift of the system, is nonpositive by assumption, and the second has a finite sum, so M is summable. M^+ has only this second term and hence is summable as well, and since V is bounded below (by 0), this implies that V^* is bounded below as well.

Thus V^* is a supermartingale and is bounded below, so it converges almost surely. Now $V - V^*$ is a submartingale, and it is bounded above, since V is bounded above and V^* is bounded below. So by the submartingale convergence theorem $V - V^*$ converges almost surely. Since V^* also converges almost surely, it follows that V converges almost surely.

The last step in showing that V converges to 0 is to argue that there cannot be positive probability that it has a strictly positive limit. Intuitively, if the system remains nears such a point at a large date t, the "deterministic force" will dominate the noise term and push the system in toward 0. For a formal argument, suppose that there is positive probability of the event that V is bounded away from 0. This implies that θ is bounded away from zero as well, and hence for some $\varepsilon > 0$ that $\text{sgn}(\theta_t)F(\theta_t) < -\varepsilon < 0$, and so for some $\delta > 0$, $\text{sgn}(\theta_t)V'(\theta_t) < -\delta < 0$. Since V is smooth, we have

$$M(\theta_t) = E[V(\theta_{t+1}) - V(\theta_t)|\theta_t]$$

$$= E\left[V\left(\theta_t + \frac{F(\theta_t) + \eta_{t+1}}{(t+1)}\right) - V(\theta_t)|\theta_t\right]$$

$$= E\left[V'(\theta_t)\left(\frac{F(\theta_t) + \eta_{t+1}}{(t+1)}\right)\right] + o\left(\frac{1}{t^2}\right).$$

Since V' and F have opposite signs and are bounded away from 0 whenever V is, we can conclude that along any path where V is bounded away from 0,

$$M(\theta_t) < \frac{-\lambda}{t+1} < 0,$$

for sufficiently large t and some $\lambda > 0$.

Define $\bar{V}(\theta_t) = V(\theta_t) - \sum_{s=1}^{t-1} M(\theta_s)$. Note that $\bar{V}$ is a martingale and that on any path $\bar{V}(\theta_t) \geq V^*(\theta_t)$ for all t. Since V^* has a finite limit almost surely, $\bar{V}$ does not have positive probability of converging to $-\infty$. If V remains bounded away from zero, the fact that the upper bound above on M is negative and that V is bounded below (it is nonnegative) implies that $\bar{V}$ converges to $+\infty$. Thus, if V has positive probability of remaining bounded away from zero, we will have $\lim_{t\to\infty} E\bar{V}(\theta_t) = \infty$ which contradicts the fact that $\bar{V}$ is a martingale. Since we already established that V converges, the fact that it cannot remain bounded away from zero with positive probability implies that it converges to zero.   ∎

References

Arthur, B., Y. Ermol'ev, and Y. Kanioskii. 1983. A generalized urn problem and applications. *Cybernetica* 19: 61–71.

Auer, P., N. Cesa-Bianchi, Y. Freund, and R. Schapire. 1995. Gambling in a rigged casino: The adversarial multi-armed bandit problem. *36th Annual IEEE Symposium on Foundations of Computer Science*. New York: IEEE Computer Society Press.

Banos, A. 1968. On pseudo-games. *Annals of Mathematical Statistics* 39: 1932–45.

Benaim, M., and M. Hirsch. 1996a. Asymptotic pseudo-trajectories, chain-recurrent flows, and stochastic approximation. *Journal of Dynamics and Differential Equations* 8: 141–74.

Benaim, M., and M. Hirsch. 1996b. Learning processes, mixed equilibria and dynamical systems arising from repeated games. Mimeo. University of California at Berkeley.

Blackwell, D. 1956a. Controlled random walks. *Proceedings International Congress of Mathematicians 1954*, vol. 3. Amsterdam: North Holland, pp. 336–38.

Blackwell, D. 1956b. An analog of the minmax theorem for vector payoffs. *Pacific Journal of Mathematics*, 6: 1–8.

Borgers, T., and R. Sarin. 1995. Learning through reinforcement and replicator dynamics. Mimeo. University College London.

Borgers, T., and R. Sarin. 1996. Naïve reinforcement learning with endogenous aspirations. Mimeo. University College London.

Bullard, J., and J. Duffy. 1994. Using genetic algorithms to model the evolution of heterogenous beliefs. Mimeo. Federal Reserve Bank of St. Louis.

Canning, D. 1991. Social equilibrium. Mimeo. Cambridge University.

Cheung, Y., and D. Friedman. 1994. Learning in evolutionary games: Some laboratory results. Mimeo. University of California, Santa Cruz.

Edwards, W. 1961. Probability learning in 1000 trials. *Journal of Experimental Psychology* 62: 385–94.

Er'ev, I., and A. Roth. 1996. On the need for low rationality cognitive game theory: Reinforcement learning in experimental games with unique mixed strategy equilibria. Mimeo. University of Pittsburgh.

Foster, D., and R. Vohra. 1995. Asymptotic calibration. Mimeo. Wharton School.

Friedman, E., and S. Shenker. 1995. Synchronous and asynchronous learning by responsive learning automata. Mimeo. Duke University.

Fudenberg, D., and D. K. Levine. 1995a. Consistency and cautious fictitious play. *Journal of Economic Dynamics and Control* 19: 1065–90.

Fudenberg, D., and D. K. Levine 1995b. Conditional universal consistency. forthcoming, *Games and Economic Behavior*.

Fudenberg, D., and D. Kreps. 1993. Learning mixed equilibria. *Games and Economic Behavior* 5: 320–67.

Fudenberg, D., and J. Tirole. 1991. *Game Theory*. Cambridge: MIT Press.

Goldberg, D. E. 1989. *Genetic Algorithms in Search, Optimization and Machine Learning*, Reading, MA: Addison Wesley.

Hannan, J. 1957. Approximation to Bayes' risk in repeated plays. In *Contributions to the Theory of Games*, vol. 3, ed. by M. Dresher, A. W. Tucker, and P. Wolfe. Princeton: Princeton University Press, pp. 97–139.

Harsanyi, J. 1973. Games with randomly disturbed payoffs. *International Journal of Game Theory* 2: 1–23.

Holland, J. H. 1975. *Adaptation in Natural and Artificial Systems*. Ann Arbor: University of Michigan Press.

Hurkens, S. 1994. Learning by forgetful players: From primitive formations to persistent retracts. Tilberg Universtiy.

Jordan, J. 1993. Three problems in learning mixed-strategy equilibria. *Games and Economic Behavior* 5: 368–86.

Kaniovski, Y., and P. Young. 1995. Learning dynamics in games with stochastic perturbations. *Games and Economic Behavior* 11: 330–63.

Kushner, H. J., and D. Clark. 1978. *Stochastic Approximation Methods for Constrained and Unconstrained Systems.* New York: Springer.

Lee, W. 1971. *Decision Theory and Human Behavior.* New York: Wiley.

Ljung, L., and T. Söoderstrom. 1983. *Theory and Practice of Recursive Identification.* Cambridge: MIT Press.

Luce, R., and H. Raiffa. 1957. *Games and Decisions.* New York: Wiley.

Majure, W. 1994. Fitting learning and evolutionary models to experimental data. Mimeo. Harvard University.

Massaro, D., and D. Friedman. 1990. Models of integration given multiple sources of information. *Psychological Review* 97: 22–252.

Megiddo, N. 1980. On repeated games with incomplete information played with non-Bayesian Players. *International Journal of Game Theory* 9: 157–67.

Myerson, R. 1991. *Game Theory.* Cambridge: Harvard University Press.

Narendra, K., and M. Thatcher. 1974. Learning automata: A survey. *IEEE Transactions on Systems, Man and Cybernetics* 4: 889–99.

Pemantle, R. 1990. Non-convergence to unstable points in urn models and stochastic approximations. *Annals of Probability* 18: 698–712.

Price, T. C. 1997. Using co-evolutionary programming to simulate strategic behaviour in markets. Mimeo. Imperial College.

Sanchirico, C. 1996. A probabilistic model of learning in games. *Econometrica* 64: 1375–93.

Siegel, S., and D. A. Goldstein. 1959. Decision-making behavior in two-choice uncertain outcome situations. *Journal of Experimental Psychology* 57: 37–42.

Thurstone, L. 1927. Psychophysical analysis. *American Journal of Psychology* 28: 368–89.

Van Huck, J., R. Battalio, and F. Rankin. 1996. On the evolution of convention: Evidence from coordination games. Mimeo. Texas A&M University.

Young, P. 1993. The evolution of conventions. *Econometrica* 61: 57–83.

5   Adjustment Models with Persistent Randomness

5.1   Introduction

In the stochastic approximation processes discussed in the previous chapter, the adjustment in the agents' assessments in period t is of order $1/t$, so the effect of the random terms eventually vanishes, and the long-run behavior of the system corresponds to that of a deterministic system in continuous time. In such models the sorts of adjustment processes that make sense all have the property that strict equilibria are locally stable: If the state converges to a strict Nash equilibrium, it stays.there.[1] As with the equilibrium refinements literature, these models offer little guidance in predicting which of several strict equilibria is most likely to be observed.[2]

This chapter consider systems in which the step size and effects of random terms both remain constant over time so that the system is stochastic even in the limit. Recently Foster and Young (1990) suggested that such processes can be used to select between strict equilibria of a game. Foster and Young studied a continuous-time stochastic system based on the replicator dynamic; we discuss their model in section 5.9, along with the related papers of Cabrales (1993) and Fudenberg and Harris (1992). Most of this chapter, however, discusses the much larger literature on discrete-time, autonomous, finite-population "stochastic adjustment" models that follow the papers Kandori, Mailath, and Rob (1993) and Young (1993). In light of the use of the term "mutation" to motivate the study of the ESS concept and the asymptotic stability of the replicator

---

1. The foregoing rather loosely identifies Nash equilibria of a game with states of the dynamic process. A more precise formulation would be "the states in which the aggregate (over players) distribution of play corresponds to a strict equilibrium are locally stable steady states."

2. This is a slight exaggeration. One might believe that the likelihood of observing various equilibria is correlated with the relative sizes of their basins of attraction, but this implicitly supposes a more-or-less uniform prior over possible initial positions.

dynamics, it may be worth emphasizing that the classical evolutionary games literature considers only deterministic systems and that the "mutations" considered there are one-time events.[3] If one thinks of "mutations" as real and recurring, although unlikely, phenomena, it might seem more appropriate to include them explicitly in the model; this is the basic point of the stochastic adjustment literature.

The literature on these stochastic adjustment models is diverse and offers a variety of results on different types of games and adjustment procedures. However, there is one important result on 2×2 games that deserves emphasis, since it obtains in many (but not all)[4] such models: This is the selection of the risk-dominant equilibrium as the unique long-run steady state. Of particular importance is the connection (and lack of connection) of risk dominance to Pareto efficiency. In pure coordination games the two concepts are the same. However, in general games, risk-dominant equilibria may fail to be Pareto efficient. The conclusion from the study of stochastic adjustment models is that learning procedures tend to select equilibria that are relatively robust to mutations (risk-dominant equilibria), and this is a different criterion than Pareto efficiency.

5.2   Overview of Stochastic Adjustment Models

Before turning to the details of the individual papers, it is helpful to have in mind an outline of the sort of procedure the papers generally follow. This procedure, described just below, relies heavily on the idea of the ergodicity of a Markov process, so understanding just what ergodicity entails is crucial; for this reason the appendix provides a brief review of ergodicity in finite Markov chains.

The procedure has several steps:

Step 0. Specify a "state space." Typically this is either the number of agents of each player population using each action (as in a model of anonymous random matching) or the actions played by each individual agent. The latter case is relevant if different agents of the same player population can behave differently, as in models of local interaction where each agent only interacts with his "neighbors." The state may also include

---

3. Foster and Young (1990) and Fudenberg and Harris (1992) are exceptions that consider stochastic differential equations models of evolution.
4. For example, the work of Ely (1995) shows that when location is endogenous, there is a tendency toward Pareto efficiency. Binmore, Samuelson, and Vaughan (1994) also challenge this result, but they use an unusual form for the stage game that makes their results hard to compare with other work in the area.

information about the actions played in previous periods. For the time being, we will specialize to the case of a finite state space and discrete time, which is the simplest case mathematically and also the one that has received the most attention in the literature.[5]

Step 1. Specify an "intentional" or "unperturbed" adjustment dynamic, such as the best-response dynamic or the replicator dynamic. Often this process is deterministic, although the unperturbed model may incorporate randomness from the outcome of the random matching procedure or because each agent's opportunity to adjust its action arrives randomly. However, the process should be "deterministic enough" that the states corresponding to each of the strict Nash equilibrium are steady states. Typically the adjustment process also has the "converse" property that only Nash equilibria are steady states in one-shot, simultaneous-move games.[6] Finally, for the techniques described below, the unperturbed dynamic should be time independent, which rules out fictitious play.[7]

As in previous chapters, we will denote the state space by Θ; the Markov transition matrix of the intentional process will be denoted by P. Then, if θ, $\xi \in \Theta$, the element $P_{\theta\xi}$ of this matrix is the probability that the state is θ at date $t + 1$ conditional on the state being ξ at date t. With this convention, probability distributions over states are represented by column vectors φ and $\varphi_{t+1} = P\varphi_t$.[8]

Step 2. Introduce a "small noise" term; this might correspond to "mistakes," "mutations," or the replacement of old players by new ones. Parameterizing the amount of noise by ε gives us a new Markov operator P^ε on the same state space. P^ε should be a continuous function of ε, and P^ε should converge to P as $\varepsilon \to 0$; this condition is usually quite natural.

However, the stochastic approximation arguments do not hold for all continuous operators P^ε, since, for example, the "null" noise operator $P^\varepsilon = P$ is continuous in ε. What is important is that there be "enough" noise in the system. More precisely, the Markov system corresponding to P^ε should be ergodic. In particular, this means that it has a unique invariant distribution; that is, a unique distribution φ_ε^* such that $\varphi_\varepsilon^* = P^\varepsilon \varphi_\varepsilon^*$.

---

5. The approach described here has also been applied to continuous-time, continuous-state processes.
6. In chapter 7 we consider stochastic evolution when the extensive form is nontrivial.
7. The basic ideas could be transferred to fictitious play but require different analytical tools. In addition there are variants on fictitious play that are time independent.
8. This follows a standard convention in probability theory. Frequently this literature adopts the opposite convention that probability distributions over states are row vectors and that the transition probability matrix is the transpose of the matrix considered here.

	A	B
A	2, 2	0, 0
B	0, 0	1, 1

Figure 5.1
Symmetric coordination game

With a finite state space there are very simple sufficient conditions for this; some are discussed in the appendix to this chapter. One important condition is that $[P^\varepsilon]^n$ is strictly positive for some integer n. Often the mutation process is defined in such a way that the ergodicity of P^ε is obvious.

Step 3. Verify that $\lim_{\varepsilon \to 0} \varphi_\varepsilon^* \equiv \varphi^*$ exists, and determine what it is.[9] Since by definition $\varphi_\varepsilon^* = P^\varepsilon \varphi_\varepsilon^*$, and $P^\varepsilon \to P$, a standard continuity argument shows that $\varphi^* = P\varphi^*$; that is, φ^* is an invariant distribution for the unperturbed process P. Calculating φ^* is ordinarily the hardest step. As we will see, there are various ways of doing this that do not require the explicit calculation of the φ_ε^*.

Step 4. Check whether φ^* is a point mass. If it is, then the corresponding strategy profile is the "stochastically stable equilibrium" in the terminology of Foster and Young. This terminology makes sense when φ^* is a point mass, since the only point masses that are invariant distributions of the unperturbed process P are steady states, and we have supposed that only Nash equilibria are steady states of the unperturbed process. In other words, if φ^* is a point mass, it must correspond to a Nash equilibrium.[10]

Example 5.1 (Variant of Canning 1992) The deterministic unperturbed process corresponds to simultaneous-move Cournot adjustment: There are two populations, player 1's and player 2's, with one agent in each population; each period each player chooses a best response to the action his opponent played in the previous period. The stage game is the symmetric coordination game with payoffs shown in figure 5.1 so that (A, A) and (B, B) are both equilibria. The Markov matrix may be written as

---

9. Since the space of distributions over Θ is compact, we know that this sequence has at least one accumulation point. With arbitrary perturbed processes, the sequence may have several accumulation points, so the limit may not exist, but in general, the perturbed processes considered in the literature guarantee the existence of a limit.

10. However, if φ^* is not a point mass, it need not be a Nash equilibrium. For this reason Canning's (1992) use of the term "equilibrium distribution" to mean "invariant distribution" is unfortunate.

$$P = \begin{bmatrix} 1 & 0 & 0 & 0 \\ 0 & 0 & 1 & 0 \\ 0 & 1 & 0 & 0 \\ 0 & 0 & 0 & 1 \end{bmatrix} \begin{matrix} \text{States} \\ A, A \\ A, B \\ B, A \\ B, B \end{matrix}$$

and the only steady states are (A, A) and (B, B). However, $(0, 1/2, 1/2, 0)$ is an invariant distribution corresponding to the two-cycle between (A, B) and (B, A).

Now we add noise in the form of a minimum probability ε for each action. That is, when player 1, say, prefers to play A (because player 2 played A last period), player 1 must play B with probability at least ε. Likewise, when player 1 played B last period, there is probability ε that player 2 plays A so that $\text{pr}(BA|BA) = \varepsilon^2$, $\text{pr}(AA|BA) = (1 - \varepsilon)\varepsilon$, and so on. The perturbed system has the Markov matrix

$$P^\varepsilon = \begin{bmatrix} (1 - \varepsilon)^2 & (1 - \varepsilon)\varepsilon & (1 - \varepsilon)\varepsilon & \varepsilon^2 \\ (1 - \varepsilon)\varepsilon & \varepsilon^2 & (1 - \varepsilon)^2 & (1 - \varepsilon)\varepsilon \\ (1 - \varepsilon)\varepsilon & (1 - \varepsilon)^2 & \varepsilon^2 & (1 - \varepsilon)\varepsilon \\ \varepsilon^2 & (1 - \varepsilon)\varepsilon & (1 - \varepsilon)\varepsilon & (1 - \varepsilon)^2 \end{bmatrix}.$$

This system is ergodic, with (unique) invariant distribution $(1/4, 1/4, 1/4, 1/4)$. This is not an equilibrium and *not* a description of play in any period, although it does correspond to the asymptotic limit of the empirical joint distribution of strategy profiles. (That is, in the long run, each of the four strategy profiles will occur $1/4$ of the time.)

This example raises the question of when is it reasonable to hope that limit distribution is a point. Freidlin and Wentzell's (1984) basic insight is that the limit distribution is concentrated on a subset of the ω-limit sets of the deterministic process.[11] If the deterministic process has stable cycles, then there is no reason to expect that adding noise will take them away. For this reason the stochastic adjustment approach has been applied to classes of games where the deterministic dynamics have no stable cycles. The leading and simplest such class is a homogeneous population playing a symmetric 2×2 game with two strict equilibria.[12]

---

11. Recall from chapter 1 that the ω-limit sets of a dynamic process are the points that are reached infinitely often from at least one initial condition. In the deterministic finite-state case we consider here, the only ω-limits are steady states and cycles.

12. Asymmetric populations playing such games can cycle as in the persistent mis-coordination in the example illustrated in figure 2.3.

5.3   Kandori-Mailath-Rob Model

In Kandori-Mailath-Rob a single population of N players plays a symmetric 2×2 game. Denote the two actions by A and B. We will focus on the most interesting case, in which there are strict equilibria at (A, A) and (B, B), and a mixed equilibrium in which the probability of strategy A is α^*. We will assume that α^* is less than $1/2$ so that the best response to $(1/2A, 1/2B)$ is to play A; this means that the equilibrium at (A, A) is risk dominant.

Step 0. State space of the process. The state of the system θ_t at date t is the number of players using strategy A.

Let $u_A(\theta_t)$ and $u_B(\theta_t)$ denote the payoffs from playing strategies A and B, respectively, against the mixed strategy $(\theta_t/N, (N - \theta_t)/N)$ corresponding to a randomly drawn player from a population where θ_t players are playing strategy A.

Step 1. Deterministic process. Kandori-Mailath-Rob take $\theta_{t+1} = P(\theta_t)$, where the only condition on the adjustment dynamics is that $\mathrm{sgn}(P(\theta_t) - \theta_t) = \mathrm{sgn}(u_A(\theta_t) - u_B(\theta_t))$ at all states where not all agents are using the strategy with the highest current payoff. They call such a dynamic "Darwinian." In the two-action games they consider (but not more generally) Darwinian dynamics are "aggregate monotonic" in the sense of the Samuelson and Zhang paper discussed in chapter 4. Moreover, in symmetric two-action games with a single (i.e., homogeneous) population, the basins of attraction of the steady states under any Darwinian dynamic are completely determined by the best-response functions and so are independent of the particular Darwinian dynamic specified.

Kandori-Mailath-Rob suggest that the Darwinian adjustment process be thought of as arising from a model setting where each period some players observe the state of the system and choose the strategy that is the best response to the last period's state. There are two small points that might cause concern about this interpretation at first sight, but neither one turns out to matter:

a. Players include themselves in computing the play of a randomly drawn opponent. (If players only look at their opponents, then for a given θ_t the distribution of opponents' play depends on which strategy the player is currently using.) However, for reasonably large N this should not matter, and at the cost of a bit more notation, it is easy to extend the conclusions below to this more realistic case where agents do not count themselves in the sample.

b. The most obvious model that leads to the purely deterministic process considered here is the one where all players adjust each period. This yields the best-response dynamic

$$\theta_{t+1} = BR(\theta_t) = \begin{cases} N & u_A(\theta_t) > u_B(\theta_t), \\ \theta_t & \text{for } u_A(\theta_t) = u_B(\theta_t), \\ 0 & u_A(\theta_t) < u_B(\theta_t). \end{cases}$$

This is also the case where the results are easiest. However, it is not the case on which Kandori, Mailath, and Rob want us to focus: If all players adjust each period, it is not obvious why players should choose their actions to maximize payoffs given the previous period's state. Kandori, Mailath, and Rob note that the myopic response makes more sense if only a few players adjust each period so that the current state is more or less locked in for a while. Indeed, if only 1 player adjusts each period, and players are sufficiently impatient, then as in the alternating-move Cournot model, myopic response is optimal and indeed consistent with perfect-foresight equilibrium. On the other hand, if the one player who has the opportunity to adjust his play is chosen at random from the population, then the adjustment process will be stochastic: Whether the state changes depends on whether the player who gets to adjust is currently playing the best response. However, the analysis of the model will show that this does not matter, since only the speed of this modified process is stochastic and not its direction.

The more important interpretational issues are the same as in the alternating-move Cournot process, namely the requirement of myopic responses, which depend on a combination of impatience and lock-in that may not be plausible in the desired applications of the model. We also question the authors' view that the model describes an interesting process of learning: Since the players who adjust are perfectly informed of the current state, and this is all they care about, it is not clear what they might be learning about. At best this model must be viewed as a rough approximation to a model in which players are less perfectly informed. As should be clear, our preference is for models that have a stronger learning theoretic foundation.

In our opinion, myopic best responses can be best viewed as the limit, as the "memory" shrinks, of systems where players choose best responses to the empirical distribution of play over the last few periods. As we will see in discussing Young (1993), such bounded-memory systems can be analyzed with the techniques we discuss in this chapter. Since for reasonably long memories such systems do seem like learning systems, the distinction between fictitious playlike models and myopic ones is not hard and fast but rather turns on how long a memory length is reasonable. Moreover the stochastically stable set can depend on the memory length in some games; it does not do so in the 2×2 games considered by Kandori, Mailath, and Rob.

Step 2. Add noise; verify ergodicity. Suppose that each period, after players have computed their intended adjustments and before the game is actually played, each player "mutates" or is replaced with probability 2ε. Mutants are equally likely to initially adopt either strategy, after which they follow the deterministic adjustment process until they "mutate" again. Note that all players have a chance of mutating, and not just those who are "consciously adjusting" their play. For example, even if only one player adjusts at a time, there is a positive probability that the entire population mutates at once.

Ergodicity follows from the fact that every state has a positive probability of mutating into any other state. Note that if only some players adjust each period, and only these can mutate (so that mutations look like trembles), then the system is no longer strictly positive but is still ergodic. (See the appendix for sufficient conditions for ergodicity.)

Step 3. Computing the limiting distribution. Let N^* be the least integer greater than $N\alpha^*$; if $\theta_t \geq N^*$, the best response is to play action A. Recall that $\alpha^* < 1/2$.

Proposition 5.1 If N is large enough that $N^* < N/2$, then the limit φ^* of the invariant distributions is a point mass on the state $\theta_t = N$ corresponding to all agents using action A.

This result is easiest to prove for the case of the best-response dynamic, for then the long-run behavior of the system can be determined by analyzing a two-state process. (This was also noted by Canning 1992.) The key idea is that each steady state has a basin of attraction, and intentional play depends only on which of these two basins the state is in and not its location within the basin. The only way to move from one basin to the other is through simultaneous mutation by a number of players. Moreover, it takes more players to mutate to move from the basin of the risk-dominant equilibrium A to the basin of B than vice versa. As the probability of mutation ε gets small, the probability of M simultaneous mutations or more is of order ε^M. Since it takes fewer mutations to get from A to B than vice versa, this means that the odds of moving from A to B become infinitely greater than the odds of moving from B to A. This in turn means that the process must spend much more time in the A basin than the B basin and that the invariant distribution places far more weight on A than on B.

Proof of Proposition 5.1   Let $D_A = \{\theta_0 \geq N^*\}$ be the basin of attraction of state N (all agents use action A) under the deterministic process P, and let D_B be the basin of state 0 (all agents use action B). All states θ_0 in D_A have the same value of $BR(\theta_t)$ and hence lead to the same probability distribution over states next period. The same is true for all states in D_B. Hence, to compute the invariant distribution, it suffices to know the distribution over the two basins. This distribution in turn is determined by the relative probabilities of transitions from one basin to the other. We define $q_{BA} = prob(\theta_{t+1} \in D_B | \theta_t \in D_A)$ and $q_{AB} = prob(\theta_{t+1} \in D_A | \theta_t \in D_B)$. Then we solve

$$\begin{bmatrix} \varphi_1 \\ \varphi_2 \end{bmatrix} = \begin{bmatrix} 1 - q_{AB} & q_{AB} \\ q_{BA} & 1 - q_{BA} \end{bmatrix} \begin{bmatrix} \varphi_1 \\ \varphi_2 \end{bmatrix}$$

to find that $\varphi_2/\varphi_1 = q_{BA}/q_{AB}$.

The last step then is to compute the limit of this ratio as $\varepsilon \to 0$. If $\theta_t \in D_A$, the intended state is N. In order for θ_{t+1} to be in D_B, there will need to be at least $N - N^*$ mutations into strategy B. Since each of the N players has a chance of mutating, the probability of a transition with exactly $N - N^*$ transitions is, from the binomial formula, equal to

$$\binom{N}{N^*} \varepsilon^{N-N^*} (1 - \varepsilon)^{N^*}.$$

There can also be transitions with more than $N - N^*$ simultaneous mutations, but these will be much less likely as the probability ε of mutation goes to 0. For example transition with $N - N^* + 1$ mutations has probability that is of order $N - N^* + 1$ in ε.

In a similar way we can compute that any transition from D_B to D_A must involve at least N^* simultaneous mutations, and N^* simultaneous mutations have probability

$$\binom{N}{N^*} \varepsilon^{N^*} (1 - \varepsilon)^{N-N^*}.$$

Substituting into the equation for φ_2/φ_1, we conclude that

$$\frac{\varphi_2}{\varphi_1} = \frac{\varepsilon^{N-N^*}(1-\varepsilon)^{N^*} + O(\varepsilon^{N-N^*+1})}{\varepsilon^{N^*}(1-\varepsilon)^{N-N^*} + O(\varepsilon^{N^*+1})}$$

so that the ratio goes to 0 as ε goes to 0.   ∎

It is important to note that the same conclusion would follow if we supposed that mutants are more likely to choose action B than action A. That is, we could suppose that the probability of mutation is $\varepsilon_A + \varepsilon_B$, with $\varepsilon_B = k\varepsilon_A$ for any positive k; this would change the ergodic distribution for any fixed value of ε_A but would not alter the conclusion that the ergodic distribution converge to a point mass on "all A" in the limit as the mutation probability goes to 0. In order to change this conclusion, the ratio $\varepsilon_A/\varepsilon_B$ would need to go to 0 in the limit. If we do not restrict the ratio $\varepsilon_A/\varepsilon_B$ in the limit, and allow the mutation rates to depend more generally on the state, then as Bergin and Lipman (1996) show the limiting distribution may place any weights on the two Nash equilibria.

5.4   Discussion of Other Dynamics

The best-response dynamics are easy to analyze because it is transparent that only two states need to be considered to compute the invariant distribution. When the deterministic process P evolves more slowly, then computation of the invariant distribution for fixed $\varepsilon > 0$ requires inverting the $N+1 \times N+1$ matrix P^ε. This is harder in practice than in theory. Fortunately the insight of Freidlin and Wentzell (1984) shows that the two-state calculation is sufficient to compute the limit of the invariant distribution for any deterministic process whose only steady states are 0 and N.

As we remarked earlier, Freidlin and Wentzell's insight is that in the limit of very infrequent perturbations, the stochastic system will spend most of its time in the ω-limit sets of the deterministic process. Consequently it suffices to consider the much smaller Markov system whose states are the ω-limit sets of the original deterministic process. Intuitively, as the perturbations become rare, the time interval between perturbations becomes very long, so that after each shock the system moves near an ω-limit before the next shock arrives. In 2×2 games with two strict equilibria, the only steady states of any one-dimensional myopic adjustment process are 0 and N,[13] so the general case reduces to that of the best-response dynamic.[14]

Let us develop the general result, since it has proved useful in the more complicated systems arising from other games.[15] Consider a one-parameter family $P^\varepsilon \to P$ of ergodic Markov chains on a fixed state space. In order to determine the limit of the corresponding ergodic distributions φ^ε, we need to know the relative sizes of the transitions probabilities $P^\varepsilon_{\theta\xi}$ that are converging to 0. In the example studied above, the elements of P^ε that converge to zero have the form ε^c, where c is the number of mutations required to move from one state to another so that the number of mutations corresponds to the order (in ε) of the corresponding transition. We will generalize this by defining the cost of a transition to be its order in ε, so that probabilities proportional to ε have cost 1, probabilities proportional to ε^2 have cost 2, and so on. Formally, we define the *cost* $c(\theta|\xi)$ *of a transition* to state θ given state ξ as

$$c(\theta|\xi) \equiv \lim_{\varepsilon \to 0} \left(\frac{\log P^\varepsilon_{\theta\xi}}{\log \varepsilon} \right).$$

Our basic assumption is that this limit exists for every pair θ, ξ. Notice that since $\log \varepsilon$ is negative, the bigger the probability of transition, the smaller is the cost. Notice also that if the transition has positive probability in the limit system ($P_{\theta\xi} > 0$), then its cost $c(\theta|\xi)$ is 0.

We now consider moving from an ω-limit set $\omega \subseteq \Theta$ to another set $A \subseteq \Theta$, which need not be an ω-limit set. This move may take place in several steps, so we consider a path $\vec{\theta} = (\theta_0, \theta_1, \theta_2, \ldots, \theta_t)$ where $\theta_0 \in \omega$ and $\theta_t \in A$ and where consecutive states in the path are not required to be distinct. We look for paths that result in the highest probability of transition; this is the same as looking for paths with the least cost. (It does not matter which state in ω is used to begin the path, since every θ_0 is in the same limit set and transitions within a limit set have a cost of 0.) Since the probability of a path is the product of the transition probabilities, the cost

---

13. For simplicity it is supposed that there is no integer that exactly corresponds to the mixed equilibrium.

14. If there were an integer $z = \alpha^* N$, then there would also be a third steady state corresponding to the mixed equilibrium. It can be shown that this equilibrium would have zero weight under the limiting distribution, but most papers in the literature suppose that there is no such integer z for simplicity.

15. Freidlin and Wentzell developed the basic ideas in what follows. Young (1993), and Kandori, Mailath, and Rob (1993), and Kandori and Rob (1995) have developed further implications of these ideas in discrete-time, discrete-state systems.

of the path is the sum of the transition costs $\sum_{\tau=1}^{t} c(\theta_\tau | \theta_{\tau-1})$. This leads us to define

$$\vec{c}(A|\omega) \equiv \min_{\vec{\theta}: \theta_0 \in \omega, \theta_t \in A} \sum_{\tau=1}^{t} c(\theta_\tau | \theta_{\tau-1}).$$

Our goal is to analyze transition costs between ω-limit sets of the process P. Let Ω denote these ω-limit sets. The direct application of Freidlin and Wentzell's technique that we will now present requires that one first determine every member of Ω. Later we will discuss Ellison's less general sufficient condition for stochastic stability that makes do without this step.

Given a finite set Ω and an $\omega \in \Omega$, an ω-tree is a tree on the set Ω in the sense normally used in game theory[16] *except* that the direction of motion is the reverse of the usual one. So the paths start at many initial nodes and converge at a single "root" which is the unique terminal node of the tree that is the ω node in an ω-tree. Let H_ω denote the set of all ω-trees, and for any ω-tree h, let $h(\omega)$ denote the successor of ω, and let $D(\omega')$ denote the basin of ω' in the limit dynamic P. Note that $\vec{c}(D(h(\omega'))|\omega') = \vec{c}(h(\omega')|\omega')$ because the cost of transitions within a basin of attraction is 0.

The following result of Young (1993) draws heavily on work of Freidlin and Wentzell (1982), which we discuss in appendix B; we state Young's result in the text because it is the easiest to use in the applications we discuss in this chapter. Kandori, Mailath, and Rob (1993) do not state this result formally, but they use essentially the same argument in establishing their main theorem.

Proposition 5.2 (Young 1993) The limit φ^* of the invariant distributions φ_ε exists, and is concentrated on the limit sets ω that solve $\min_{\omega \in \Omega} \min_{h \in H_\omega} \sum_{\omega' \in \Omega/\omega} \vec{c}(D(h(\omega'))|\omega')$.[17]

---

16. That is, a directed graph that branches out. See, for example, Kreps (1990) or Fudenberg and Tirole (1991) for a formal definition.

17. The basis of this result is Freidlin and Wentzell's lemma 5.1 in appendix B, which gives an explicit formula for the ergodic distribution of the perturbed dynamics. This formula shows that the relative probabilities of any two states is a ratio of polynomials in the transition probabilities; Young observes that when these probabilities themselves are assumed to be polynomial in ε, the relative probabilities are also polynomial in ε so that the limit distribution exists. The formula given in the proposition follows from the observation that the states with positive probability under the limit distribution are those whose probability in the φ_ε^* is of the lowest order in ε. Kandori, Mailath, and Rob (1993) give an argument similar to that of Young.

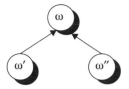

Figure 5.2
Simple three-node ω-tree

Note also that the formula sums over all paths for a given ω-tree as opposed to only counting the cheapest such path. For example, in the simple three-node ω-tree shown in figure 5.2 the formula sums $\tilde{c}(D(\omega)|\omega')$ and $\tilde{c}(D(\omega)|\omega'')$. Appendix B to this chapter gives some intuition for this summation and for proposition 5.2

In complex systems the cost in proposition 5.2 may be hard to compute, not least because the computation may require identification of every ω-limit set, but in simple examples it is not too hard. For example, in the Kandori-Mailath-Rob case above, the cost of moving from one state to another is just the number of mutations required to get there, so the cost of moving from one steady state to the basin of another is the minimum number of mutations required for the move.[18] Specifically, the limit set, $\Omega = \{0, N\}$, consists of the two steady states. The only 0 ω-tree is $N \to 0$, and $\tilde{c}(D(N)|0) = N - N^*$; the only N ω-tree is $0 \to N$ and $\tilde{c}(D(0)|N) = N^*$, so the problem is reduced to that of the best-response dynamic.

5.5   Local Interaction

In the Kandori-Mailath-Rob model, when the mutation rate is close to 0, although the states spends most of its time at the risk-dominant equilibrium, it is likely to stay at the other equilibrium for a long time if it begins near to it. Indeed, Ellison (1993) argues that for plausible payoff values, and $N = 50$ or 100 players, the system changes basins so infrequently that for practical purposes its behavior (for the first 10^5 to 10^{20} periods, depending on the size of the payoff differences) is determined by the initial condition.

---

18. We should mention that we write cost as we write transition probabilities, with the target state first and the state we condition on second. This is the standard convention in probability theory. Unfortunately, the existing literature in this area uses the opposite convention.

To explain why stochastic adjustment processes might select the risk-dominant equilibrium in an economically relevant time frame, Ellison (1993) develops an alternative model in which the players interact only with their neighbors. Here a few players playing the risk-dominant strategies can spread to the entire population quite rapidly, so the ergodic distribution may be a much more interesting description of actual play. Ellison uses this result to argue that "the nature of the matching process is crucial to ... whether historical factors or risk dominance will determine play."

In the Ellison model the N players are evenly spaced along a circle, and each player is matched against a randomly chosen opponent from his two nearest neighbors in a symmetric 2×2 game.[19] Each agent must select a single action to use against both opponents. As in Kandori-Mailath-Rob, players are perfectly informed of last period's state and hence of the last period's distribution of opponents' play. Players are assumed to choose their actions to maximize their expected payoff against this distribution, so the unperturbed dynamic is a "local" version of the best-response dynamic. As before, both "all A" and "all B" are steady states; the difference is in how these steady states respond to mutations. As in Kandori-Mailath-Rob, mutations are modeled as the replacement of a player with a newcomer who is equally likely to choose either action.

The key observation is that in the case of local interactions, the steady state "all B" can be upset by a small number of mutations. In this case it is easy to see that any cluster of two adjacent agents playing A will spread and eventually take over the entire population: Each of the two agents in the cluster assigns probability at least $1/2$ to his next opponent playing A and so sticks with A; moreover each of the two agents on the boundary of a cluster of A's assigns probability $1/2$ to his next opponent playing A and so switches from B to A. This means that random events that shift the process from the state "all B" to the basin of the state "all A" have an arrival rate of order ε^{-2} independent of the total population size N. In contrast, in the "uniform matching" model of Kandori, Mailath, and Rob, the arrival rate is $\varepsilon^{-\alpha^* N}$. This insight is not quite a proof, but it does suggest why the convergence speed will be much faster in the local interaction model.

Before discussing speeds of convergence, we should first check that as in Kandori-Mailath-Rob, the limit of the ergodic distribution as the

19. Ellison also considers the case of interactions with the $2K$ nearest neighbors. His strongest results in this case are in his 1995 paper.

mutation rate goes to zero is a point mass on "all A." We again apply the process outlined above.

Step 0. State space. Since the location of the agents matters, the state space here is the set $\Theta = \{A, B\}^N$ of N vectors whose components specify the actions of the individual agents.

Steps 1. Deterministic process. We begin by examining the deterministic system in order to compute the ω-limit sets of the intentional adjustment process and characterize their basins of attraction. Note that under the unperturbed dynamic, the number of players playing A can never decrease, for if j players play A at date t, all of their neighbors play A at $t + 1$. Moreover a cluster of two adjacent A's leads to "all A." Notice that in addition to the steady states "all A" and "all B," when N is even, there is one other ω-limit set, namely the two-cycle between the states "*ABAB* ...," "*BABA* ...." We can see that the steady states and basins of attraction of this process are as follows:

ω_1: "All B;" the basin of this state is simply the state itself.

ω_2: Only exists if N is even; this is the two-cycle just mentioned. Its basin includes at least the two states in the cycle.

ω_3: "All A;" the basin of this state includes at least all states with two adjacent A's and any state with a string "*ABBA*."

Step 2. Adding mutations. It is a simple observation that the system is ergodic.

Step 3. Computing the limiting distribution. To compute φ^*, compute $\min_{\omega \in \Omega} \min_{h \in H_\omega} \sum_{\omega' \neq \omega} \vec{c}(D(h(\omega'))|\omega')$. Ellison shows that for N even, the minimum cost is 2 and that it is given by the ω_3-tree $\omega_1 \to \omega_2 \to \omega_3$; for N odd, the minimum cost is 1.

We will explain this computation in the more complicated case of N even. First we check that the cost of the tree $\omega_1 \to \omega_2 \to \omega_3$ is indeed 2. Given ω_1 (all B) a single mutation leads to "*ABB* ..."; the deterministic process then goes to the two-cycle ω_2, so the cost of the transition $\omega_1 \to \omega_2$ is 1. From either point in the two-cycle ω_2, a single mutation then leads to a state with two adjacent A's; the deterministic process then goes to ω_3. Thus the cost of $\omega_2 \to \omega_3$ is 1 as well, and the total cost of the tree is 2.

We must now check that 2 is actually the minimum cost. First note that there are two other ω-trees with root ω_3, $\omega_2 \to \omega_1 \to \omega_3$ and the ω-tree shown in figure 5.3. In both cases the cost of ω_3 given ω_1 is greater than one: A single mutation leads to the cycle not the steady state at "all A,"

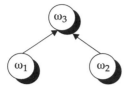

Figure 5.3
Third ω-tree

so two mutations adding adjacent A's are needed to get into the basin of ω_3. In the first case we must add in the cost of ω_1 given ω_2, which is $N/2$ (since the number of A's cannot decrease). In the second case we must add in the cost of ω_3 given ω_2, which we already noted is 1. In both cases the cost exceeds 2.

Finally we must consider ω-trees with roots ω_1 and ω_2. We claim that (if $N > 4$) these have cost higher than 2. Any ω_1-tree must have a path from ω_3 to ω_1; since the deterministic process never decreases the number of A's, this cost is at least N. For the same reason cost of any ω_2-tree is $N/2$. Thus the stochastically stable set is "all A."

In light of Kandori-Mailath-Rob this conclusion is not surprising, but one should note that this dynamic and the Kandori-Mailath-Rob dynamic need not have the same stochastically stable sets in 3×3 (or larger) games. The reason for this is simple: In the two-neighbor model the stochastically stable set is determined by the best response to the six possible configurations of neighbors, while the stochastically stable set with uniform matching and a large population depends on how players respond to every mixed strategy that can be generated by some state of the aggregate population. As a consequence the stochastically stable set with uniform matching may depend on the details of the payoffs that do not matter in the two-neighbor model.[20]

Returning to 2×2 games, the interesting observation is that the convergence times are faster under local interaction. This is most easily seen in simulations: Supposing the system starts in state "all B," how long does it take to get to state "all A"? This depends on the payoffs (which determine α^* and hence how many mutations are needed in Kandori-Mailath-Rob) and also on N and on the probability ε of mutation. Note that with

---

20. Ellison gives an example of this case, based on an example of Young (1993), to show how the equilibrium selected under uniform matching can depend on the details of the payoff matrix.

Table 5.1
Waiting times in the global interaction case

	$\varepsilon = 0.025$	$\varepsilon = 0.05$	$\varepsilon = 0.1$
$N = 50$	10^{14}	10^{9}	10^{5}
$N = 100$	10^{27}	10^{17}	10^{9}

Table 5.2
Waiting times in the local interaction case with 2 neighbors

	$\varepsilon = 0.025$	$\varepsilon = 0.05$	$\varepsilon = 0.1$
$N = 50$	11	8	6
$N = 100$	11	8	6

Table 5.3
Waiting times in the local interaction case with 12 neighbors

	$\varepsilon = 0.025$	$\varepsilon = 0.05$	$\varepsilon = 0.1$
$N = 50$	460	46	11

only two neighbors, all agents want to play A if they have at least one neighbor playing A, so the speed of convergence is the same for all values of $\alpha^*(< 1/2)$. With more than two neighbors, this is no longer the case, and convergence can be faster in games where α^* is smaller.

We now compare rates of convergence between the global and local interaction cases for $\alpha^* = 1/3$. In the Kandori-Mailath-Rob global interaction case with the best-response dynamic, the expected waiting time until everyone plays A can be computed analytically. They are displayed in table 5.1, where the entries are the expected waiting time for passage from the state "all B" to the state "all A." By way of contrast, in the two-neighbor local interaction case, the expected waiting times until 75% of the population plays A with two neighbors can be found numerically from a simulation, as shown in table 5.2. The expected waiting time with 12 neighbors for 75% A is displayed in table 5.3.

Ellison confirms these simulations with an analytic result. Finite-state Markov processes always converge at an exponential rate given by the second largest eigenvalue of the transition probability matrix (the largest eigenvalue is always 1). Ellison computes this eigenvalue to determine how rapidly the system converges from the initial condition to the ergodic distribution. For the Kandori-Mailath-Rob model Ellison shows that the exponential rate is $\varepsilon^{\alpha^* N}$, which is intuitive, since this is the probability of the required number of mutations. In contrast, with two-neighbor matching the exponential rate for small ε is approximately independent of N and is of order ε.

5.6   Radius and Coradius of Basins of Attraction

So far we have characterized the stochastically stable set using Freidlin and Wentzell's technique of constructing "trees" that link the limit sets of the unperturbed stochastic process, assigning a cost to each ω-tree, and then determining which ω-tree has the lowest cost. This approach has the advantage that it can, in principle, always be applied, but it has two related drawbacks. First, the method may require that one determine *all* of the limit sets of the unperturbed process. This determination was straightforward in the systems Kandori-Mailath-Rob and Young considered but can be difficult in systems with a large number of limit sets. Second, determining the least-cost ω-tree can be a complicated graph-theory problem. Recently Ellison (1995) has provided an alternative, and much simpler, sufficient condition for a set to be stochastically stable. This sufficient condition is not necessary, so the technique is not useful in all cases, but when it does apply, it is has the additional benefit of yielding the rate of convergence as well as the identity of the limit set.

Ellison's condition is based on two concepts, the *radius* and *coradius* of a limit set, which are defined in terms of the costs of various transitions. We continue to use $\omega \in \Omega$ for ω-limit sets of the limit dynamic P and $D(\omega)$ for the basin of ω. The *radius of* ω is just the cost of leaving $D(\omega)$. Let us also denote $\sim D \equiv \Omega \backslash D$. Formally,

$$R(\omega) \equiv \bar{c}(\sim D(\omega)|\omega).$$

In the Kandori-Mailath-Rob model the least-cost path away from a steady state is a direct jump; that is, the path considered has only two elements, the initial state in ω and the subsequent state which is not in $D(\omega)$. This is true more generally if (1) the shocks take the form of i.i.d. mutations and (2) in the basin of each limit set ω, $\min_{\theta \notin D(\omega)} c(\theta|\theta_t)$ is non-decreasing under the limit dynamic. The first condition says that we can measure cost by the number of mutations required to reach a given point so that, for example, the cost of a three-state sequence that has two mutations in the first period and one in the second is the same as the cost of a three-mutation transition. Condition 2 requires that the deterministic dynamic cannot decrease the cost of getting out of the basin.

When the least-cost path is a direct jump, the way to show that the radius equals some particular r is to first exhibit a direct jump out of the basin with cost r and then argue that any direct jump of lower cost must remain in $D(\omega)$.

Intuitively the radius measures how easy it is for perturbations to push the system out of $D(\omega)$ and hence captures the expected time the system remains in $D(\omega)$ each time this basin is entered. From this perspective the other datum we need is a measure of how quickly mutations return the system to $D(\omega)$ from states outside of it.

The simplest such measure is the *coradius* of a limit set. The *coradius* of ω, denoted $CR(\omega)$, is defined by

$$CR(\omega) = \max_{\theta} \vec{c}(\omega|\theta).$$

This expression will be used to give a bound on the wait until the system returns to $D(\omega)$ that is useful in some applications, but the bound is not tight; section 5.7 discusses the tighter bound given by the "modified coradius."

Proposition 5.3 (Ellison 1995) If there is a limit set ω such that $R(\omega) > CR(\omega)$, then every stochastically stable state is contained in ω.

Proof This is a consequence of the more general proposition 5.5 below.

As one application of this result, consider extending the sort of "Darwinian dynamics" studied by Kandori-Mailath-Rob to symmetric, two-player, $M \times M$ games as follows: Say that the deterministic dynamic P is "best-response-respecting" if $[P(\theta)]_i > \theta_i$ whenever the ith pure strategy is a best response to the mixed strategy corresponding to θ. This is a very weak form of monotonicity; it reduces to KMR's "Darwinian" condition in 2×2 games.[21] A symmetric equilibrium (A, A) is "p-dominant" (Morris, Rob, and Shin 1995) if A is a strict best response to any mixed strategy that places probability at least p on A.[22] In 2×2 games $1/2$-dominance is equivalent to risk dominance; in $N \times N$ games it is more restrictive than the pairwise risk-dominance notion[23] proposed by Harsanyi and Selten.   ∎

---

21. Small but obvious modifications of the definition and of proposition 5.4 are required to handle the case where each player responds to the distribution corresponding to the play of the other $N - 1$ agents in the population.

22. Note that p-dominance for a given p implies p'-dominance for all $p' \le p$.

23. One strategy pairwise risk dominates another one if it risk dominates it in the 2×2 game formed by deleting all other strategies.

Proposition 5.4 If (A, A) is a 1/2-dominant equilibrium, then for all sufficiently large populations the stochastically stable set obtained by perturbing any best-response-respecting dynamic is a point mass on all agents playing A.

Proof Since A is 1/2-dominant, the radius of "all A" is at least $N/2$. The coradius of "all A" is bounded by the number of mutations required to directly jump to a point in the basin of all A. Since A is 1/2-dominant, it suffices that the fraction of A's be slightly less than 1/2, which suggests that the coradius should be less than qN for some $q < 1/2$. Due to the finite population size the least integer greater than qN may actually be greater than $(N-1)/2$, but this can be avoided by taking N sufficiently large.   ∎

This proof is essentially the same as that for the 2×2 case studied in Kandori-Mailath-Rob. Although the hypothesis could be weakened using the notion of modified coradius discussed below, it is sufficient to include several results from the literature. First, Kandori and Rob (1995) show that in pure coordination games the Pareto-optimal equilibrium is selected; in such games the Pareto-optimal equilibrium is 1/2-dominant.

Second, Kandori and Rob (1993) consider symmetric coordination games with the "total bandwagon property" that the best responses to any distribution are in the support of that distribution (so that action A cannot be a best response to a distribution in which all agents use B or C) and the "monotone share property," which says that if S' is a strict subset of S, then the (unique) mixed-strategy equilibrium $m^*(S)$ with support S gives each pure strategy in S' a strictly smaller probability than does the (unique) mixed-strategy equilibrium with support S'. For generic payoffs the only ω-limit sets in these games are the states where all agents choose the same action. Kandori and Rob show that their assumptions on the payoff functions imply that the cheapest path from one ω-limit set to another is a direct jump to the corresponding basin, as opposed to a path that first jumps to some third equilibrium, so the modified coradius and the radius are the same. This allows Kandori and Rob to determine the stochastically stable equilibrium in the case of three actions by explicitly solving for the least-cost ω-tree, but the minimization is too complicated to be solved in general. Instead, Kandori and Rob show that if, in addition to their assumptions, there is a single equilibrium that pairwise risk dominates all of the others, then that equilibrium is stochastically stable. It is straightforward to check that the equilibrium in question must be 1/2-dominant. Moreover pairwise risk dominance and the total bandwagon property are enough to imply 1/2-dominance; the monotone share assumption is not needed.

Third, Ellison's analysis extends immediately to I-player games played by a single population of players, provided that 1/2-dominance is extended to mean that action A is 1/2-dominant if it is a best response to any mixed-strategy profile in which each opponent gives probability at least 1/2 to A. (We should point out that we have not seen a definition of 1/2-dominance for I-player games in the literature.) Note that this reduces to the original definition in two-player games because the payoff to action A against a mixed strategy of the opponent is linear in the opponent's randomizing probabilities. This extension of 1/2-dominance reveals the structure behind Kim's (1996) analysis of symmetric I-person coordination games in which each player has only two actions. In contrast to two-player, two-action games, I-player two-action games need not have a 1/2-dominant action. However, Kim assumes that a player's payoff depends only on his own action and the total number of opponents playing the same action, and that the payoff to using an action is increasing in the number of opponents that use it; this implies that there are only two pure Nash equilibria, the ones in which all players play the same action. Moreover the action that is the best response when each opponent randomizes 1/2-1/2 is also the best response to any profile in which each opponent gives the action probability at least 1/2; in other words that action is 1/2-dominant. In particular, except in one knife-edge case, one of the two pure equilibria in a game of this type must be 1/2-dominant. This explains why Kim finds that the long-run equilibrium is the one that is 1/2-dominant in the sense defined above.[24]

5.7   Modified Coradius

The coradius gives an upper bound on the expected time until a return to ω, but a tighter bound called the *modified coradius* is available, and it turns out to be useful in a variety of settings. The insight behind the idea of the modified coradius is that the most probable path from one basin of attraction to another need not involve jumps due to perturbations in consecutive periods provided that the intermediate points are themselves steady states. In this case the system may simply remain at the intermediate

---

24. Kim also shows that for this class of models, other dynamic adjustment procedures, for example, rational expectations with lock-in, lead to a different conclusion about which equilibrium is selected in the very long run.

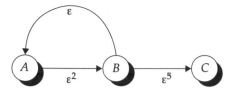

Figure 5.4
Coradius example

steady state for a while, before moving on to the next steady state, and this is far more likely to happen than two jumps in consecutive periods.

With this motivation we now define the *modified coradius* of a limit set. Let $\omega_1(\vec{\theta}), \omega_2(\vec{\theta}), \ldots, \omega_I(\vec{\theta})$ be the sequence of limit sets through which the path $\vec{\theta}$ passes, with the convention that a limit set can appear on the list several times but not consecutively. The modified coradius is just

$$CR^*(\omega) = \max_{\theta \notin D(\omega)} \min_{\vec{\theta}|\theta_0 = \theta, \theta_t \in \omega} \sum_{\tau=1}^{t} c(\theta_\tau|\theta_{\tau-1}) - \sum_{i=2}^{I-1} R(\omega_i(\vec{\theta})).$$

Note that by construction $CR^*(\omega) \leq CR(\omega)$.

The definition of the modified coradius involves several subtleties, all of them linked to the fact that the modified coradius is only useful in obtaining a bound on the worst-case expected waiting time. First of all, while the modified coradius provides a correct upper bound on the worst-case waiting time, the bound need not be tight. Moreover the modified coradius at limit sets ω' that are not maximizers of the expression above does not bound the corresponding waiting time, nor does the modified coradius give a correct bound at every ω where the maximum waiting time is obtained. We will not explain all of these complications here, but the example shown in figure 5.4 should at least indicate why the modified coradius might provide a better bound than the unmodified one in some simple cases. In figure 5.4 $P_{BA} = \varepsilon^2$, $P_{AB} = \varepsilon$, $P_{BC} = \varepsilon^5$, and $c(B|A) = 2$, $c(A|B) = 1$, $c(B|C) = 5$. Consequently the coradius of C is the sum of cost going from A to C, equal to 7. According to this calculation the amount of time to get from A to C should be on the order of ε^{-7}. The modified coradius subtracts from this the radius of B, namely 1, resulting in a cost of 6, suggesting a waiting time of ε^{-6}. How long does it actually take to get from A to C in this example? The system has probability of ε^2 of moving from A to B. Once at B, it is likely to remain for quite some time. However, it is more likely to return to A than move on to C. Indeed, the system must return ε^{-4} times to A on average before moving on to C. Each trip from A to B back to A takes roughly ε^{-2} periods, so the length of time before hitting C is roughly $\varepsilon^{-4}\varepsilon^{-2} = \varepsilon^{-6}$. This is the calculation made by the modified coradius.

Proposition 5.5 (Ellison 1995) If there is a limit set ω such that $R(\omega) > CR^*(\omega)$, then

1. every stochastically stable state is contained in ω,

2. for any $\theta \notin \omega$, the expected waiting time until ω is reached, starting at θ, is of order (at most) $\varepsilon^{-CR^*(\omega)}$ as $\varepsilon \to 0$.

Sketch of Proof Let φ_ε denote the unique invariant distribution corresponding to an ε perturbation. For part 1 it is enough to show that $\varphi_\varepsilon(\theta)/\varphi_\varepsilon(\omega) \to 0$ as $\varepsilon \to 0$ for all $\theta \notin D(\omega)$. As a first step toward this goal, we claim that

$$\frac{\varphi_\varepsilon(\theta)}{\varphi_\varepsilon(\omega)} = \frac{\text{E\{Number of } \theta \text{ occurrences before reaching } \omega|\theta\}}{\text{E\{Number of } \omega \text{ occurrences before reaching } \theta|\omega\}} \qquad (*)$$

where the expectation in the numerator is with respect to the ergodic distribution. The distribution in the denominator is more complicated, since it requires using an expectation over states in the set ω conditional on the state having entered the set ω; fortunately all that will matter about this distribution is that it can be bounded below uniformly over all distributions on ω.

To see why $(*)$ is correct, consider the auxiliary two-state (non-Markov) process formed by taking realizations of the original process and mapping state θ to state 1 and every state in ω to state 2, and omitting all periods in which other states occur. For example, if the original process is in state θ in periods 1 and 2, in some state θ' outside of ω in period 3, in ω in periods 4 and 5, and in state θ in period 6, then the first five realizations of the auxiliary process are $(1, 1, 2, 2, 1, \ldots)$. The relative frequency of 1's and 2's in the auxiliary process is the same as the relative frequency of θ and ω in the original one, and moreover in the auxiliary process these relative frequencies are simply the relative sizes of the run lengths.

Examining equation $(*)$, the numerator of the RHS is at most the waiting time to reach ω from θ, and the denominator is bounded below by a nonvanishing constant times the minimum over states in ω of the expected waiting time to reach a state outside of $D(\omega)$. Thus the proof of both parts of the theorem boils down to showing that the waiting time to leave $D(\omega)$, starting in ω, is approximately $\varepsilon^{-R(\omega)}$ while the waiting time to reach ω is of order $\varepsilon^{-CR^*(\omega)}$.

We will not prove these facts here, though the proof of the first is not hard. We recommend instead that the reader check them in simple two- or three-state examples.   ■

As a final application, suppose that a 2×2 game with $1/4 < \alpha^* < 1/2$ is played in a model of local interaction on a two-dimensional lattice. Specifically, consider an $N_1 \times N_2$ lattice on the surface of a torus, and suppose that the limit system P is given by each player choosing the strategy that is a best response to the distribution of strategies used by his four immediate neighbors in the previous period.[25] Unlike Ellison's one-dimensional model, this system has a large number of steady states. Define a *vertical stripe* to be a location in the first dimension such that all players at that location play the same strategy. If there are only two actions, A and B, with A being $1/2$-dominant, then any state formed of vertical stripes is a steady state provided that there are at least two adjoining B-stripes between each A-stripe. We can similarly form equilibria consisting of horizontal stripes. Yet another type of steady state is for all players to play B except for 2×2 rectangles of players playing A surrounded by opponents playing B.

Now consider perturbing the dynamic with the now-familiar stochastic replacements: Each period each player being replaced with i.i.d. probability ε. What is the stochastically stable set? This model, unlike the one-dimensional model of Ellison (1993), does not have the "contagion" property, where a one-time occurrence of a few mutations (only 2 in the two-neighbor model) is enough to send the system from "all A" to "all B." Instead, starting from "all B," four simultaneous adjacent mutations sends the system to a steady state with a 2×2 rectangle of A's. Clearly the program of first determining all of the limit sets of this dynamic and then finding the least cost ω-trees that connect them would require a great deal of computation. However, Ellison shows that the limit distribution is a point mass on all players using the $1/2$-dominant action and moreover that the expected waiting time is of order ε^{-3}, where 3 is the modified coradius of all A.

This shows that the fast convergence times of the one-dimensional model do not require that model's property of contagion. Instead, "fast convergence" obtains because the system can move from "all B" to "all A"

---

25. As in previous papers on local interaction, for example, the Ellison (1993) paper discussed earlier and Blume (1993) who studied the play of 2×2 games in an infinite two-dimensional lattice, this assumes that players are constrained to use the same action when paired with each of their neighbors.

by a sequence of jumps from one steady state to another, with each jump having waiting time at most ε^{-3}. This suggests that, ceteris paribus, convergence times will be quicker in models with many intermediate steady states than in models where direct jumps between pure-strategy equilibria are the quickest paths.

5.8   Uniform Random Matching with Heterogeneous Populations

Kandori, Mailath, and Rob (1993) considered a single homogeneous population of agents playing a 2×2 symmetric game. As we saw, in that model the stochastically stable outcome is the risk-dominant equilibrium for any "Darwinian" adjustment dynamics. However, KMR acknowledge that that this robustness to the specification of the adjustment dynamics does not extend to the case where there are distinct populations of player 1's and player 2's, a case analyzed by Hahn (1995).

Hahn's model follows Kandori-Mailath-Rob in every detail except that he assumes there are two populations and allows the game played to be asymmetric. Recall in Kandori-Mailath-Rob the two actions are denoted A and B. Hahn defines the state space so that the state $\theta_t = (\theta_t^1, \theta_t^2)$ at time t is now the number of agents in each of the two populations who are playing A. Following Kandori-Mailath-Rob, Hahn assumes that the unperturbed dynamic has the following form:

$$\theta_{t+1}^i = \theta_t^i + f^i(\theta_t),$$

where the f^i satisfy $\mathrm{sgn}(f^i) = \mathrm{sgn}(u^i(A, \theta_t^{-i}) - u^i(B, \theta_t^{-i}))$ as well as boundary and montonicity conditions.

Continuing to follow Kandori-Mailath-Rob, suppose that the game has two strict equilibria and equilibrium in mixed strategies, denoted $(\alpha^{*1}, \alpha^{*2})$. Since there are two populations, though, the system has two dimensions, and not one, with two stable steady states corresponding to the pure-strategy equilibria and an unstable saddle at the mixed equilibrium. One expects that since this equilibrium is unstable, it should have probability 0 in the ergodic distribution; to simplify Hahn, supposes that the equilibrium mixing ratios cannot be attained in any state.[26]

As throughout this chapter, the long-run behavior of the perturbed system with very small mutation rates is determined by computing the

---

26. Since there are only finitely many agents in each population, this assumption is satisfied for generic payoffs.

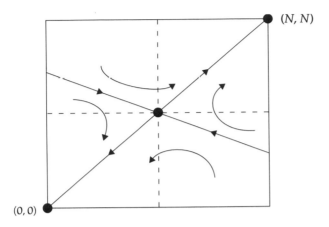

Figure 5.5
Two-population phase portrait

number of mutations required to jump in and out of two basins. Moreover under Hahn's conditions the lowest-cost transition is the immediate
one:

In other words, to determine the stochastically stable outcome, we need
only determine the basins of the two equilibria and compute the minimum
distance of each state corresponding to a pure-strategy equilibrium to the
basin of the other. At this point the difference with the one-population
model emerges: In the one-dimensional system the basins of the two
equilibria under any "Darwinian" dynamics are the sets $\{\theta | \theta < \alpha^* N\}$ and
$\{\theta | \theta > \alpha^* N\}$. In contrast, even strengthening the "Darwinian" assumption
to the monotone assumption does not pin down the location of the basins
in the two-dimensional case corresponding to two populations of players.[27] This can easily be seen by reference to figure 5.5. The "Darwinian"
assumption implies that the lower left-hand region lies in the basin of (0,
0), where all players play B and that the upper right-hand region lies in
the basin of (N, N) where all players play A, but it does not pin down the
eventual destinations of paths that start in the other two regions. In the
upper left-hand box, for example, all trajectories have θ^1 increasing and
θ^2 decreasing until the first time that either $\theta_t^1 < \alpha^* N$ or $\theta_t^2 > \alpha^* N$, but
which of these occurs first depends on the relative speeds of adjustment
of the two components of the state variable in this region. Moreover

---

27. In a similar paper Romaldo (1995) notes that the Darwinian assumption does not determine the basins of attraction in one-population models with three or more actions per player.

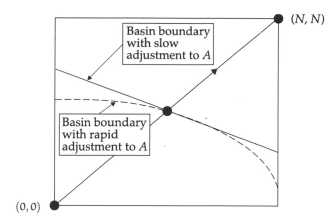

Figure 5.6
Two-population phase portrait with differential adjustment rates

the details of this specification can matter for the long-run outcome, for the shortest path from (0, 0) to the basin of (N, N) need not be along the diagonal connecting the two equilibria. As an example of the possibilities this generates, suppose that both populations adjust faster toward strategy A when A is optimal than they do toward B when B is optimal:

$$\begin{cases} \theta_{t+1}^i - \theta_t^i = \beta^A & \text{if } \theta_t^j > \alpha^{*j}N, \\ \theta_{t+1}^i - \theta_t^i = \beta^B & \text{if } \theta_t^j < \alpha^{*j}N, \end{cases}$$

with $\beta^A > \beta^B$. Then, if the game is symmetric (or nearly so), the stochastically stable outcome is the state (N, N) where all agents play A. This change in the basin when the adjustment rates change is illustrated in figure 5.6.

Hahn's focus is on asymmetric game like battle of the sexes, in which player 1 prefers the equilibrium (A, A) and player 2 prefers (B, B). He gives an upper bound on the relative speeds of adjustment that is sufficient for the equilibrium selected to be invariant to other details of the dynamic.

5.9 Stochastic Replicator Dynamics

As we remarked in the introduction to this chapter, the evolutionary games literature traditionally considers only deterministic systems, with "mutations" being an unmodeled explanation for restricting attention to stable steady states. If one believes that "mutations" are real and recurring phenomena, it might seem more appropriate to include them explicitly in the model. From this viewpoint an obvious way to study the effects of stochastic shocks is to introduce a stochastic term into the standard replicator equations, and indeed the first paper to study a stochastic adjustment model, Foster and Young (1990), did exactly that.

As noted by Fudenberg and Harris (1992), there is an important difference between stochastic replicator dynamics and the finite-population models discussed earlier in the chapter: If the noise has continuous sample paths, the evolutionary system will too. Consequently the "cost" of transitions between the basins of various equilibria, and thus the nature of the long-run distribution, can depend on the "strength" or size of the "flows" (i.e., the deterministic part of the dynamics) and not just on the directions of movement. This contrasts with the finite-population models discussed so far, where the transitions can occur by "jumps" and the transition costs depend on the shapes of the various basins but not on the exact specification of the deterministic process within the basins. In the analogy used by Fudenberg and Harris, the various ω-limit sets can be viewed as "ponds" with the deterministic process corresponding to various "streams" of water. In the models driven by many simultaneous individual mutations, the state moves from one pond to another by "jumping upstream" *over* the flow, so the strength or speed of the stream does not matter; in models with continuous sample paths, the state must "swim" against the flow, and the identity of the stochastically stable set is determined by comparing the relative size of expressions that involve integrals of both the noise and deterministic forces.

Foster and Young (1990) start with the single-population replicator model, and add a Wiener process with no cross-covariance and a general state-dependent variance to arrive at the system of stochastic differential equations of the general form

$$d\theta_t(s) = \theta_t(s)[u_t(s) - \bar{u}_t] + \sigma(s|\theta)\, dW_t(s),$$

where each $W(k)$ is a standard Wiener process, and as in chapter 3, the arguments of the variables denote the actions.

If the variance functions $\sigma(s|\theta)$ do not shrink quickly enough as the boundary is approached, then solutions to this system have positive probability of hitting the boundary of the state space in finite time, so the boundary behavior of the system matters. Foster and Young specify that the system has instantaneous reflection at the boundary.[28] They then give a general description of how to compute the limit of the long-run distributions as the variances of the Wiener processes shrink to 0, and use it to argue that in the case where the $\sigma(s|\theta)$ are constant, the distributions in 2×2 coordination games converge to a point mass on the Pareto-efficient and risk-dominant equilibrium.[29]

Instead of adding stochastic terms directly to the replicator equations for population shares, Fudenberg and Harris (1992) take a different methodological approach. They add the stochastic terms to the equations governing the absolute population sizes and then derive the corresponding equations for the evolution of population shares. That is, they start with the standard deterministic equations

$$\dot{\phi}_t(s) = \phi_t(s)u(s, \theta_t)$$

for the evolution of population size[30] and then suppose that the payoff to strategy s at date t is given by $u(s, \theta_t) + \sigma\, dW_t(s)$, where the W are independent standard Wiener processes. For notational simplicity we set the variance coefficient to be the same for each strategy. The resulting stochastic differential equation then becomes

$$d\phi_t(s) = \phi_t(s)u_t(s, \theta)\, dt + \phi_t(s)\sigma\, dW_t(s).$$

The formulation using payoff shocks has the advantage of being consistent with a nonnegligible amount of noise in models with continuum of agents, while i.i.d. shocks to individual agents might be expected to become almost deterministic in the aggregate as the population becomes large, just as the transition and convergence times in Kandori, Mailath, and Rob (1993) grow exponentially with the population

28. Roughly speaking, instantaneous reflection in a continuous-time stochastic system means that when the system hits the boundary, it continues to move with the same speed but discontinuously reverses the direction with which it hit the boundary. This is a reasonable model of some systems in mechanics, but Fudenberg and Harris argue that it is not well motivated as a model of strategy adjustment.

29. In symmetric 2×2 coordination games, the risk-dominant equilibrium must also be Pareto dominant. Unfortunately, Foster and Young's proof of the general result cites a chapter of Freidlin and Wentzell that does not apply to their problem. Foster and Young have recently written a corrigendum that addresses this issue.

30. As we discussed in chapter 3, this formulation allows the possibility that payoffs and hence population growth rates may be negative, but the growth rate in the replicator dynamics can be thought of as the net difference between births and deaths.

size.[31] As we see below, this formulation, in which variations in play are caused by variations in payoffs, can have very different implications than the "mutations" of KMR; it is not clear to us that either source of noise should be expected to always overwhelm the other one.

The stochastic system for the evolution of population shares can be derived by applying Ito's lemma applied to the function

$$\theta_i(s) = \frac{\phi(s)}{\sum_{s'} \phi(s')}.$$

This yields, in the 2×2 case, the equations

$$d\theta_t(s) = \theta_t(s)\theta_t(s')[(u_t(s) - u_t(s'))\,dt + (\sigma^2(\theta_t(s') - \theta_t(s)))\,dt + \sqrt{2}\sigma\,d\tilde{W}_t],$$

where $\tilde{W} = (W(s) - W(s'))/\sqrt{2}\sigma$ is another standard Wiener process.

Observe that the deterministic part of the system (the coefficient of dt) is not the same as in the deterministic replicator dynamics but includes an additional term corresponding to the weighted difference of the variances. In addition, when the shocks to the underlying payoff process have a constant variance, the shocks to the population shares have variance that shrinks as the boundary is approached. It is easily seen that the boundary is never reached in finite time, so the boundary behavior is irrelevant. This should be intuitive: Regardless of the realization of the payoff shocks, and of the resulting absolute sizes of the population using each strategy, the share of each strategy is, by definition, nonnegative.

Fudenberg and Harris solve for the long-run behavior of this system in 2×2 games.[32] If the game has two strict equilibria, the system is not ergodic. Rather, the system converges with probability 1 to one of the

---

31. While we emphasize that some form of correlation seems necessary to explain non-negligible noise in a model with a continuum of players, Binmore, Samuelson, and Vaughan (1995) note that a stochastic differential equation can be used to approximate the limit of the long-run distribution of a discrete-time, finite-population model in which only one agent moves at a time so that the limiting sample paths are continuous. The stochastic differential equation arises when the limit is taken in the following order: First time goes to infinity, then period length goes to 0, then population size grows to infinity, and finally a mutation rate goes to 0. The resulting stochastic differential equation is not used to model a situation with nonnegligible noise but only to compute the long-run limit of the system as the noise become negligible.

32. In contrast to most of the papers discussed in this chapter, the results in Fudenberg and Harris are not based on the perturbation methods of Freidlin and Wentzell but rather on an analysis of stochastic differential equations by Skorokhod (1989). Unfortunately, that analysis becomes very difficult in higher-dimensional systems, so it may not prove as useful in further work.

two pure equilibria, but the relative probabilities depend on the initial condition. Intuitively, since the replicator dynamics says that the absolute growth rate of a small population must be small, the assumed shocks to payoffs do not do very much to perturb the population shares in the neighborhood of a point where almost everyone is using the same action.

Fudenberg and Harris go on to consider a further modification of the replicator dynamics intended to capture the effects of a deterministic flow of mutations (or more generally an inflow of new players), as in Boylan (1994). This flow serves to keep the system from approaching the boundaries and thus makes the system ergodic. Moreover the ergodic distribution can be found by calculating an integral that depends on the strength of the flow and the variance of the system (e.g., see Skorokhod 1989). In 2×2 games with two strict equilibria, the limit of the ergodic distribution as the variances of the payoffs and the flow of "mutations" both go to 0 is a point mass on the risk-dominant strategy. While this seems to demonstrate the robustness of the Kandori, Mailath, and Rob result, the degree of confirmation implied may be less than it appears, since the equilibrium selected depends on the strength of the flows of the unperturbed adjustment process at each state and not only on the direction of adjustment. More precisely there are many "Darwinian" processes with the same basin of attraction as replicator dynamic that select the risk-dominated equilibrium; an easy but artificial example is a process with very rapid adjustment in the basin of the dominated equilibrium and very slow adjustment in the basin of the dominant one.

Cabrales (1993) extends Fudenberg and Harris's analysis to general n-player games and shows that even the stochastic replicator dynamics need not select the equilibria with the largest basin of attraction in symmetric one-population models of games with more than two players. The proof follows from computing the integral alluded to above. The technical reason that the answer here is different is that the payoff to a given strategy is a linear function of the population fractions in a two-player game, but with more than two players it is a higher-order polynomial. To obtain a more satisfactory explanation, we must relate this observation to the foundations of the models. The driving force in the models we discussed in previous sections is the probability that enough players simultaneously "mutate" that the remaining players wish to switch as well. Since the fraction required depends only on the size of the basin, the size of the basin determines the stochastically stable outcome. In contrast, the driving force in models with shocks to payoffs is the probability of a sufficiently large change in payoffs that players choose to change their action. In a symmetric two-player game these two criteria are identical because payoffs are linear in the population fraction playing each action, but in n-player games payoffs are polynomial in the population fraction playing different actions.

To get an intuition about why the polynomial dependence of utility on population fractions makes a difference, consider the stag-hunt game, where the two strategies are "Hare," which pays 1 regardless of opponents' play, and "Stag," which pays $a > 1$ if *all* opponents play Stag but pays 0 otherwise.[33] If there are only two players, the Pareto-dominant equilibrium "all Stag" is risk dominant if and only if $a > 2$, but for any $a > 2$ "all Hare" is risk dominant if the number of players n is large enough that $a < 2^{n-1}$. Now consider the simple case where only the payoff to "all Stag" is stochastic and where the fractions playing Stag and Hare are bounded below by $\varepsilon_S, \varepsilon_H > 0$ due to the inflow of new players. At the state "all Stag," the payoff to Stag is $a(1 - \varepsilon_H)$ and the payoff to Hare is 1, so the payoffs would need to change by $a(1 - \varepsilon_H) - 1$ to make Hare the optimal choice. At the state "all Hare," the payoff to Hare is 1 and the payoff to Stag is $a\varepsilon_S$, so payoffs would need to change by $1 - a\varepsilon_S$ to make Stag optimal. Thus, regardless of the number of players, the change in payoffs required for a shift from Stag to Hare is larger than that for the reverse shift iff $a(1 - \varepsilon_H) - 1 - (1 - a\varepsilon_S) > 0$, such as if $a - 2 > a(\varepsilon_H - \varepsilon_S) \approx 0$. This highlights the differing effects of the sources of noise in the two formulations.

Appendix A: Review of Finite Markov Chains

We consider discrete-time, finite-state Markov processes with Markov transition matrix P. Then, if $\theta, \xi \in \Theta$, the element $P_{\theta\xi}$ of this matrix is the probability that the state is θ at date $t + 1$ conditional on the state being ξ at date t. With this convention, probability distributions over states are represented by column vectors φ and $\varphi_{t+1} = P\varphi_t$. Note that this system is "autonomous" or "stationary," meaning that P does not depend on the time t. This rules out processes such as fictitious play where the step size shrinks over time.

What can be said about the long-run behavior of the system? Under certain conditions developed below, this behavior is described by its

---

33. In Rousseau's story all players must work together in order to catch the stag. This game is quite similar to the example of a team problem that Cabrales used in his paper.

"invariant distribution." We say that φ is an *invariant distribution* if $P\varphi = \varphi$.

Every finite Markov chain has at least one invariant distribution (P is a continuous operator on the compact convex set $\Delta(\Theta)$), but in general, this distribution need not be unique. Consider, for example, the deterministic process corresponding to the Markov operator $P = I$ (the identity matrix). Here every probability distribution is an invariant distribution. Notice, however, that only the point masses on a single state make sense as descriptions of the long-run behavior of this system; the other invariant distributions are rather descriptions of which beliefs would be "stable" (constant over time) for an outside observer whose initial beliefs are exogenous and who cannot observe the system itself.

This example shows that some conditions are needed in order to be able to interpret the invariant distributions as sensible descriptions of long-run behavior. A system is *ergodic* if it satisfies all of the following three conditions:

1. The invariant distribution $\hat{\varphi}$ is unique.

2. Convergence of time averages

$$\lim_{T\to\infty}\left(\frac{1}{T}\right)\sum_t 1(\theta_t = \theta) = \hat{\varphi}(\theta)$$

almost surely, where the indicator function $1(\cdot)$ is equal to one if the condition is true, and zero otherwise.

3. Convergence of the date-t distributions:

$$\forall\varphi, \lim_{t\to\infty} P^t\varphi = \hat{\varphi}.$$

Some examples will help clarify the implications of these conditions. Looking first at the uniqueness of an invariant distribution, suppose that

$$P = \begin{bmatrix} 0 & 1 \\ 1 & 0 \end{bmatrix}$$

This system cycles back and forth between the two states. It also has the unique invariant distribution $\hat{\varphi} = [1/2, 1/2]$. The extent to which this is a good description of long-run behavior is given by properties 2 and 3. Property 2, the convergence of the long-run average, means that the system spends half of its time in each state. This property is satisfied by the example. Property 3 would mean that even if the initial state is known perfectly, beliefs about the state at a sufficiently far distant time are 50-50. This property is not satisfied by the example: If the initial condition is known, then it is possible to predict exactly where the system will be at each future time, since it is deterministic.

Two examples show how a system that is not ergodic may be perturbed slightly so that it is. The first is a perturbation of the identity map

$$\begin{bmatrix} 1-\varepsilon & \varepsilon \\ \varepsilon & 1-\varepsilon \end{bmatrix},$$

which can be described as a persistent state: The system tends to remain in the current state but has a slight chance of moving to the other state. The second is a perturbation of a deterministic two-cycle

$$\begin{bmatrix} \varepsilon & 1-\varepsilon \\ 1-\varepsilon & \varepsilon \end{bmatrix},$$

which can be described as a near cycle. This system cycles (switches to the other state) with high probability, but with a small probability it instead remains in the current state. Although it may not be immediately obvious, both of these systems are ergodic.

Taking their ergodicity as given for the moment, notice that these examples show that even if the system is ergodic, the beliefs of a player who observes the system as it evolves need not correspond to the ergodic distribution: In particular, while condition 3 says that knowing yesterday's state does not help with forecasting the system's long-run behavior, knowing yesterday's state can help forecast today's, as it does in the two examples here. Put differently, convergence to the invariant distribution does not imply the convergence of the time-t distributions over outcomes conditional on history until that point, but only the convergence of the unconditional distributions.

The easiest sufficient condition for ergodicity is the "strict positivity" condition that $P > 0$. The two examples above satisfy this condition, as do most of the models in this chapter. A weaker sufficient condition is $P^n > 0$ for some n. Another condition weaker than strict positivity is that there is a state that can be reached from any other state and such that, when this state is reached, there is a positive probability of remaining there the next period. That is, there exists a state θ such that for any θ' there exists a time n such that

1. $(P^n)_{\theta\theta'} > 0$,
2. $P_{\theta\theta} > 0$.

This condition may be understood in terms of the notion of a *recurrent class*, which is a stochastic analogue of the invariant sets of the deterministic theory: A subset of states is recurrent if it has the property that once it is reached, the state must remain in the set with probability one. A recurrent class has the stronger property that it is a minimal recurrent set. Property 1 above implies that there is only one recurrent class, since recurrent classes must be disjoint and all contain the special state θ. Property 2 says that there is a positive probability of remaining in this state from one period to the next. This rules out deterministic cycles and leads to the conclusion that the recurrent class is "aperiodic."

More generally, if there is a unique recurrent class, then there is a unique invariant distribution, and this is sufficient for the time averages to converge. Consequently the first two conditions for ergodicity are satisfied. (In some treatments ergodicity is defined by the first two conditions alone.) The addition of the condition that the recurrent class is aperiodic ensures that the distant future is not terribly sensitive to current conditions, a condition known as mixing, and this leads to the final condition for ergodicity, the convergence of the long-run distribution.

An example shows how the weak condition may be satisfied even when the transition matrix is not strictly positive. Consider two sequences of short-run players playing a two-player game; each individual plays only once but knows what happened in the past $K > 1$ periods. Each player i "intends" to choose the strategy that maximizes his expected payoff against the distribution corresponding to the last K periods of play. The realized strategy is the intended one with probability $1 - \varepsilon$, and some fixed strategy $\hat{s}^i$ with probability ε. Here the state is the realized strategy profiles in the last K periods, so not all transitions are possible in a single period. (For example, if $K > 1$, the transition from a history of both players always playing "1" to a history of both players always playing "2" is impossible in a single period.) Moreover, if (s^{1*}, s^{2*}) is a profile of strictly dominated strategies, the state has probability 0 of being in "K observations of (s^{1*}, s^{2*})" in any period after the first. However, the state "K observations of $(\hat{s}^1, \hat{s}^2)$" satisfies the two-part condition for ergodicity given above.

Appendix B: Stochastic Stability Analysis

The basis of proposition 5.2 is the following result of Freidlin and Wentzell which characterizes the invariant distribution of any finite-state irreducible Markov chain in terms of the trees defined in the text, where

here the trees include all states θ and not just those that are the ω-limit sets of some (as yet unspecified) deterministic system. Let $(\theta', \theta'') \in h_\theta$ mean that the tree h_θ has a transition from θ' to θ''.

Lemma 5.1 (Freidlin and Wentzell 1982)   If Q is an irreducible finite-dimensional matrix, the unique invariant distribution μ of Q is given by

$$\mu_\theta = \frac{Z_\theta}{\sum_{\theta'} Z_{\theta'}},$$

where $Z_\theta = \sum_{h_\theta \in H_\theta} \prod_{(\theta', \theta'') \in h_\theta} Q_{\theta'' \theta'}$ and H_θ is the set of all θ-trees.

The proof of this lemma is not very revealing, since it consists of simply verifying that the distribution constructed is indeed invariant. Intuitively the reason that the formula involves a sum over all the h_θ-trees is that each ω-tree represents one way that the state might arrive at θ; each path is then weighted by its probability. Of course the weight attached to a transition from θ' to θ depends on the probability of θ' as well as on the conditional probability of the transition, which is just another way of saying that invariant distribution is a fixed point. A brute-force computation of the distribution would involve inverting the matrix Q, and thus introducing a term corresponding to $1/\det(Q)$; this corresponds to the summation in the denominator of the expression for μ_θ.

With lemma 5.1 in hand, we now turn to our case of interest where the perturbed matrices P^ε play the role of the irreducible matrix Q so that the transition probabilities $Q_{\theta'' \theta'}$ are approximately $k_{\theta'' \theta'} \varepsilon^{c(\theta'' | \theta')}$, where the $k_{\theta'' \theta'}$ are independent of ε. Inspecting the formula $\mu_\theta = Z_\theta / \sum_{\theta'} Z_{\theta'}$ shows that the support of the limit distribution will be concentrated on the states θ for which Z_θ is the lowest order in ε. Furthermore the order of

$$Z_\theta = \sum_{h_\theta \in H_\theta} \prod_{(\theta', \theta'') \in h_\theta} Q_{\theta'', \theta'} = \sum_{h_\theta \in H_\theta} \left[\prod_{(\theta', \theta'') \in h_\theta} k_{\theta'' \theta'} \right] \varepsilon^{\left(\sum_{(\theta', \theta'') \in h_\theta} c(\theta'' | \theta') \right)}$$

will be determined by the lowest-order elements in the summation, so

$$o(Z_\theta) = \arg \min_{h_\theta \in H_\theta} \varepsilon^{\sum_{(\theta', \theta'') \in h_\theta} c(\theta'' | \theta')}.$$

Thus we conclude that the limit distribution is concentrated on the states whose trees have the lowest cost.

Freidlin and Wentzell use this fact to determine the invariant measures of some continuous-time systems on $\mathcal{R}^n$ with "small" stochastic parts by approximating the system of interest with a finite-state system in discrete time. However, the direct application of their result to discrete-time systems with a large number of states requires one to consider all of the states of the process. The appeal of proposition 5.2 is that it shows that it is sufficient to build trees whose elements are the ω-limit sets of the unperturbed process P. It is easy to see that if state θ' is in the basin $D(\theta)$ of state θ under P, then transitions from θ' to θ have cost 0 and can be ignored in computing the minimum. Therefore, if we construct a tree on the ω-limit sets whose cost is $\min_{\omega \in \Omega} \min_{h \in H_\omega} \Sigma_{\omega' \in \Omega/\omega} \vec{c}(D(h(\omega'))|\omega')$, we can construct a tree of the same cost over all the states adding an initial step in which every state θ is mapped to its ω-limit. The final step is to verify that no other tree on the whole state space can have lower cost than $\min_{\omega \in \Omega} \min_{h \in H_\omega} \Sigma_{\omega' \in \Omega/\omega} \vec{c}(D(h(\omega'))|\omega')$. This is done by a straightforward but tedious "tree surgery" argument which we will omit.

References

Bergin, J., and B. Lippman. 1995. Evolution with state dependent mutations. Mimeo. Queens University.

Binmore, K., L. Samuelson, and K. Vaughn. 1995. Musical chairs: Modelling noisy evolution. *Games and Economic Behavior* 11: 1–35.

Blume, L. 1993 The statistical mechanics of strategic interaction. *Games and Economic Behavior* 5: 387–424.

Boylan, R. 1994. Evolutionary equilibria resistant to mutations. *Games and Economic Behavior* 7: 10–34.

Cabrales, A. 1993. Stochastic replicator dynamics. Mimeo. University of California at San Diego.

Canning, D. 1992. Average behavior in learning models. *Journal of Economic Theory* 57: 442–72.

Ellison, G. 1993. Learning, local interaction, and coordination. *Econometrica* 61: 1047–71.

Ellison, G. 1995. Basins of attraction and long-run equilibria. Mimeo. Massachusetts Institute of Technology.

Ely, J. 1995. Local conventions. Mimeo. Northwestern University.

Foster, D., and P. Young. 1990. Stochastic evolutionary game dynamics. *Theoretical Population Biology* 38: 219–32.

Freidlin, M., and A. Wentzell. 1984. *Random Perturbations of Dynamical Systems*. New York: Springer.

Fudenberg, D., and C. Harris. 1992. Evolutionary dynamics with aggregate shocks. *Journal of Economic Theory* 57: 420–41.

Fudenberg, D., and J. Tirole. 1991. *Game Theory*. Cambridge: MIT Press.

Futia, C. 1982. Invariant distributions and the limiting behavior of Markovian economic models. *Econometrica* 50: 377–408.

Hahn, S. 1995. The long run equilibrium in an asymmetric coordination game. Mimeo. Harvard University.

Kandori, M., and R. Rob. 1993. Bandwagon effects and long run technology choice. Mimeo, DP 93-F-2. University of Tokyo.

Kandori, M., and R. Rob. 1995. Evolution of equilibria in the long run: A general theory and applications. *Journal of Economic Theory* 65: 383–414.

Kandori, M., G. Mailath, and R. Rob. 1993. Learning, mutation and long run equilibria in games. *Econometrica* 61: 27–56.

Kim, Y. 1993. Equilibrium selection in n-person coordination games. *Games and Economic Behavior* 15: 203–77.

Kreps, D. 1990. *A Course in Microeconomic Theory*. Princeton: Princeton University Press.

Morris, S., R. Rob, and H. Shin. 1993. p-dominance and belief potential. *Econometrica* 63: 145–58.

Romaldo, D. 1995. Simularities and evolution. Mimeo. Harvard University.

Skorohod, A. V. 1989. *Asymptotic Methods in the Theory of Stochastic Differential Equations*, trans. by H. H. McFadden. Providence, RI: American Mathematical Society.

Young, P. 1993. The evolution of conventions. *Econometrica* 61: 57–83.

**Extensive-Form Games
and Self-confirming
Equilibrium**

6.1 Introduction

So far we have limited attention to simultaneous-move games, where a player's strategy is simply a choice of a single uncontingent action. In such games it is natural to assume, as we have done, that at the end of each play of the game each player observes the strategies used by each of his opponents. We now wish to consider learning in nontrivial extensive-form games. The most natural assumption in many such contexts is that agents observe the terminal nodes (outcomes) that are reached in their own plays of the game, but that agents do not observe the parts of their opponents' strategies that specify how the opponents would have played at information sets that were not reached in that play of the game.[1] The only setting we can imagine in which players observe more information than the realized terminal node is if the players are forced to write down and commit themselves to contingent plans, and even in that case the most natural interpretation is that the game has been changed to one in which the "actions" are commitments to strategies of the original game. On the other hand, in many settings players will not even observe the realized terminal node, as several different terminal nodes may be consistent with their observation. For example, in a first-price sealed-bid auction players might observe the winning bid but not the losing ones. We say more about this possibility below. In large population settings we will also assume that agents observe no signals at all about the outcomes of matches they do not participate in. This is the case in most game theory experiments, but it is less compelling as a description of real-world games,

---

1. Recall that each terminal node is associated with a unique path through the tree, and so with a unique sequence of actions.

since in many cases agents may receive information about the outcomes in other matches.

Given that players do not observe play at unreached information sets, it is possible for the observed outcome to converge while the players maintain incorrect beliefs about off-path play. As a result the learning process can converge to outcomes that cannot be generated by any Nash equilibrium of the game. We first illustrate this in section 6.2 with an example. After setting up the basic notation of an extensive-form game in section 6.3, we recapitulate the simple learning model of chapter 2 in the extensive-form setting in section 6.4. Section 6.5 introduces a weakening of Nash equilibrium, *self-confirming equilibrium*, that allows differences in beliefs off the equilibrium path. The stability of this concept of equilibrium in the basic learning model is explored in section 6.6. In section 6.7 we weaken the notion of self-confirming equilibrium to allow the possibility that when there is a large population of players who share a single role, different players who play the same role may have different beliefs off the equilibrium path.

We also consider several possible ways of strengthening self-confirming equilibrium. In section 6.8 we consider the possibility that opposing players randomize (or "tremble"). This gives players more information about certain forms of off-path play, so the resulting equilibrium notion, called consistent self-confirming equilibrium, allows "fewer" departures from Nash equilibrium play. We consider the exact connection between consistent self-confirming equilibrium and Nash equilibrium in section 6.9. Finally players may know (or be fairly confident of) one another's payoffs and use this knowledge to deduce restrictions on the likely play of their opponents. For example, players may judge it very unlikely that their opponents would play dominated strategies. This leads to the concept of rationalizable self-confirming equilibrium, which we explore in section 6.10.

6.2   An Example

The possibility of non-Nash outcomes persisting in the long run is illustrated in the following example from Fudenberg and Kreps (1988):

Example 6.1 (Fudenberg and Kreps 1988)   In the three-player game illustrated in figure 6.1, player 3 moves last and cannot tell whether he has the move because player 1 played D_1 or because player 1 played A_1 and player 2 played D_2. Suppose that player 1 expects player 3 to play R

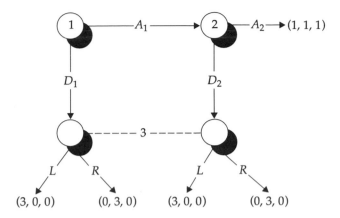

Figure 6.1
Fudenberg-Kreps example

with probability exceeding 2/3, and player 2 to play A_2 with high probability, while player 2 expects player 3 to play L with at least this same 2/3
probability and expects player 1 to play A_1.[2] Given these beliefs, it is
myopically optimal for players 1 and 2 to play A_1 and A_2, and the first-
period outcome will be (A_1, A_2). Moreover, provided that player 1's initial
beliefs about the play of players 2 and 3 are independent (i.e., are a product distribution), the observed outcome gives player 1 no reason to
change his beliefs about the play of player 3—player 1 becomes all the
more convinced that 2 plays A_2. Likewise, if player 2's initial beliefs are a
product distribution, player 2's beliefs about player 3 remain unchanged
as well. Consequently the outcome in the second and subsequent periods
will also be (A_1, A_2), so this outcome is a steady state. However, it is not a
Nash equilibrium out-come: Nash equilibrium requires players 1 and 2 to
make the same (correct) forecast of player 3's play, and if both make the
same forecast, at least one of the players must choose D.

---

2. For a more precise specification, suppose that players 1 and 2 form and update their beliefs
as follows: Player 1's prior beliefs over the mixed strategies of players 2 and 3 are given by
$\text{Prob}[\pi_2(A_2) \leq p, \pi_3(R) \leq q] = p^{100}q^{100}$; player 2's beliefs are given by $\text{Prob}[\pi_1(A_1) \leq p, \pi_3(L) \leq q] = p^{100}q^{100}$. Given these beliefs, player 1 assigns marginal probability
$\int_0^1 100q^{100}\, dq = 100/101$ that 3 chooses R, and assigns this same probability to player 2
choosing A_2; player 2 assigns probability 100/101 to the event that 1 plays A_1 and assigns
this same probability to 3 playing L. Consequently the myopic best responses for players 1
and 2 are A_1 and A_2, and this is the first-period outcome. Moreover, given the product
structure of the beliefs, neither player 1 nor player 2 is led to change his beliefs about player
3, so the outcome is a steady state. Section 6.3 gives a more general discussion of the extension of fictitious play to extensive-form games.

This example shows that learning can lead to non-Nash steady states unless there is some mechanism that leads players to have correct beliefs about off-path play. In this chapter we focus on settings where Nash outcomes cannot be expected because there are no such mechanisms. In the next chapter we examine one important reason why off-path learning might occur: Players might not be myopic and consequently might choose to "experiment" with off-path actions that have a lower current period payoff in order to gain information that can be used in future plays. It is also possible that players can learn off-path play from on-path observations if they believe on-path and off-path play are sufficiently correlated. While we do not wish to rule out such correlation, we do not wish to assume it, since we are not convinced that it is more reasonable than the opposite polar case of independent beliefs. We will discuss this point further when we revisit example 6.1.

6.3   Extensive-Form Games

We will examine extensive-form games with I players; the game tree X, with nodes $x \in X$, is finite. Terminal nodes are $z \in Z$. For notational convenience, we represent Nature by player 0, and suppose that Nature moves only at the initial node of the tree. Information sets, denoted by $h^i \in H$, are a partition of $X \backslash Z$. The information sets where player i has the move are denoted by $H^i \subset H$. The feasible actions at information set $h^i \in H$ are denoted $A(h^i)$. We continue to use $-i$ for all players except player i so that, for example, H^{-i} are information sets for all players other than i. A pure strategy for player i, s^i, is a map from information sets in H^i to actions satisfying $s^i(h^i) \in A(h^i)$. S^i is the set of all such strategies; mixed strategies are $\sigma^i \in \Sigma^i$. Each player except Nature receives a payoff that depends on the terminal node; this payoff is denoted $r_i(z)$.

In addition to mixed strategies, we define behavior strategies $\pi^i \in \Pi^i$. These are probability distributions over actions at each information set for player i. For any given mixed strategy σ^i for player i, and any information set for that player, we can define a behavior strategy by Kuhn's theorem; we denote this as $\hat{\pi}(\cdot | \sigma^i)$. For any given behavior strategy π it is also useful to define the induced distribution over terminal nodes $\hat{\rho}(\pi)$. We will also use the shorthand notation $\hat{\rho}(\sigma) \equiv \hat{\rho}(\hat{\pi}(\sigma))$.

We assume that all players know the structure of the extensive form and their own payoff function, so the only uncertainty each player faces concerns the strategies the opponents will use.[3] To avoid complications, we suppose that the distribution of Nature's moves is known; any unknown but exogenous distributions can be represented as arising from the choice of a "dummy" player. To model the "strategic uncertainty" about players' strategies, we let μ^i be a probability measure over Π^{-i}, the set of other players' strategies. As discussed in chapter 2, assuming that the support is Π^{-i} and not $\Delta(\Pi^{-i})$ implies that players are certain that opponents do not correlate their play and will maintain that belief regardless of any evidence to the contrary. That is, any correlating devices that may be available to any subset of the players are explicitly included in the description of the extensive form. We are somewhat concerned by this restriction, but we impose it anyway to limit the number of complications that need to be addressed.

Again following chapter 2, the beliefs, which are distributions over strategies, must be integrated to obtain the player's predictions about expected play. For example, the probability that i assigns to terminal node z being reached when he plays π^i is $\gamma^i(z|\pi^i,\mu^i) = \int_{\Pi^{-i}} \hat{\rho}(z|\pi^i, \pi^{-i})\mu^i[d\pi^{-i}]$. This allows us to compute the expected utility $u^i(\pi^i,\mu^i) = \sum_z r^i(z)\gamma^i(z|\pi^i,\mu^i)$.

For any mixed profile σ, we let $\bar{H}(\sigma) \subset H$ be the information sets that are reached with positive probability when σ is played. Note that this set is entirely determined by the distribution over terminal nodes ρ, so we may equally well write $\bar{H}(\rho) = \bar{H}(\sigma)$ where $\rho = \hat{\rho}(\sigma)$, or $\bar{H}(\pi) = \bar{H}(\sigma)$ where $\pi = \hat{\pi}(\sigma)$. We denote by $H(s_i)$ (or $H(\pi_i)$) the set of information sets that can be reached when player i plays s_i, that is, the set $\{h^i|\exists s^{-i} \, s.t. \, h^i \in H(s^i, s^{-i})\}$; this is also called the *reachable* information sets under s_i (or π_i). For any subset $J \subset H$ and any profile σ we may define the subset of behavior strategies consistent with players other than i playing σ_{-i} at the information sets in J by $\Pi^{-i}(\sigma^{-i}|J) \equiv \{\pi^{-i}|\pi^i(h^i) = \hat{\pi}(h^j|\sigma^j), \forall h^j \in H^{-i} \cap J\}$.

6.4   A Simple Learning Model

We now consider an extensive-form analog of the generalized version of fictitious play discussed in chapter 2. To keep things simple, at this point we will suppose that there is only one agent in each player role and that

---

3. One way to model cases where players are uncertain of the structure of the extensive form is to include a move by Nature in which the extensive form is chosen. This permits a player who is consistently outguessed when he *thinks* he is playing the simultaneous-move game "matching pennies" to eventually infer that his opponent is somehow observing and responding to the player's choice.

all agents are completely myopic; both of these restrictions will be relaxed in chapter 7.

Each play of the game results in a particular terminal node z being reached. We assume that all players observe this terminal node. Thus at the start of round t all players know the sequence $(z_1, z_2, \ldots, z_{t-1})$; this is called the *history at t*, and is denoted h_t. Similarly h_∞ denotes an infinite history of play; when a particular infinite sequence h_∞ has been fixed, h_t will mean the first t observations in that sequence. (Note that h^i are information sets, while h_t are histories.) A *belief rule* for player i is a function from histories to beliefs μ^i. In a slight abuse of notation we will denote this function by μ^i as well so that $\mu_t^i(h_t)$ denotes player i's beliefs at date t given history h_t.[4]

Our next step is to specify how players update their beliefs and choose their actions in the course of the dynamic learning process.

6.4.1 Beliefs

To model beliefs, we will extend the strategic-form definition of asymptotic empiricism (given in chapter 2) to the current setting of extensive-form games.[5] Following Fudenberg and Kreps (1995a), we suppose that player i's estimates of play at a given information set for player j converges to the empirical distribution of play at that information set as the number of observations of play at that information set converges to infinity.

To make this more precise, let $\hat{H}(h_\infty)$ denote the information sets that are reached a positive fraction of the time along history h_∞, and let $d(h^j|h_t)$ be the empirical distribution of play at information set h^j.

Definition 6.1 Player i's belief rule is *asymptotically empirical in the extensive form* if for every $\varepsilon > 0$, infinite history h_∞, $j \neq i$, and information set $h^j \in \hat{H}(h_\infty) \cap H^j$,

$$\lim_{t \to \infty} \mu_t^i(h_t)(\{\pi^{-i} | \|\pi^j(h^j) - d(h^j|h_t)\| < \varepsilon\}) = 1.$$

---

4. To model the situation where players need not observe the terminal node at the end of each round, we could suppose that each player i observed some element $\lambda^i(z)$ of a partition of the z's, where each player's own payoff function is measurable with respect to his partition. This sort of more general learning model is implicit in the equilibrium concept proposed by Battigalli (1987).

5. Recall that the strategic-form definition said that players' beliefs about each opponent's strategy converged to the empirical marginal distribution over that strategy.

In one-shot simultaneous-move games this definition reduces to that of asymptotic empiricism in the strategic form *provided* that the assessments are assumed to be the product of independent marginals. To see this, suppose that player 1 and player 2 each have a single information set, and those information sets are reached a positive fraction of the time. Then the probability that any third player assigns to the event (1 and 2 both play L) must converge to the product of the corresponding empirical marginal distributions, even if the empirical *joint* distribution is correlated.

6.4.2 Behavior Given Beliefs

For simplicity, we will assume here that players are completely myopic and that in each period they choose a strategy that is a best response to their current beliefs. More precisely, we suppose that the strategy chosen by player i at date t is a maximizer of $u^i(\pi^i, \mu_t^i) = \sum_z r^i(z)\gamma_t^i(z|\pi^i, \mu_t^i)$. We should emphasize that this is an ex ante notion of maximization, as is the definition of asymptotic myopia in strategic-form games given in chapter 4: With this notion of maximization, a maximizing strategy may prescribe an action that is suboptimal at an information set that has probability 0 given π^i, μ_t^i.

Note also that this assumption is more restrictive than it was in the case of strategic-form games, for in the context of extensive-form games myopia is *not* an implication of large population models with random matching. Such models do imply that players should not sacrifice utility in the current match to influence play in future matches, but in the present setting there is an additional reason that players might choose to sacrifice current utility, namely to gain information that may be useful in future play. That is, players might choose to "experiment" in order to learn more about their opponents' strategies.

To see this, consider the game in figure 6.2. Suppose that player 1's beliefs μ^1 are that with probability 1/2 player 2 plays u in every period,

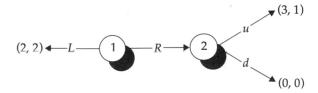

Figure 6.2
Selten game

and with probability 1/2 player 2 plays d in every period. Then player 1's current assessment of 2's play corresponds to the mixed strategy (1/2, u, 1/2, d), and the expected payoff from R is 1.5, which is less than the payoff to L. Hence a myopic player 1 would play L in the first period. Since this results in no new information about player 2's play, player 1 would then play L in all subsequent periods as well. However, if player 1 plays R a single time, he will learn exactly how player 2 is playing, so the decision rule "play R in the first period, and play R thereafter if and only if 2 plays u" has probability 1/2 of yielding 3 in every period and probability 1/2 of yielding 0 in period 1, followed by 2 at all future dates, which will have a higher present value provided that player 1's discount factor is not too small.

This shows that we should not expect players to behave myopically in the initial periods of the game, since they may choose to "experiment" with strategies that do not maximize their short-run expected payoff. However, the results we will present extend to situations where players satisfy the much weaker condition of "asymptotic myopia," meaning that they *eventually* stop experimenting and play to maximize their current period's payoff. Fudenberg and Kreps (1995a,b) formulate several variants of this condition and use it in place of the exact myopia we assume here.[6] From the literature on the "bandit problem," we would expect that players with any discount factor less than 1 would eventually stop experimenting and be "asymptotically myopic" in this sense. Chapter 7 discusses the results of Fudenberg and Levine (1993b) who show that this is true for Bayesian present-value maximizers in a closely related model of learning in extensive-form games.

To summarize this section, then, we will be interested in fictitious playlike processes in which the strategies chosen in each period are a best response to expected play in that period and where beliefs about opponents' actions are asymptotically empirical in the extensive form.

---

6. In fact a major concern of that paper is formulating and investigating definitions of "asymptotic myopia" that seem general enough to be plausible while still strong enough that the experimentation does not "show up" in the long-run outcome. Another issue that that paper addresses, and we will skip over, is the extent to which very weak forms of asymptotic myopia may conflict in spirit with some strengthenings of asymptotic empiricism that might otherwise seem natural. For example, one might require beliefs to correspond to the empirical distribution at all information sets that are reached infinitely often, even those that are reached with vanishing frequency. (Note that Bayesian updating from a full-support prior has this property.)

6.4.3 Equilibrium Notions

A number of notions of "conjectural," "subjective," or "self-confirming" equilibrium have been introduced to capture the relationship between steady states of a learning process in an extensive-form game and equilibria of the static game. The notion originates in Hahn (1977) in the context of production economies and is discussed in Battigalli (1987) in the context of a game.[7] Self-confirming equilibrium in which only the terminal nodes of the game are observed is developed in Fudenberg and Levine (1993a) and in Fudenberg and Kreps (1995a). The notion of subjective equilibrium is developed in the context of repeated games in Kalai and Lehrer (1993). There are also some related concepts that include elements of rationalizability; we discuss these later in this chapter. All of these definitions are intended to capture and generalize some version of the point raised by example 6.1, namely that each time the game is played players get only incomplete information about the strategies used by their opponents, so incorrect beliefs about off-path play can persist. Our presentation follows Fudenberg and Kreps (1995a) with the goal of providing analogs of the results in chapter 2 on the relationship between steady states of this learning process and equilibria of the underlying game.

Nash equilibrium is usually defined as a strategy profile such that each player's strategy is a best response to his or her opponents. For our purposes, though, it is instructive to give an equivalent definition that parallels the way in which we will define self-confirming equilibrium.

Definition 6.2 A *Nash equilibrium* is a mixed profile σ such that there exist beliefs μ^i and for each $s^i \in \text{supp}(\sigma^i)$,

1. $u^i(s^i|\mu^i) \geq u^i(\hat{s}^i|\mu^i)$ for all $\hat{s}^i \in S^i$,
2. $\mu^i(\Pi^{-i}(\sigma^{-i}|H)) = 1$.

In this definition condition 1 requires that each player's strategy be optimal given his beliefs about the opponents' strategies. The second condit ion requires that each player's beliefs are correct at every information set.

If, as we suppose, players observe only the terminal nodes that are reached, and not how opponents would have played at unreached information sets, then even if player i continually plays σ^i, he will only observe opponents' play at information sets in $\bar{H}(\sigma)$ and will not learn about his

---

7. Battigalli's concept allows more general "signals" that correspond to the partitions discussed in note 3 above.

opponents' play at other information sets. This leads us to the following equilibrium concept.

Definition 6.3 (Fudenberg and Levine 1993a) A unitary self-confirming equilibrium is a mixed profile σ such that there exist beliefs μ^i such that for each $s^i \in \text{supp}(\sigma^i)$,

1. $u^i(s^i|\mu^i) \geq u^i(\hat{s}^i|\mu^i)$ for all $\hat{s}^i \in S^i$,
2. $\mu^i(\Pi^{-i}(\sigma^{-i}|\bar{H}(\sigma))) = 1$.

6.5 Stability of Self-confirming Equilibrium

We turn now to stability analysis in the simple learning model introduced above. As in chapter 4, say that a profile is *unstable* if for every positive ε, players' behavior is almost surely more than ε away from the profile infinitely often.

Proposition 6.1 (Fudenberg and Kreps 1995a) If σ is not a self-confirming equilibrium, then it is unstable with respect to any behavior rules that are myopic with respect to asymptotically empirical assessments.

The intuition for this is simple: If play converges to σ, then by the strong law of large numbers, we expect that every information set in the support of σ will be reached a nonvanishing fraction of the time and that the distribution of actions at such information sets will converge to that generated by σ. Asymptotic empiricism then implies that players' assessments converge to σ along the path of play, and a standard continuity argument shows that some player eventually perceives a benefit to deviating from σ.

This result only shows that *strategy profiles* cannot converge to a limit that is not a self-confirming equilibrium; it does not preclude a situation in which the strategy profiles fail to converge while the *outcome* converges to a limit that cannot be generated by any self-confirming equilibrium. Since only outcomes are observed, it is of some interest to know that the proposition can be extended: Say that an outcome ρ is unstable if there is an $\varepsilon > 0$ such that there is probability 0 that the distribution of outcomes generated by the players' strategies is always within ε of ρ.

Proposition 6.2 (Fudenberg and Kreps 1995a) If outcome ρ is not generated by any self-confirming equilibrium, then it is unstable with respect to any behavior rules that are myopic with respect to asymptotically empirical assessments.

Note that this result compares the probability law generating outcomes to the specified outcome distribution ρ, as opposed to comparing the observed empirical distribution to ρ, but arguments in the spirit of the strong law of large numbers can be combined with proposition 6.2 to show that there is probability 0 that the empirical distribution of outcomes remains within ε of ρ.

The discussion of example 6.1 already gives an example of a stable profile that is not a Nash equilibrium. A more formal statement of this requires a definition of local stability that allows for randomness:

Definition 6.4   A strategy profile π is *locally stochastically stable* under a given behavior rule (and initial condition) if there is positive probability that the strategy profile chosen by the players converges to π.

Proposition 6.3   Every self-confirming strategy profile π is locally stochastically stable for some behavior rules that are myopic with respect to asymptotically empirical assessments.

The proof of this parallels the construction in chapter 4 in which players start out with a strong prior belief in the particular equilibrium and maintain that belief unless they receive overwhelming evidence to the contrary.

6.6   Heterogeneous Self-confirming Equilibrium

In chapter 7 we will discuss learning in the extensive form in a model where players are randomly matched with one another and observe only the results of their own match, as in most game theory experiments. In this case there is no reason that two subjects assigned the same player role should have the same prior beliefs. Moreover, given that players only observe the outcomes in their own matches, if two subjects have always played different pure strategies, their beliefs may remain different.[8] Fudenberg and Levine (1993a) introduce the following weaker notion of self-confirming equilibrium to capture this notion.

Definition 6.5   A *heterogeneous self-confirming equilibrium* is a mixed profile σ such that for all $s^i \in \text{supp}(\sigma^i)$ there exist beliefs μ^i such that

1. $u^i(s^i|\mu^i) \geq u^i(\hat{s}^i|\mu^i)$ for all $\hat{s}^i \in S^i$,
2. $\mu^i(\Pi^{-i}(\sigma^{-i}|\bar{H}(s^i, \sigma^{-i}))) = 1$.

---

8. On the other hand, we would expect all players to eventually have the same beliefs if they observe the aggregate distribution of outcomes in the whole population.

This definition allows different beliefs to be used to rationalize each pure strategy in the support of σ^i, and it allows the beliefs that rationalize a given strategy to be mistaken at information sets that are not reached when the strategy is played but are reached under a different strategy that is also in the support of σ^i. A simple example from Fudenberg and Levine (1993a) shows how this allows outcomes that cannot arise with unitary beliefs:

Example 6.2 (Fudenberg and Levine 1993a)   Consider again the game in figure 6.2. The game has two types of Nash equilibria: the subgame perfect Ru and the equilibria in which player 1 plays L and player 2 plays d at least 1/3 of the time. However, there is no Nash equilibrium in which player 1 randomizes between L and R, nor is there a unitary self-confirming equilibrium of that form. This is a consequence of proposition 6.6 in section 6.8 below, which gives conditions for the outcomes of unitary SCE to coincide with the set of Nash outcomes, but the argument can be made directly in this example: If a single player 1 randomizes between L and R, unitary SCE requires that he know how player 2 responds to R, and since player 2 is reached a positive fraction of the time, player 2's will always play u.

There is, however, a heterogeneous self-confirming equilibrium in which player 2 always plays u while player 1's strategy assigns positive probability to both L and R. To see that this satisfies definition 6.5, let the beliefs associated with L be that 2 plays d and the beliefs associated with R be that 2 plays u. Then the beliefs associated with R are correct, while the beliefs associated with L are not refuted by the information revealed when L is played. This corresponds to a situation in which some player 1's have correct beliefs and play R, while other player 1's fear that 2 plays d and so chose not to give 2 the chance to move, which prevents them from learning that their beliefs are mistaken.

Note that in a one-shot simultaneous-move game, all information sets are on the path of every profile, so the sets $\bar{H}(s^i, \sigma^i)$ are all of H, and even heterogeneous self-confirming equilibrium requires that beliefs be exactly correct. Hence in these games all self-confirming equilibria are Nash.

6.7   Consistent Self-confirming Equilibrium

So far we have considered various ways of weakening the notion of equilibrium to capture steady states of a learning process where the entire opponents' strategy is not observed. We now wish to consider ways in which we can strengthen the notion of self-confirming equilibrium to reflect additional information that may be available to players. Our first considerations is what happens when a player faces an opponent whose hand "trembles," or equivalently (in our random matching context) the player faces a sequence of different opponents, a small fraction of whom have different preferences. In this case the player in question will learn not only what will happens on the equilibrium path but also what will happen at all information sets that are actually reachable given his own strategy.

Definition 6.6 A *consistent unitary self-confirming equilibrium* is a mixed profile σ such that for all i there exist beliefs μ^i such that for each $s^i \in \text{supp}(\sigma^i)$,

1. $u^i(s^i|\mu^i) \geq u^i(s'^i|\mu^i)$ for all $\hat{s}^i \in S^i$,
2. $\mu^i(\Pi^{-i}(\sigma^{-i}|H(\sigma^i)) = 1$.

Consistent self-confirming equilibria have stronger properties and are more "Nash-like" than inconsistent self-confirming equilibrium. (Note that the non-Nash outcome in example 6.1 relies on inconsistent beliefs.) Although consistency may be a reasonable condition to impose in some circumstances, such as those mentioned above, the main uses of the condition so far have been consequences of the fact that in some classes of games, all self-confirming equilibria are necessarily consistent.

Obviously Nash equilibrium requires consistency: Since Nash equilibrium requires that all players have correct beliefs, it requires in particular that any two players agree about the play of a third. However, not all inconsistent beliefs lead to departures from Nash equilibrium. In particular, in order for inconsistent beliefs of players 1 and 2 about the play of player 3 to support an outcome that cannot occur in a Nash equilibrium, both player 1 and player 2 need to be able to *unilaterally* deviate from the path of play and cause the information set in question to be reached, which is only possible if player 3 is unable to distinguish between deviations by the two players. Fudenberg and Levine (1993a) define a class of games in which this cannot happen.

Definition 6.7 A game has *observed deviators* if for all players i, all strategy profiles s, and all deviations $\hat{s}^i \neq s^i$, $h^i \in \bar{H}(\hat{s}^i, s^{-i}) \backslash \bar{H}(s)$ implies that there is no $\hat{s}^{-i}$ with $h^i \in \bar{H}(s^i, \hat{s}^{-i})$.

What this definition requires is that if a deviation by player i leads to a new information set off the equilibrium path, there is no deviation by i's opponents that leads to the same information set. Games of perfect information satisfy this condition, as do repeated games with observed actions.

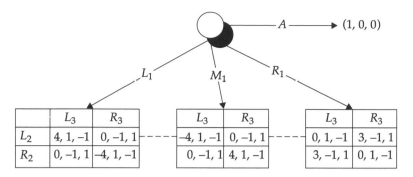

Figure 6.3
Example where untested correlation matters

More generally, the conditions are satisfied by all multistage games with observed actions, as defined by Fudenberg and Tirole (1991). Moreover Fudenberg and Levine establish that two-player games of perfect recall satisfy this condition: With two players, both players must know whether it was their deviation or their opponents' that led them to a particular information set.

Proposition 6.4 (Fudenberg and Levine 1993a)   In games with observed deviators, self-confirming equilibria are consistent self-confirming.

The idea is that with observed deviators, the information sets off the equilibrium path that are reachable when a player's opponents deviates (as described in the definition of consistency) cannot be reached when the player himself deviates, so beliefs about play at such information sets are irrelevant.

6.8   Consistent Self-confirming Equilibria and Nash Equilibria

Even consistent self-confirming equilibria, however, need not be Nash. There are two reasons for this difference. First, consistent self-confirming equilibrium allows a player's uncertainty about his opponents' strategies to be correlated, while Nash equilibrium requires that the beliefs be a point mass on a behavior strategy profile.

Example 6.3 (Untested correlation)   In the game in figure 6.3 player 1 can play A, which ends the game, or make any other of three moves, all leading to a simultaneous-move game by player 1's opponents, player 2 and player 3, neither of whom observes player 1's move. In this game A is

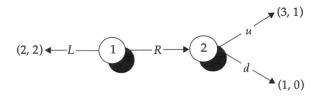

Figure 6.4
Public randomization in a Selten game

not a best response for player 1 to any behavior strategy of his opponents, but it is a best response to the correlated distribution with puts equal weight on (L_2, L_3), (R_2, R_3).[9] Making use of this observation, we see that in fact the only Nash equilibrium of this game has player 1 playing R_1 and players 2 and 3 giving both actions equal probability. However, player 1 can play A in a consistent self-confirming equilibrium provided his beliefs are the correlated distribution given above.

The non-Nash outcome in this example arises because of player 1's correlated uncertainty about the play of players 2 and 3. Note well that the support of player 1's beliefs is the (uncorrelated) mixed strategies of players 2 and 3, so that player 1 does not believe that the actual play of his opponents is correlated. Rather, the correlation lies in player 1's subjective uncertainty about his opponents' play. In the opposite case, when beliefs over behavior strategies induce a probability distribution over outcomes consistent with independent play by opponents, we refer to beliefs as *independent*.

Of course subjective correlation can only arise in games with three or more players. There is a second way that consistent self-confirming equilibria can fail to be Nash that arises even in two-player games. This is because the heterogeneous self-confirming concept allows each s_i that player i assigns positive probability to be a best response to different beliefs. The most immediate consequence of these differing beliefs is a form of convexification, as in the following example.

Example 6.4 (Public randomization)   In the game in figure 6.4, player 1 can end the game by moving L, or he can give player 2 the move by choosing R. Player 1 should play L if he believes 2 will play D, and he should play R if he believes 2 will play U. If player 1 plays R with positive probability, player 2's unique best response is to play U, so there are two Nash equilibrium outcomes, (L) and (R, U). The mixed profile $((1/2L,$

9. This is verified in Fudenberg and Levine (1993a).

$1/2R)$, U) is a self-confirming equilibrium whose outcome is a convex combination of the Nash outcomes: Player 1 plays L when he expects player 2 to play D, and R when he expects 2 to play U; when he plays L his forecast of D is not disconfirmed. (Note that this equilibrium is independent.)

Although we are unaware of a formal proof, we believe that in all two-player games of perfect information the only possible heterogeneous self-confirming equilibria are public randomizations over Nash equilibrium. Absent the restriction to perfect information, self-confirming equilibria in two-player games can involve more than convexification over Nash equilibria. The idea is that by embedding a randomization over equilibria as in example 6.4 in the second stage of a two-stage game, we can induce one player to randomize in the first stage even though such randomization cannot arise in Nash equilibrium. Moreover this randomization may in turn cause the player's opponent to take an action that would not be a best response without it.

Both the off-path correlation of the first example and the "extra randomization" of the second one can occur in the *extensive-form correlated equilibria* defined by Forges (1986). These equilibria, which are defined only for games whose information sets are ordered by precedence, are the Nash equilibria of an expanded game where an "autonomous signaling device" is added at every information set. The joint distribution over these signals is assumed to be independent of the actual play of the game, and common knowledge to the players, and the player on move at each information set h is told the outcome of the corresponding device before he chooses his move. Extensive-form correlated equilibrium includes Aumann's (1974) correlated equilibrium as the special case where the signals at information sets after stage 1 have one-point distributions and so contain no new information. The possibility of signals at later dates allows the construction of extensive-form correlated equilibria that are not correlated equilibria, as in Myerson (1986).

Proposition 6.5 (Fudenberg and Levine 1993a)   For each consistent self-confirming equilibrium of a game whose information sets are ordered by precedence, there is an equivalent extensive-form correlated equilibrium.

Here equivalent means they have the same distribution over terminal nodes, that is, the same outcome. Note that the converse is false in general: Even "ordinary" correlated equilibria need not be self-confirming, as is easily seen by considering one-shot simultaneous-move games, where self-confirming equilibrium reduces to Nash.

Corollary 6.1 In two-player games every self-confirming equilibrium outcome is the outcome of an extensive-form correlated equilibrium.

The discussion and examples above show that there are at least three possibilities that allow non-Nash outcomes to occur in a self-confirming equilibrium: Two players may have different (i.e., inconsistent) beliefs about the play of a third one, subjective correlation in a players' beliefs about the play of two or more opponents, and multiple (heterogeneous) beliefs for a single player role. The following result shows that these are the only reasons that a non-Nash outcome can be self-confirming.

Proposition 6.6 (Fudenberg and Levine 1993a) Every consistent self-confirming equilibrium with independent, unitary beliefs is equivalent to a Nash equilibrium.

The idea, as in the proof of proposition 6.3, is simply to specify that each player's off-path actions are exactly those that the player's opponents believe would be played. The assumption of unitary beliefs ensures that there is only a single equilibrium path associated with each player i. The consistency condition implies that all of player i's opponents have the same beliefs about player i's off-path play, and the independence condition ensures that these do not reflect implicit "threats" to use correlated strategies.

6.9   Rationalizable SCE and Prior Information on Opponents' Payoffs

Because self-confirming equilibrium allows beliefs about off-path play to be completely arbitrary, it (like Nash equilibrium) corresponds to a situation in which players have no prior information about the payoff functions of their opponents. This may be a good approximation of some real-world situations; it is also the obvious assumption for analyzing game theory experiments in which subjects are given no information about opponents' payoffs. In other cases, both in the real world and in the laboratory, it seems plausible that players do have some prior information about their opponents' payoffs. In an effort to capture this idea, Dekel, Fudenberg, and Levine (1996) introduce the notion of "rationalizable self-confirming equilibrium."

Consider in particular the game in example 6.4, shown in figure 6.4. Self-confirming equilibrium allows 2 to play d so long as 2's information set is not reached in the course of play. As noted by Selten (1965), 2 can thus "threaten" to play d, and thus induce 1 to play L. However, this threat is not "credible" if 1 knows 2's payoff function, for then player 1 should realize that player 2 would play u if ever her information set is reached. For this reason in many settings the weak rationality condition used by Nash and self-confirming equilibrium incorporates too little information about opponents' payoffs.

Although Selten used this example to motivate subgame perfection, it is important to note that the argument given in the last paragraph, taken on its own, only justifies the much weaker conclusion that a player should not use a strategy that is not a best response at the information set in question. In particular, this argument does not provide a rationale for subgame perfection's requirement that expectations about play in an off-path proper subgame should be a Nash equilibrium of that subgame. Dekel, Fudenberg, and Levine (1996) propose that the appropriate use of information about opponents' payoffs is through a version of extensive-form rationalizability. The idea is that players should exclude certain strategy profiles from consideration before they observe any information about how the game is actually being played.

The key issue involved in modeling this idea is determining what sort of prior information about payoffs should be considered, since this will determine which strategy profiles are ruled out by the players. One possibility would be to consider predictions consistent with common certainty about payoffs. However, it is well known that predictions of this type are not robust to even a small amount of uncertainty. Since we believe that exact common certainty is more prior information than is reasonable, we focus instead on the strongest restrictions on players' beliefs that are robust to small amounts of payoff uncertainty. Past work suggests that this assumption should be that payoffs are almost common certainty in the sense of Monderer and Samet (1989).[10] This is captured by a preliminary concept called rationalizability at reachable nodes that incorporates almost common certainty of the payoffs and as a result is robust to the introduction of a small amount of uncertainty. In particular, players believe that their opponents' actions will maximize their presumed payoff functions so long as the opponents have not been observed to

---

10. This can be seen, for example, by relating the results of Dekel and Fudenberg (1990) and Börgers (1994). More specifically, Dekel and Fudenberg applied the FKL notion of robustness to show, roughly speaking, that the tightest robust solution concept that does not impose the common prior assumption is given by deleting one round of weakly dominated strategies and then iteratively deleting strongly dominated strategies. Subsequently Börgers (1994) showed that this solution concept is characterized by almost common certainty of caution and of payoffs/rationality in the strategic form.

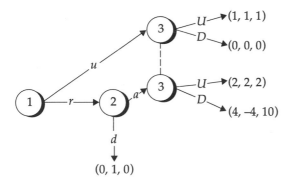

Figure 6.5
Dekel-Fudenberg-Levine example

deviate from anticipated play, but once an opponent has deviated, this restriction is no longer imposed.[11]

Before getting into the details, consider the following example which illustrates some of the possibilities that occur when rationalizability is combined with self-confirming equilibrium. An example from Dekel, Fudenberg, and Levine (1996) shown in figure 6.5 illustrates the issues involved.

In this example (u, U) is a Nash outcome (and so certainly self-confirming), since 2's information set is off the equilibrium path and so he may play d. Intuitively, however, if this were the long-run outcome of as learning process, player 1 should realize that 2 knows that 3 is playing up, and player 1 can use this knowledge and his knowledge of player 2's payoffs to deduce that 2 will play a.

6.9.1 Notation

To deal formally with rationalizability and self-confirming equilibrium, it is necessary to introduce additional notation concerning beliefs in extensive-form games. An *assessment* a^i for player i is a probability distribution over nodes at each of his information sets. A *belief pair* for player i is a pair $b^i = (a^i, \pi^{i:-i})$ consisting of i's assessment over nodes a^i and i's expectations of opponents' play $\pi^{i:-i} = (\pi^{i:j})_{j \neq i}$. Notice that we are now imposing the independence restriction that a player must believe that his opponents play independently of one another. The belief $b^i = (a^i, \pi^{i:-i})$ is

---

11. This assumes, in addition to almost common certainty of the payoffs, that the payoffs are determined independently, so the signal refers only to the deviator's payoffs.

consistent (Kreps and Wilson 1982) if the assessment a^i can be derived from full support approximations to $\pi^{i:-i}$.

Given a consistent belief by player i, player i's information sets give rise to a decision tree in a perfectly natural way. Moreover each information set has associated with it a well-defined subtree that follows after that information set. Each behavior strategy induces a strategy in that subtree in a natural way. A behavior strategy is a *conditional best response at h^i* by player i to consistent beliefs b^i if the restricted strategy is optimal in subtree that follows h^i. (This implicitly supposes that the player will play optimally at subsequent nodes, so a choice that will yield 1 given optimal future play, and 0 otherwise, is just as good as a choice that guarantees a payoff of 1.)

6.9.2   Belief-Closed Sets and Extensive-Form Rationalizability

The basic idea of rationalizability, due to Bernheim (1984) and Pearce (1984), is that based on his knowledge of the payoffs, each player should have a consistent sequence of conjectures about how his opponent thinks he thinks he should play, and so forth. One method of formalizing this idea is to assign to each player a set of strategy-belief pairs. Each strategy should be a best response to the corresponding beliefs, and each belief in this set should be "rationalized" by the existence of strategies that are in the set of consistent strategy-belief pairs for other players. It is convenient to separate out this latter idea of "belief-closedness" in a separate definition. When combined below with the requirement that the strategies be best responses to beliefs, we get a definition of rationalizability.

Definition 6.8   The collection of sets of strategy-belief pairs $SB^1, \ldots,$ SB^n is *belief-closed* if $(\pi^i, (a^i, \pi^{i:-i})) \in SB^i$ implies that $\pi^{i:j}$ arises from a mixture over the set $\{\tilde{\pi}^j | (\tilde{\pi}^j, b^j) \in SB^j \text{ for some } b^j\}$.

In words, if i believes that j can choose some behavior strategy, then that strategy must be in j's set of possible choices. As we indicated above, the elements of the sets SB^j are better viewed as "things that player i might think player j will do" than as "things j is likely to do ex ante." For example, if j's strategy specifies an action at some off-path information set that is not optimal given j's specified payoffs, the interpretation is that this is something i plausibly thinks that j would do if that information set is reached.

As a preliminary step it is useful to provide an equivalent definition of self-confirming equilibrium that incorporates the notion of belief-closedness; the point is that without the additional requirements we introduce below, belief-closedness itself has no force.

Proposition 6.7 *Profile $\hat{\pi}$ is a unitary self-confirming equilibrium if and only if there is a collection of sets of strategy-belief pairs, $SB^1, \ldots, SB^n$, such that for all players i,*

1. *if $(\pi^i, b^i) \in SB^i$, then π^i is a best response to b^i at information sets that are reached with positive probability under $(\pi^i, \pi^{i:-i})$;*

2. *every $(\pi^i, b^i) \in SB^i$ has the distribution over outcomes induced by $\hat{\pi}$;*

3. *$SB^1, \ldots, SB^n$ is belief-closed.*

Next we use belief-closedness to give a version of rationalizability for extensive-form games.[12]

Definition 6.9 *A collection $SB^1, \ldots, SB^n$ is rationalizable at reachable nodes if for all I,*

1'. *if $(\pi^i, b^i) \in SB^i$, then π^i is a best response to b^i at information sets reachable under π^i;*

3. *$SB^1, \ldots, SB^n$ is belief-closed.*

Note that condition 1' strengthens condition 1 above by requiring optimal play at a larger set of information sets. Note also that since this definition is in the spirit of rationalizability, it does not suppose that there is a commonly known path of play, so it does not impose an analogue of condition 2 in proposition 6.7. For reasons of robustness which we discuss further below, this notion does not require rationalizability at all nodes.

To combine these concepts, rationalizable self-confirming equilibrium strengthens the optimality condition in the definition of self-confirming equilibrium by adding the requirement that the chosen strategy be a best response at all reachable information sets rather than merely all information sets that are reached with positive probability.

Definition 6.10 *Profile $\hat{\pi}$ is a rationalizable self-confirming equilibrium if there is a collection $SB^1, \ldots, SB^n$ such that for all players i,*

1'. *if $(\pi^i, b^i) \in SB^i$, then π^i is a best response to b^i at information sets reachable under π^i;*

---

12. Related notions can be found in Basu (1988), Reny (1992), Rubinstein and Wolinsky (1994), and Greenberg (1994).

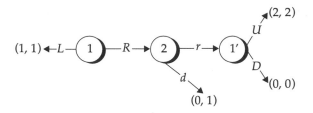

Figure 6.6
A robustness example

2. every $(\pi^i, b^i) \in SB^i$ has the distribution over outcomes induced by $\hat{\pi}$;

3. $SB^1, \ldots, SB^n$ is belief-closed.

Turning back to the game of example 6.4, in figure 6.4, we see that the rationalizable self-confirming equilibrium notion captures what we wanted: L is not part of any beliefs that are rationalizable at reachable nodes. To see this, observe that 2's information set is always reachable, so condition 1' implies that the only strategy in SB^2 is u. From condition 3 player 1 must believe this, so he plays R.

6.9.3 Robustness

An important feature of rationalizable self-confirming equilibrium is that a strategy need not be optimal at information sets that the strategy itself precludes. The reason that we do not wish to impose optimality at such information sets is that this stronger requirement is not robust to the presence of a small amount of payoff uncertainty. To see this, consider the game in figure 6.6.

In this game the outcome L occurs in the Nash equilibrium (LD, d) but not in any subgame-perfect equilibrium. However, in the game of incomplete information in figure 6.7, where payoffs are very likely to be as in figure 6.6, the outcome L occurs in a sequential equilibrium. So requiring optimality at all information sets rules out the outcome L in figure 6.6 but not in 6.7; hence this requirement is not robust to small payoff uncertainties.[13] It is easy to see that by construction rationalizable self-confirming

---

13. Just as in previous work related to this notion of robustness, one may be able to identify a smaller set of robust predictions if one feels confident that certain forms of payoff uncertainty are much less likely than others. We say more about this in the next section. For more on the idea of robustness, see Fudenberg, Kreps, and Levine (1988) and Dekel and Fudenberg (1990).

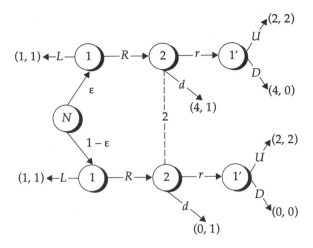

Figure 6.7
Incomplete information version of figure 6.6

equilibrium achieves our objectives in figure 6.6: Since player 1's second information set is not reachable when 1 plays L, the outcome L can occur in a rationalizable self-confirming equilibrium.

6.9.4   Example 6.1 Revisited

Ordinary self-confirming equilibrium allows two players to disagree about the play of the third. This example demonstrates the intuitive idea that the possibilities for such disagreements are reduced when players must believe that opponent's play is a best response at reachable nodes. Consider the version shown in figure 6.8 of the extensive-form game Fudenberg and Kreps (1988) used to show that mistakes about off-path play can lead to non-Nash outcomes. Here the outcome (A, a) is self-confirming for any values of x and y. It is supported by player 1 believing that player 3 will play R and player 2 believing that player 3 will play L. However, because 3's information set is reachable, this outcome is not a rationalizable self-confirming equilibrium if both x and y have the same sign: If $x, y > 0$, then players 1 and 2 forecast that 3 will play R, and so 2 plays d; if $x, y < 0$, then 3 plays L, so 1 plays D. However, if x and y have opposite signs, then (A, a) is a rationalizable self-confirming equilibrium outcome, since 1 and 2 are not required to have the same beliefs about player 3's off-path assessment of the relative probability of the two nodes, and player 1 can think that 3's assessment makes R optimal, while player 2 can think that 3's assessment induces her to play L. This example shows

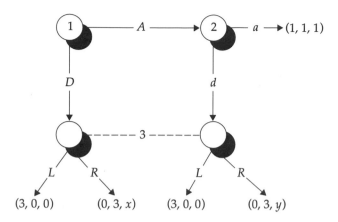

Figure 6.8
Variation on the Fudenberg-Kreps example

that even a sequentially rationalizable self-confirming equilibrium need not be Nash.

6.9.5 *Experimental Evidence*

Perhaps the best motivation for rationalizable self-confirming equilibrium is a pair of experiments by Prasnikar and Roth (1992) on the "best-shot" game in which two players sequentially decide how much to contribute to a public good. The only rationalizable self-confirming equilibrium of this game is its backward-induction solution in which the first mover contributes nothing; there is also an imperfect Nash equilibrium in which the first mover contributes and the second does not. Prasnikar and Roth ran two treatments of this game. In the first one, players were informed of the function determining opponents' monetary payoffs. Here, by the last few rounds of the experiment, the first movers had stopped contributing, which is the prediction made by rationalizable self-confirming equilibrium. In the second treatment, subjects were not given any information about the payoffs of their opponents. In this treatment, even in the later rounds of the experiment, many first movers contributed to the public good. This is not consistent with rationalizable self-confirming equilibrium, but it is consistent with an (approximate, heterogeneous) self-confirming equilibrium (Fudenberg and Levine 1997). Thus these experiments provide evidence that information about other players' payoffs makes a difference and that this difference corresponds to the distinction between self-confirming equilibrium and rationalizable self-confirming equilibrium.

References

Aumann, R. 1974. Subjectivity and correlation in randomized strategies. *Journal of Mathematical Economics* 1: 67–96.

Basu, K. 1988. Strategic irrationality in extensive games. *Mathematical Social Sciences* 15: 247–60.

Battigalli, P. 1987. Comportamento razionale ed equilibrio nei giochi e nelle situazioni sociali. Undergraduate thesis. Bocconi University.

Bernheim, D. B. 1984. Rationalizable strategic behavior. *Econometrica*, 52: 1007–28.

Dekel, E., and D. Fudenberg. 1990. Rational behavior with payoff uncertainty. *Journal of Economic Theory* 52: 243–67.

Dekel, E., D. Fudenberg, and D. K. Levine. 1996. Payoff information and self-confirming equilibrium. Mimeo, HIER D.P. 1774. Harvard University.

Forges, F. 1986. An approach to communication equilibrium. *Econometrica* 54: 1375–85.

Fudenberg, D., and D. K. Levine. 1993a. Self-confirming equilibrium. *Econometrica* 61: 523–45.

Fudenberg, D., and D. K. Levine. 1993b. Steady state learning and Nash equilibrium. *Econometrica* 61: 547–73.

Fudenberg, D., and D. K. Levine. 1997. Measuring subject's losses in experimental games. *Quarterly Journal of Economics* 112: 507–36.

Fudenberg, D., and D. M. Kreps. 1988. Learning, experimentation and equilibrium in games. Mimeo. Stanford University.

Fudenberg, D., and D. M. Kreps. 1995a. Learning in extensive games, I: Self-confirming equilibrium. *Games and Economic Behavior* 8: 20–55.

Fudenberg, D., and D. M. Kreps. 1995b. Learning in extensive games, II: Experimentation and Nash equilibrium. Mimeo. Harvard University.

Fudenberg, D., and J. Tirole. 1991. *Game Theory*. Cambridge: MIT Press.

Fudenberg, D., D. M. Kreps, and D. K. Levine. 1988. On the robustness of equilibrium refinements. *Journal of Economic Theory* 44: 354–80.

Greenberg, J. 1994. Social situations without commonality of beliefs: Worlds apart but acting together. Mimeo, W.P. 8/94. McGill University.

Hahn, F. 1977. Exercises in conjectural equilibrium. *Scandinavian Journal of Economics* 79: 210–26.

Kalai, E., and E. Lehrer. 1993. Rational learning leads to Nash equilibrium. *Econometrica* 61: 1019–46.

Kreps, D., and R. Wilson. 1982. Reputation and imperfect information. *Journal of Economic Theory* 50: 253–79.

Myerson, R. 1986. Bayesian equilibrium and incentive compatibility: An introduction. In *Social Goods and Social Organization: Essays in Honor of Elisha Pazner*, ed. by L. Hurwicz, D. Schmeidler, and H. Sonnenschein. Cambridge: Cambridge University Press.

Pearce, D. 1984. Rationalizable strategic behavior and the problem of perfection. *Econometrica* 52: 1029–50.

Prasnikar, V., and A. E. Roth. 1992. Considerations of fairness and strategy: Experimental data from sequential games. *Quarterly Journal of Economics* 107: 865–88.

Reny, P. 1992. Rationality in extensive-form games. *Journal of Economic Perspectives* 6: 103–18.

Rubinstein, A., and A. Wolinsky. 1994. Rationalizable conjectural equilibrium: Between Nash and rationalizability. *Games and Economic Behavior* 6: 299–311.

Selten, R. 1965. Spieltheoretische Behandlung eines Oligopmodells mitnachfragetragheit. *Zeitschrift für die gesampte Staatswissenschaft* 121: 301–24.

7

Nash Equilibrium, Large Population Models, and Mutations in Extensive-Form Games

7.1 Introduction

As we have seen, there is no presumption that simple learning in extensive-form games leads to Nash equilibrium outcomes, even when the learning process converges. However, a convergent learning process *will* converge to a Nash equilibrium outcome if it generates "enough" learning about off-path play. This chapter explores the related issues of just how much information is "enough" and what sorts of forces might lead to "enough" information being available. While we discuss several explanations, our focus is on the idea that players sometimes deliberately "experiment" with actions that do not maximize the current period's expected payoff in order to gain information about how their opponents react to these little-played actions.

As the first step in this chapter, we address the question of how much information about opponents' play is "enough" to rule out all but Nash equilibrium outcomes. The usual definition of Nash equilibrium implies that players know the entire strategy profile used by their opponents, or equivalently the distribution of actions that would occur at any information set. However, this is more knowledge than is necessary, since a given player's beliefs about play at some information sets may have no impact at all on how he chooses to play. Instead, it suffices that players have correct beliefs at those information sets that are "relevant" to them. We formalize this idea in section 7.2.

Section 7.3 develops sufficient conditions on exogenously specified behavior (in the spirit of fictitious play) that lead to Nash equilibirum. Section 7.4 then examines these assumptions, how they might be relaxed, and the connection between learning in games and in multi-armed bandit problems. Section 7.5 considers a model of fully rational, Bayesian learning in which experiementation rates are endogenous. In order to avoid some of the problems discussed in section 7.4, this is done in the context of a model of steady-state learning in large, heterogeneous populations. This model also provides a foundation for heterogeneous self-confirming equilibrium.

One obvious question in this area that has so far been little explored is the extent to which it is possible to establish convergence to a refinement of Nash equilibrium. Section 7.6 discusses the work of Noldeke and Samuelson (1993) that relates the stochastically stable outcomes of a particular learning process to the subgame-perfect equilibria in a special class of games.

We conclude with a discussion of cheap-talk games and return to the idea (discussed in chapter 3) that players can give a "secret handshake," a signal that they intend to carry out a particular action. We give a critical overview of the literature on evolutionary dynamics in this game and suggest that future work on this topic should take account of the extensive-form nature of the game.

7.2 Relevant Information Sets and Nash Equilibrium

Self-confirming equilibrium need not be Nash because some players may have incorrect beliefs about off-path play. However, to conclude that a particular self-confirming equilibrium is Nash, it is not necessary to assume that every player's beliefs are correct at every information set. In particular, since Nash equilibrium tests only for unilateral deviations, a player's beliefs about what would happen if some other player deviated are irrelevant. To capture this, Fudenberg and Kreps (1995b) introduce the following definition:

Definition 7.1   An information set h is *relevant to player i at profile π_** if there is some π^i such that (π^i, π_*^{-i}) assigns positive probability to h; the set of all such information sets is denoted $\hat{H}^i(\pi_*)$.

As in chapter 6, let $\Pi^{-i}(\pi_*|J) \equiv \{\pi^{-i}|\pi^j(h^j) = \pi_*^j(h^j|\sigma^i), \forall h^j \in H^{-i} \cap J\}$ be the subset of behavior strategies consistent with players other than i playing according to π_* at the information sets in J.

Proposition 7.1 (Fudenberg and Kreps 1995b)   A strategy profile π_* is a Nash equilibrium if there exist beliefs μ^i such that for all i,

1. $u^i(\pi_*^i|\mu^i) \geq u^i(\pi^i|\mu^i)$ for all π^i,
2. $\mu^i(\Pi^{-i}(\pi_*|\hat{H}^i(\pi_*)) = 1$.

This shows that it is sufficient for Nash equilibrium that beliefs be correct at relevant information sets. It is obvious that even this condition is not necessary.

However, the result does show that in order for a non-Nash profile to be unstable in a learning model, it is sufficient that beliefs become approximately correct at information sets that are relevant given the profile.

This in turn raises the question of when that will be the case. Intuitively, beliefs about play at an information set will be correct if that information set is reached sufficiently often, so players have "enough" observations about play at the information set to outweigh their possibly incorrect priors. Moreover, unless we are prepared to make assumptions about the *strength* of the players' prior convictions (i.e., the size of the fictitious initial sample in fictitious play), "enough" observations means infinitely many of them. Of course any assumption that implies a positive probability that a myopically suboptimal action will be played infinitely often is inconsistent with optimal behavior in the discounted multi-armed bandit problem; with a full-support prior the optimal solution has probability 1 that experimentation ceases in finite time, with a positive probability of "locking onto" the objectively "wrong" arm. (The appendix reviews the classic multi-armed bandit problem.)

Consequently any assumptions that imply probability 1 of all relevant information sets being reached infinitely often, regardless of the priors (and consequently probability 0 of convergence to a non-Nash self-confirming outcome), are not consistent with optimal behavior in the discounted bandit problem. The reason for interest in such assumptions is that they do correspond to the limit of behavior in the bandit problem as the discount factor goes to 1. Intuitively, as players become more patient, the value of information increases, so they do more experiments, and the probability of locking onto the wrong arm converges to 0. As a result the "sufficient experimentation" conditions in the following section should be interpreted as an idealization of the limit behavior as the discount factor tends to 1.

7.3 Exogenous Experimentation

Fudenberg and Kreps (1995b) develop sufficient conditions for instability of non-Nash equilibrium and local stability of Nash equilibrium in a model of boundedly rational behavior that is in the spirit of fictitious play. Their assumptions imply that if the strategies played converge, then all relevant information sets (given the limit profile) are reached infinitely often, that beliefs at these information sets converge to the empirical distribution of play there, and that the empirical distribution resembles the limit profile to which play is converging. The latter two conditions are imposed by strengthening the asymptotic myopia and asymptotic empiricism conditions developed in chapter 6; the first condition, that all relevant information sets are reached infinitely often, is obtained by imposing lower bounds on the probabilities that players "experiment" in various ways.

The reason that the experimentation condition on its own is not sufficient is that the definitions of asymptotic empiricism and myopia given in chapter 6 impose no restrictions at all on beliefs or behavior at information sets that are reached infinitely often but a vanishing fraction of the time. It is easy to strengthen the empiricism condition. Fix an infinite history h_∞, and let $H_\infty^i(h_\infty)$ be the collection of player i's information sets that are reached infinitely often along h_∞:

Definition 7.2 Player i's belief rule μ_t^i is *strongly asymptotically empirical in the extensive form* if for every $\varepsilon > 0$, infinite history h_∞, $j \neq i$, and information set $h^j \in H_\infty^j(h_\infty)$,

$$\lim_{t \to \infty} \mu_t^i(h_t)(\{\pi^{-i} | \|\pi^j(h^j) - d(h^j|h_t)\| < \varepsilon\}) = 1.$$

This condition is satisfied by Bayesian learners who believe that opponents' play corresponds to a fixed but unknown distribution (i.e., exchangeable draws) and have a nondoctrinaire prior over the set of all strategy profiles for the opponents.

For Nash equilibrium to be reached in the limit, players must engage in "enough" experimentation to learn about off-path play; in particular, the "rate" of experimentation cannot decrease too quickly. At the same time, however, these experiments must vanish quickly enough that they are a negligible component of asymptotic play. We first modify the definition of asymptotic myopia to include a limited and asymptotically negligible amount of experimentation. Let $\kappa(a, h_t)$ denote the number of time the action a has been played in the history h_t and $\kappa(h^i, h_t)$ the number of time the information set h^i has occurred.

Definition 7.3 For a particular forecast rule γ^i a behavior rule ρ^i is *strongly asymptotically myopic with experience-time limitations on experimentation* if it can be decomposed into two rules, a "myopic" rule $\hat{\rho}^i$ and an "experimentation" rule $\tilde{\rho}^i$ such that

1. $p^i(h_t)(h^i) = a^i(h_t)(h^i)\hat{p}^i(h_t)(h^i) + (1 - a^i(h_t)(h^i))\tilde{p}^i(h_t)(h^i)$ for   some $a^i(h_t)(h^i) \in [0, 1]$,

2. $\hat{p}^i$ is asymptotically myopic,

3. there is a nonnegative sequence $\eta_t \to 0$ such that $(1 - a^i(h_t)(h^i))\tilde{p}^i(h_t)(h^i)(a) > 0$ only if $\kappa(a, h_t)/\kappa(h^i, h_t) \leq \eta_{\kappa(h^i, h_t)}$.

In other words, the probability assigned to an "experimental" action must be zero unless the action has been tried infrequently.

The experience-time limitations on experimentation imply that, asymptotically, play is with high probability asymptotically myopic. In particular, the proportion of the time that i experiments at an information set must go to 0 as the number of times that the information set is reached becomes large. On the other hand, to attain Nash equilibrium, it is necessary also that there be "enough" experimentation.

Definition 7.4   For a given player i and information set h^i, the behavior rule p^i satisfies the *minimal experience-time experimentation condition* at h^i if there is a constant $\beta > 0$ and a nonnegative sequence $v_t \to 0$ with tv_t nondecreasing such that

$$p^i(h_t)\left(a \in A(h^i) \,\middle|\, \frac{\kappa(a, h_t)}{\kappa(h^i(a), h_t)} \leq v_{\kappa(h^i(a), h_t)}\right) \geq \beta.$$

In other words, actions that have been played infrequently should be tried with at least probability β.

The force of this condition can be seen from the following result:

Proposition 7.2   If player i's behavior satisfies the minimal experience-time experimentation condition at information set h^i, then for every $a \in A(h^i)$,

$$P\left(\left\{h_\infty \,\middle|\, \lim_{t \to \infty} \kappa(h^i, h_t) = \infty \quad \text{and} \quad \lim_{t \to \infty} \kappa(a, h_t) < \infty\right\}\right) = 0.$$

Roughly speaking, this says that if h^i is reached infinitely often, then every action that is feasible there must be taken infinitely often. This is a strong conclusion, and indeed it suggests that the so-called "minimal experience-time experimentation condition" may require more experimentation than is plausible. We discuss these issues in the next section. For now we note the following corollary: In a game of perfect information, if minimal experience-time experimentation is satisfied at *every* information set, then with probability 1 every information set is reached infinitely often.

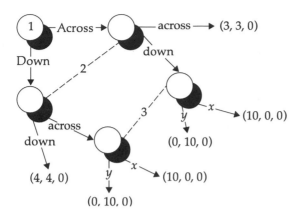

Figure 7.1
Fudenberg-Kreps example of convergence to non-Nash outcome despite "frequent" experimentation

Surprisingly these assumptions are not enough to preclude convergence to non-Nash equilibrium in games of imperfect information. The example in figure 7.1, from Fudenberg and Kreps (1995b), illustrates the potential problem. In figure 7.1, the outcome (Across, across) is not a Nash equilibrium, since for any strategy of player 3, at least one of them would prefer to deviate. Suppose that player 1 initially believes 3 will play *y*, so Across is player 1's short-run optimum, while 2 believes that 3 will play *x*, so 2's myopic best response is to play across. Suppose moreover that both players choose to "experiment" with their other, apparently suboptimal, action at dates 1, 10, 100, 1,000, and so forth. The behavior rules satisfy the minimal experience-time experimentation condition, yet player 3's information set is never reached. Fudenberg and Kreps show that this problem can be avoided with either of two additional assumptions. The following is the simpler but less palatable of the two:

Definition 7.5   The behavior rule ρ^i is *uniformly nonexperimental* iff the probability $a^i(h_t)(h^i)$ of following the nonexperimental rule $\hat{\rho}^i$ at information set h^i given history h_t is uniformly bounded below by some $\alpha > 0$.

This requires that there always be at least an α chance a player does not experiment so that experimentation by the opposing player has a chance of revealing information about his nonexperimental play. However, this assumption is inconsistent with optimal play in a bandit problem. (We discuss this in more detail below.) As an alternative, Fudenberg and Kreps suggest that stability be redefined so as to exclude histories in which the players somehow perfectly coordinate their experiments; we say more about this in the next section. The next section also explains why an analogue of uniform nonexperimentation holds in models with anonymous random matching in a large population.

Proposition 7.3 (Fudenberg and Kreps 1995b)   If beliefs are strongly asymptotically empirical, if behavior rules satisfy asymptotic myopia with experience-time limitations on experimentation, if the minimal experience-time experimentation condition holds at all information sets behavior is uniformly nonexperimental, then if π is not a Nash profile, it is unstable; if π is a Nash profile, then it is weakly stable.

It is perhaps not surprising that with the "right" amount of experimentation only Nash equilibria can be reached. Intuitively the combination of asymptotic myopia and asymptotic empiricism implies that the limit point must be self-confirming equilibria, as in chapter 6. Moreover, at least in games of perfect information, the assumption of minimal experience-time experimentation at all information sets implies that every information set is reached infinitely often. Hence in such games, if play converges, players come to have correct beliefs about play at every information set, and so the limit point must be a Nash equilibrium. In more general games, minimal experience-time experimentation need not imply that all information sets are reached, as in the example above; this is why an additional assumption is needed.

7.4   Learning in Games Compared to the Bandit Problem

The assumptions that give local stability of Nash equilibria and instability of non-Nash equilibria are quite strong. In particular, the uniform nonexperimental condition is inconsistent with Bayesian optimization in a multi-armed bandit problem. In this section we consider alternative assumptions giving the same result and discuss more generally the issue of how learning about an extensive-form game differs from learning in a bandit problem.

The classical bandit problem is a simple one-move, one-person extensive-form game with random payoffs to each action, where the distributions of payoffs for some actions are unknown, and the payoffs to the various actions are distributed independently so that observing the payoff to one action reveals no information about the distributions governing the payoffs to other choices.[1] It is well known that even in a

---

1. There is a smaller literature on bandit problems with correlated payoffs. One way of thinking about learning in extensive-form games is that it corresponds to a bandit problem with a particular and potentially complex form of correlation.

bandit problem, an impatient player may fail to optimize: If it is believed a priori that a particular arm is inferior, it may never be tried, even if it is superior. In fact, for any fixed discount factor, experimentation in a bandit problem ends in finite time with probability one.[2] However, in the limit as the discount factor goes to one, the amount of time during which experimentation takes place goes to infinity, and the probability of a sub-optimal choice goes to zero. In the previous section the basic assumption was that experimentation continues forever. This should be viewed as an effort to capture the limit of optimal play in discounted bandit problems as the discount factor tends toward one. In the remainder of this section, we will use this limit as motivation for the types of rules that we would like to allow.

As we indicated, the uniform nonexperimental condition is inconsistent with optimal play in either the discounted or undiscounted bandit problem, since the optimal solution will typically involve playing an experimental action with probability one at some histories.[3] There are several answers to this problem. One possibility, explored in more detail below, is that the probability of nonexperimentation represents a probability of meeting an opponent who is not experimenting in a matching setting. Another possibility is to drop the assumption of uniform nonexperimentation altogether. An alternative, proposed by Fudenberg and Kreps, is to modify the definition of stability to include a condition that observed play passes some simple "statistical tests" of exchangeability and independence. The idea is that if the observed histories fail the tests, then players should realize that the environment is not after all asymptotically exchangeable and independent. Fudenberg and Kreps then verify that play can converge to Nash equilibrium and satisfy the statistical tests, while play cannot both satisfy the tests and converge to a non-Nash outcome, even when uniform nonexperimentation is not required. This formulation does not address how players behave if some player's statistical test fails.[4]

We next examine the minimal experience-time condition which requires experimentation with *all* actions that have been tried infrequently. This is

---

2. A more detailed discussion of bandit problems can be found in the appendix to this chapter.

3. It is true that uniform nonexperimentation is consistent with ε-optimization in the undiscounted bandit problem, but then so is any fixed and small amount of "trembling" onto other actions. This brings us back to the point made at the end of chapter 6: Non-Nash self-confirming outcomes should be viewed as descriptions of what will happen up to some time T for sufficiently small amounts of noise.

4. Chapter 8 discusses work that does specify how players behave if they detect certain sorts of departures from the assumptions of exchangeability and independence.

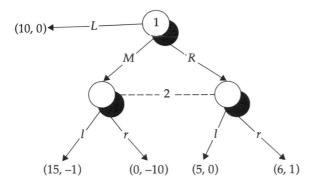

Figure 7.2
Fudenberg-Levine's example of costly experimentation

certainly the right strategy in the classic bandit problem where the pay-offs to the various arms are distributed independently. However, there are several reasons why this might not be optimal in a game. First of all, a player might have several actions, each of which leads to the same information sets of all opponents, and thus yields the same information. Since the payoffs of these actions need not be equal, it makes sense to suppose (and the optimum requires) that the player would experiment only with the action that involves the smallest expected loss.[5] The example in figure 7.2 from Fudenberg and Levine (1993) shows how this might happen. Suppose that player 1 assigns a low probability to player 2 playing *l*. In this case his immediate expected payoff is maximized by playing *L* himself. Suppose, however, that player 1 is willing to conduct a costly experiment to obtain information about player 2's play. Given player 1's beliefs, the lowest-cost way of obtaining this information is by playing *R*, and indeed it is possible that player 1 will never play *M*.[6]

---

5. But note that such considerations suggest equilibrium refinements in the spirit of Myerson's (1978) properness, since out-of-equilibrium actions tend to be taken as cheaply as possible.

6. As an aside, we note that this example also shows why optimal experimentation does not yield results in the spirit of forward induction (Kohlberg and Mertens 1986). Forward induction interprets all deviations from the path of play as attempts to gain in the current round. Since *L* strictly dominates *R*, forward induction argues that player 2 will believe that player 1 has played *M* whenever player 2's information set is reached, and hence that player 2 will play *l*; this will lead player 1 to play *M*. In contrast, in our model player 1 deviated from *L* to gain information that will help him in future rounds, and the cheapest way to do this is to play *R*. When *R* is more likely than *M*, *r* is optimal for player 2.

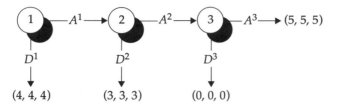

Figure 7.3
Fudenberg-Kreps minimum experience time example

There is no very easy modification of the minimal experience-time requirement that allows experimentation to be least cost. However, our discussion below of Bayesian learning in a steady-state setting takes account of the full optimization process, including the requirement that experiments be chosen with an eye to costs as well as benefits.

A second issue with the minimal experience-time experimentation condition is that we have required it to hold at all information sets. The example in figure 7.3 from Fudenberg and Kreps (1995b) shows why this is problematic. Suppose that along some history, player 1 chooses A^1 infinitely often but a vanishing fraction of the time, and that player 2 starts out with the assessment that player 3 is more likely to play D^3 than A^3. Then player 2, in periods when her information set is reached, would see A^2 as a costly but potentially worthwhile experiment. However, the experiment of playing A^2 only pays off if, first of all, player 2 learns that player 3 usually plays A^3, and *in addition* player 1 gives player 2 an opportunity to use that information by playing A^1 again in the not-too-distant future. Since player 2 has few observations on 3's play, she should assign a nonnegligible probability to the event that player 3 usually plays A^3, so she should expect that she might indeed have something to learn. However, given that player 1 plays A^1 with frequency going to 0, even a very patient, optimizing player 2 might not find it worthwhile to do any experiments with A^2. For this reason it is not sensible to require the minimal experience-time condition at every information set.

Here it is important to note that Nash equilibrium does not require that the minimal experience-time experimentation condition be satisfied at every information set. Instead, it is sufficient that the condition be satisfied at information sets that player i feels are "empirically relevant"— loosely speaking where the information set h^i is empirically relevant given an infinite history if it is reached a "sufficiently large" proportion of the times that it "might have been reached." Formally Fudenberg and Kreps (1995b) define

Definition 7.6 The behavior rule ρ^i satisfies the *modified minimal experience-time experimentation condition* or *MME* if there are a constant $\beta > 0$ and a nonnegative sequence $v_t \to 0$ with tv_t nondecreasing and a nonincreasing sequence of strictly positive numbers $\delta_k \to 0$ such that for all t and h_t, if $a_1^i, a_2^i, \dots$ is the unique sequence of actions by player i that lead to h^i and

$$\frac{\kappa(h^i(a_k^i), h_t)}{\kappa(a_k^i, h_t)} \geq \delta_{\kappa(a_k^i, h_t)},$$

then

$$\rho^i(h_t)\left(a \in A(h^i) \left| \frac{\kappa(a, h_t)}{\kappa(h^i(a), h_t)} \leq v_{\kappa(h^i(a), h_t)}\right.\right) \geq \beta.$$

The force of this condition can be seen from the following result:

Proposition 7.4 Suppose that player i's behavior satisfies the modified minimum experience-time experimentation condition and that there is a profile π_* and $\varepsilon > 0$ such that for all infinite histories h in some set Z, and all times t, at every partial history h_t the behavior rules ρ^i assign probability at least ε to every action a for which $\pi_*(a)$ is positive. Then almost surely on Z, every information set that is π_*-relevant to player i will be reached infinitely often.

Roughly speaking, the conclusion of this proposition is that every information set that "matters" to the player is reached infinitely often. Note that it allows there to be probability 1 that player 3's information set to be reached only finitely often in the example of figure 7.3, since the limit profile assigns probability 0 to player 2's information set. (Moreover it is easy to construct behavior rules that satisfy MME for all players and yet imply with probability 1 that player 3's information set is reached only finitely often.) In contrast, if every player's behavior satisfies minimal experience-time experimentation, then as we noted following proposition 7.2, player 3's information set is reached infinitely often with probability 1. However, we know from proposition 7.1 that since player 2's information set is never reached in the limit profile, player 2's beliefs about subsequent play are immaterial.

Fudenberg and Kreps show that the MME condition can be used in place of minimal experience-time experimentation to prove results in the spirit of proposition 7.3. In particular, play cannot converge to a non-Nash outcome if beliefs are strongly asymptotically empirical, behavior

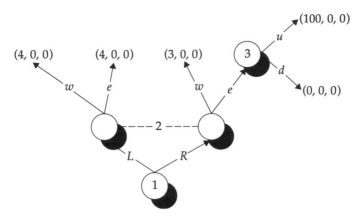

Figure 7.4
Illustration of an unrepresentative sample

satisfies MME and is asymptotically myopic with experience-time limitations on experimentation, and either players use statistical tests of independence and exchangeability or behavior play satisfies uniform non-experimentation.

Finally, although we noted that for any given discount factor, experimentation in a classic bandit problem should stop in a finite amount of time, in the setting of extensive-form games there can be histories along which players find it optimal to experiment a positive fraction of the time, even in the long run. The example in figure 7.4 illustrates the complications that may occur if certain unrepresentative samples occur. Suppose that player 1 has played both L and R many times and equally frequently. Suppose that it has just happened that when 1 played L, 2 played w half the time, but when 1 played R, 2 has always played w. Since player 1 knows that 2 has an information set, he knows that the actual probability of 2 playing e is about 1/4. Despite this, he has never actually seen player 3 play and does not know whether 3 is playing u, in which case R would be best, or whether 3 is playing d, in which case L would be best. A priori 1 may believe that 3 is likely playing d, in which case from a myopic point of view it would be best to play L. However, despite the large number of observations by player 1, there is still good reason to experiment with R, since, if 3 is playing u, it would be quite lucrative for 1 to play R. This shows that the assumption of asymptotic myopia can be inconsistent with certain unrepresentative samples. Intuitively, though, such samples should have probability 0 in the long run; Fudenberg and Levine (1993) verify this in a closely related setting.

7.5   Steady-State Learning

We now consider the Bayesian model of learning in which players believe that they face a stationary distribution of opponents' strategies. As we noted above, one possible problem with this is that in the setting where a fixed set of players are playing a game, the assumption is not true, and particularly if the system does not converge, players may be able to discover this. An alternative explored by Fudenberg and Levine (1993) is to study a model of a population of randomly matched players, with players entering and leaving the population. As players enter and leave (taking their knowledge with them), this model has a steady state in which the fraction of the population playing particular strategies remains fixed over time. The goal is to see what happens in this steady state when players are Bayesian optimizers and live for a long time.

The optimal amount of experimentation that takes place in the steady state is complicated. In practice, some experiments are more revealing than others, and more patient individuals will be more inclined to experiment than less patient individuals. Moreover the incentive to experiment depends on how lucky the individual has been with past experiments. What Fudenberg and Levine (1993) show is that when players have sufficiently long lives, their play resembles that of a self-confirming equilibrium, and if in addition players are patient enough, it resembles Nash equilibrium.

Specifically, corresponding to each player (except Nature) in the stage game is a population consisting of a continuum of players in the dynamic game. In each population the total mass of players is one. There is a doubly infinite sequence of periods, $\ldots, -1, 0, 1, \ldots$, and each individual player lives T periods. We denote the age of a player by τ. Every period $1/T$ new players enter the ith population, and we make the steady-state assumption that there are $1/T$ players in each generation, with $1/T$ players of age T exiting each period.

Every period each player i is randomly and independently matched with one player from each population $i' \neq i$, with the probability of meeting a player i' of age τ equal to its population fraction $1/T$.[7] For example, if $T = 2$, each player is as likely to be matched with a "new" player as an "old" one. Each player i's opponents are drawn independently.

Over his lifetime each player observes the terminal nodes that are reached in the games he has played but does not observe the outcomes

---

7. Boylan (1995) has shown that this deterministic system is the limit of a stochastic finite-population random matching model as the number of players goes to infinity.

in games played by others. Thus each player will observe a sequence of private histories h_τ^i.

The state of the system at a moment of time t is specified by the fraction of the population with each possible type of history $\theta_t^i(h_\tau^i)$. Let ρ^i denote the optimal strategy for a Bayesian player with a nondoctrinaire prior and discount factor δ. For any state θ it is also useful to define the actual number of people playing the strategy s^i:

$$\bar{\theta}^i(s^i) \equiv \sum_{h_\tau^i \mid \rho^i(h_\tau^i) = s^i} \theta^i(h_\tau^i)$$

With this background the deterministic dynamic in this state space can be described. We let $f^i(\theta)[h_\tau^i]$ denote the fraction of population i with private history h_τ^i at time $t + 1$ when the state at time t was θ; the dynamic in other words is given by $\theta_{t+1} = f(\theta_t)$. New entrants to the population have no experience, so

$$f^i(\theta)[h_0^i] = \frac{1}{T}.$$

Of the existing population $\theta^i(h_\tau^i)$ with a particular history, the fraction having experience $(h_\tau^i, \rho^i(h_\tau^i), z)$ is the fraction that were matched with opponents playing strategies that led to the terminal node z. Let $\hat{s}^{-i}(s^i, z)$ be the pure strategies for i's opponents that lead to the outcome z:

$$f_i(\theta)[h_\tau^i, \rho^i(h_\tau^i), z] = \theta^i(h_\tau^i) \sum_{s^{-i} \in \hat{s}^{-i}(s^i, z)} \prod_{j \neq i} \bar{\theta}^j(s^j).$$

It is clear that

$$f_i(\theta)[h_\tau^i, \rho^i(h_\tau^i), z] = 0 \quad \text{if} \quad s^i \neq \rho^i(h_\tau^i).$$

As always, we denote by $\hat{\theta}$ a steady state of the dynamical process f. We will not examine the convergence of the dynamical process to the steady state but only the steady state itself. (As in previous chapters, the *existence* of the steady state is not at issue, since the dynamical process is a continuous map from a compact state space to itself, the existence of steady states follows immediately from Brower's fixed-point theorem.)

Observe first that steady states in this model need not bear any particular relation to equilibrium of any kind. If players live short lives, they have little opportunity to learn and basically play against their priors. So the only interesting case is the limit as the length of life $T \to \infty$. Fudenberg and Levine (1993) prove two different results depending on whether or not players are patient: Generally, with long life steady states approximate heterogeneous self-confirming equilibrium; with long life and patience they resemble Nash equilibria.

The intuition for why long life leads to self-confirming equilibrium has three parts. First, any strategy s^i that is played with positive probability in the steady state must be played by a positive fraction of the population a positive fraction of their life. Second, when the lifetime is long, a player who plays a strategy a positive fraction of her life should, by combining result of Diaconis and Freedman (1990) with the central limit theorem, have approximately correct beliefs about its consequences. Third, the strategy s^i should maximize the current expected payoff of most of the players who are playing it. That is, the bulk of players using s^i do so because it is myopically optimal and not because they are experimenting. This final fact is subtle because, as we saw in the previous section, the optimal experimentation plan is relatively complicated. Combined, these facts imply that playing s_i is an approximate best response to beliefs that are approximately correct along the path of play, that is, approximately a self-confirming equilibrium.

In showing that long-life plus patience leads to Nash equilibrium, the order of limits turns out to be quite important: The discount factor must go to one much more slowly than the length of life goes to infinity. It is not currently known whether the conclusion holds for the other order of limits. The intuition of the result is that patient players do enough experimentation to learn the true best responses to the steady state. Note that the fact that in the steady state players do not choose strategies based on calendar time means that the type of incidental correlation of experiments discussed in Fudenberg and Kreps (1995b) is not a problem; in effect in the steady-state/random-matching model the uniform nonexperimental condition is satisfied provided that most players are not actually experimenting.

Note that the obvious argument is that if a player is very patient, and a strategy has some probability of being the best response, the player ought to try it and see. However, we already saw that some strategies may never be tried, even though they do have a chance of being a best response, if there is some other strategy that provides the same information at lower cost. Instead, the argument actually used by Fudenberg and Levine (1993) considers the notion that an experiment has an option value: The option is to continue with the experiment if it works. If the steady-state distributions of strategies converge to a limit that is not a Nash equilibrium, then there is a strategy being played with appreciable probability that is not optimal against the steady state. This implies that the option value for experimenting with this strategy cannot be converging to zero. On the other hand, it can be shown that Bayesian optimal play and random matching imply that most option values become small.

7.6 Stochastic Adjustment and Backward Induction in a Model of "Fast Learning"

This section discusses a model of "fast learning" in extensive games that Noldeke and Samuelson (1993) used to investigate the extent to which learning processes might tend to converge to refinements of Nash equilibrium. Fudenberg and Kreps (1988) identify several factors that suggest that results along these lines may require quite strong assumptions. First of all, beliefs must be correct at the larger class of "sequentially relevant" information sets, instead of the smaller class of relevant ones defined in section 7.2, and this can require "more experimentation" than is required by MME. For example, in games of perfect information, all information sets are sequentially relevant, and so absent a priori restrictions on the payoff functions, *every* information set must be reached infinitely often to ensure that only the backward-induction solution is stable. As shown in the discussion of figure 7.3, this in turn requires that players experiment even at information sets that are being reached a vanishing fraction of the time, and it is not obvious that even patient players would choose to do this.[8] Second, moving from subgame perfection to sequential equilibrium requires that players come to have common assessments about the relative probability of various nodes within an information set, even if the information set in question is reached with vanishing frequency.

In Noldeke-Samuelson (1993) the Kandori-Mailath-Rob type of analysis is applied to games in which each player moves at most once on any path through the tree. In such games a player's deviation from expected play cannot signal that he is likely to deviate at a subsequent information set, and so various sorts of refinements coincide. For example, trembling-hand perfection in the strategic form coincides with trembling-hand perfection in the agent-strategic form, and the notion of "rationalizability at reachable nodes" that we defined in chapter 6, which does not restricts play at

---

8. Which is not to say that we know that they would not. Indeed a related and still open question is whether this much experimentation occurs in the steady-state learning model discussed earlier in this chapter in the limit of discount factors tending toward 1. On the other hand, if there is a minimum probability of experimentation as in the model of smooth fictitious play, then this assumption would be satisfied. The issues raised by this possibility are discussed in greater detail at the end of this chapter.

information sets that the player was expected to preclude, is equivalent to the stronger notion of sequential rationalizability, which requires "rational" play at every information set.

Noldeke and Samuelson consider anonymous random matching in a finite population with a steady inflow of "mutants" or "replacement players." The analysis will first determine the behavior of the system without these stochastic shocks and then consider the system in which shocks are present but become vanishingly small. After we have done so, we will explain why the system involves much faster learning than in the models discussed earlier in this chapter.

7.6.1 The Model

Each of the finitely many agents in the model is described by a current strategy and a "conjecture" about the play of the opposing population(s). These conjectures take the form of a single behavior strategy for each population and so implicitly impose the assumption of independent beliefs we discussed in chapter 6. Further each agent's strategy is presumed to be a best response to his current conjecture, where the agent's goal is to maximize his ex ante expected payoff given his conjecture. This allows an agent's strategy to prescribe conditionally dominated actions at information sets that the player's conjecture assigns probability 0. Each period all agents are randomly matched to play the game. In particular, the probability that a given agent of player i is matched with a given agent of player j is some fixed number bounded away from 0.

At the end of period, each agent has probability μ of "learning." A learning agent observes the terminal nodes in *every* match this period and resets his beliefs at the corresponding information sets to equal this period's observation. Note that all agents who learn end the period with the same (and correct) on-path beliefs. Note also that if the agent does not get to "learn," he does not change his beliefs even if they are inconsistent with the terminal node reached in his own match this period. This strikes us as an odd aspect of the model, but it does not seem important for the results.[9]

9. In a private communication, Larry Samuelson has sketched an argument that all of the asymptotic results of the paper are unchanged if each agent learns the outcome in his own match in every period provided that agents still set their conjectures about play at each information set equal to their most recent observation there. However, that assumption is less attractive when agents only observe their own matches than if they observe all outcomes, since the agent is trying to learn the aggregate distribution of opponents' play, and he will typically play a different opponent each period.

The agent then adjusts his strategy so that it prescribes a best response to his conjectures at all of his information sets. It is assumed that there is "inertia," meaning that the agent does not change his actions at information sets where the previously chosen action is one (possibly of several) best response to the new conjecture.

This process of belief revision and strategy adjustment, in which players use only their most recent observation and ignore all previous ones, parallels that in the Kandori-Mailath-Rob papers. A new feature here is the assumption that observing play at the information sets that were reached in this period has no effect on beliefs about play at the unreached information sets.[10] From a Bayesian perspective this amounts to supposing that beliefs take the form of a product of independent distributions over play at each information set. Consequently seeing a player shift his response to a given action does not signal that the player may have changed his response to others. This is a stronger assumption than the independence across *players* that is implicit in the formulation of conjectures as strategy profiles.

The previous paragraph defines the "no-mutations" adjustment process $\Gamma(0)$. The state space of this process is the set Θ whose elements specify a strategy and conjecture for each individual agent. To extend this to a process with mutations or replacements, suppose that in each period with probability λ each agent is replaced by another one with an arbitrary conjecture and a strategy that is a best response to the conjecture, and that this replacement is independent across agents. These mutations create an ergodic system denoted $\Gamma(\lambda)$; Samuelson and Noldeke's goal is to characterize the limit of its ergodic distribution μ^λ as $\lambda \to 0$.

Two aspects of this system deserve special emphasis. First, the set of mutations or perturbations is somewhat smaller than that considered in Kandori, Mailath, and Rob, since mutants never adopt strictly dominated strategies. For this reason the transition matrix of $\Gamma(\lambda)$ is not strictly positive, but since all undominated strategies have strictly positive probability, it is easy to see that the system is indeed ergodic.[11]

---

10. In this setting it is somewhat trickier to justify the decision rules as being approximately optimal when the system changes only slowly and the agent has a small discount factor, since the most recent observed *outcomes* need not be a sufficient statistic for the entire history of outcomes. However, this is taken care of by the combination of the assumption that learning players observe the outcome in all matches and the independence assumption. Note moreover that this sort of memoryless learning makes it very hard a priori for a mixed-strategy equilibrium to be stable. This did not matter very much in the 2×2 coordination games considered by Kandori, Mailath, and Rob, where the mixed equilibrium would clearly be unstable in any sensible dynamic, but it becomes an issue when considering more general extensive-form games.

11. See the appendix to chapter 5.

Second, the mutations will be a source of "experiments" with off-path actions. Moreover, since the probability of the event "all agents learn" will in the limit $\lambda \to 0$ be infinitely larger than that of a mutation, the model will generate much more information about off-path play than if each agent only observed the outcomes of their own matches. Consequently we should expect that "less" experimentation is required to rule out non-Nash outcomes in this model than under the usual observation structure. This effect is strengthened by the assumption that when players learn, they revise their conjecture to correspond to their most recent observation, so a single experiment here can have as much force as an infinite number of them in the model of fictitious play. Indeed, we will see that the key event to consider in determining the long-run distribution is "a single player i experiments, and then all players revise their conjectures to match the outcome of the experiment before any other players change their actions." For this reason we should expect that convergence to a non-Nash outcome will be less common in this model than in those we discussed earlier in the chapter. This is also why we call the model one of (relatively) "fast learning."

7.6.2 Deterministic Dynamic

As usual, the method is to work out what happens without mutations first. In this case the outcome generated by any singleton limit set (steady state) must be the outcome of an independent and unitary self-confirming equilibrium. To see this, note that since each player has some chance of eventually learning, and a player who learns observes play in *all* matches, if play is absorbed by a single outcome, *all* players will eventually learn what that outcome is, and so all players must have correct conjectures at *all* information sets on the corresponding path. Thus the outcome must correspond to a unitary self-confirming equilibrium; the independence is imposed by assumption, as we noted above. Conversely, any independent and unitary self-confirming equilibrium corresponds to a singleton limit set.

Note that a given self-confirming *outcome* can correspond to many different steady states, since actual play at unreached information sets is arbitrary, and there are only weak restrictions on the conjectures about this off-path play. In particular, if in a steady state θ player i could deviate and send play to an unreached subgame, and no other player's deviation can cause this subgame to be reached, then any other state θ' that differs from θ only in the conjectures of players other than i about play in the subgame is also self-confirming, and consequently also a steady state.

Moreover there can be steady states in which different agents of a given player (e.g., player 1) disagree about precisely what payoff they would get if they gave player 2 the move so long as in the steady state player 2's information set is never actually reached. Thus, even though the outcome of the steady state must be a unitary self-confirming equilibrium, that outcome can also correspond to a steady state without unitary beliefs.

Due to this great multiplicity of steady states, the brute-force approach of enumerating all of the steady states of the unperturbed system and then computing minimal order trees is likely to be quite tedious. However, such calculations are not needed, since, as shown below, the large number of steady states makes it so easy for mutations to switch play from one steady state to another that we need only consider transitions that can be caused by a single mutation.

7.6.3   Dynamic with Mutations

We turn now to the case with mutations so that $\lambda > 0$. We will say that a state is *stochastically stable* if it is contained in the limit of the supports of the ergodic distributions μ^{λ} as $\lambda \to 0$.

Proposition 7.5 (Noldeke and Samuelson 1993)   If state θ is stochastically stable, so is any other steady state θ' whose basin of attraction (in $\Gamma(0)$) can be reached with a single mutation.

Intuitively, if a single mutation suffices to jump away from θ, the expected time spent in state θ is of order $1/\lambda$, and since θ' is a steady state, it will take at least one mutation before this state is left. Thus the expected time spent in θ' is at least of the same order as that spent in θ.

Using this lemma about stable states, Noldeke and Samuelson develop a necessary condition for there to be a stochastically stable outcome; that is, for the limit distribution to be concentrated on states all of which induce the same distribution over terminal nodes. From our remarks above, we see that for there to be a stable outcome, there must be a corresponding set of states, all of which lead to that outcome and such that no single mutation leads to a state with a different outcome.

Proposition 7.6 (Noldeke and Samuelson 1993)   Consider an extensive-form game in which each player moves at most once on any path of play. Suppose that an outcome is stochastically stable and that at some stochastically stable state with that outcome player i can deviate and send play to some subgame. Then no self-confirming equilibrium of the subgame can give player i a higher payoff than he received in the stochastically stable outcome.

Sketch of Proof Let z be a stochastically stable outcome generated by the stochastically stable set Θ^*. The first step is to check that every state in Θ^* is a steady state and hence self-confirming. (The idea is that non-singleton limit sets of $\Gamma(0)$ must contain states with at least two different outcomes.) Suppose next that at outcome z there is a player i who can take an action a that sends play to a subgame $G(a)$ that has a self-confirming equilibrium σ that gives the player more than he is getting in z. Fix a stochastically stable state θ', and consider the state θ where all players' strategies and conjectures agree with θ' at all information sets outside of $G(a)$, in which player i has the same strategy and conjecture as in θ', and such that strategies and conjectures of all players who have an information set in $G(a)$ correspond to σ. Since θ' corresponds to a self-confirming equilibrium, so does θ.

Now consider a mutation that makes one agent of player i play into this subgame, and then suppose that all player i's learn before any agent of any other player type and before any further mutations. This sends the system to a new state, whose outcome is some z' that is different than the outcome z we started with. Moreover, since play in $G(a)$ is a self-confirming equilibrium of the subgame, the learning mechanism cannot further adjust actions or conjectures in this subgame. Since player i's payoff in this subgame is greater than it had been under the initial outcome z, and since at z player i can force play into the subgame, the learning process starting at z' cannot lead back to z. Since a single mutation suffices to send the system away from z, and at least one mutation will be required to return to z, z cannot be the unique outcome in the support of the ergodic distribution of the perturbed system.   ∎

Corollary 7.1 In a multistage game with observed actions in which each player moves at most once on any path of play, any stochastically stable outcome must be a subgame-perfect equilibrium.[12]

---

12. Noldeke and Samuelson assert that this conclusion follows without the restriction to multistage games, but as Larry Samuelson has pointed out to us, their proof is incorrect. However, no counterexample has been found, and it remains an open question whether this restriction is really needed. To see why it might not be, note that while the inconsistent self-confirming equilibrium (A_1, A_2, L_3) in figure 6.1 is a steady state of the unperturbed learning process, it is not locally stable: A single mutation by a player 1 onto D_1 sends the unperturbed dynamic to the Nash equilibrium (D_1, A_2, A_3). This raises the yet unproved conjecture that all locally stable outcomes must correspond to Nash equilibria

Proof From proposition 6.4, in multistage games every unitary self-confirming equilibrium with independent beliefs has the same outcome as a Nash equilibrium. Thus proposition 7.6 and the fact that every stochastically stable outcome is self-confirming implies that a stochastically stable outcome must be a Nash equilibrium outcome with the additional property that no player can deviate and send play to a subgame where that player gets a higher payoff in some self-confirming equilibrium. The conclusion then follows from the fact that every subgame-perfect equilibrium of any subgame is self-confirming. ∎

Three aspects of these results deserve emphasis. First, on a technical level, the proof is greatly simplified by the fact that a single mutation suffices to leave the basins of many steady states. Noldeke and Samuelson use the same proof technique in a subsequent paper on learning dynamics in a "screening" model. This technique is useful in these papers because of the assumption that a player who learns observes play in all matches. Thus the key event in both models is "a single mutation onto a previously unused action, followed by *all* agents of a given player learning." The nature of the learning process means that the single mutation onto a previously unplayed action can have dramatic consequences.

As of this writing, the technical argument has not been extended to other types of learning processes. However, the second and more general point made by these papers is that dynamics in extensive-form games should be expected to be more sensitive to various forms of noise and perturbation than are dynamics in static games with strict equilibria, and we expect that point to hold quite generally.

Third, and relatedly, the sensitivity to perturbations suggests that many games will not have a stochastically stable outcome. This can be seen in the strength of proposition 7.6, and is illustrated in the figure 7.5, which is a three-player "centipede" game in which each player in succession

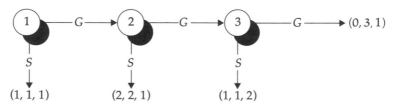

Figure 7.5
Three-player centipede

chooses between G (Go) and S (Stop); if any player chooses S the game ends, and in any case the game ends after player 3's move. The unique subgame perfect equilibrium is (G, S, S) with outcome (G, S); profile (G, S, G) has the same outcome. This would also need to be in the stochastically stable set if (G, S, S) is. But, at the state corresponding to (G, S, G), where all player 3's play G, if all player 2's learn simultaneously, while none of the player 1's do, the state switches to (G, G, G). Suppose that in the following period all player 1's learn and no other players do. This sequence of events, which relies only on the "learn" draws, has positive probability under the unperturbed no-mutations dynamics and leads to the steady state (S, G, G) with outcome S, so outcome (G, S) is not stable.

In contrast to this example, suppose that the subgame-perfect equilibrium gives all players a higher payoff than any other outcome. In this case it is stochastically stable. Noldeke and Samuelson prove a slightly stronger theorem. Consider the outcome of a subgame-perfect equilibrium in a game of perfect information. This outcome is the unique stochastically stable outcome if no player has an action that can send play to a subgame in which some terminal node gives that player a higher payoff than he received in equilibrium.

Since it is so unlikely to be satisfied, the notion of a single point being stochastically stable is not that useful. One conclusion we can draw from this is to accept the idea that limit sets may fail to be single points.

7.7 Mutations and Fast Learning in Models of Cheap Talk

This section discusses the application of fast learning with mutations to the cheap-talk 2×2 coordination game we discussed in chapter 3. Recall the structure of the game: There are two stages of play. In the first stage players simultaneously announce messages, which will be treated as signals of their "intended action" L or R; in the second stage they play the coordination game with payoffs given in figure 7.6. Talk is cheap in the sense that announcing an action has no direct effect at all on the realized payoffs, which depend only on the second-stage choices.

	L	R
L	2, 2	−100, 0
R	0, −100	1, 1

Figure 7.6
Coordination example

In chapter 3 we observed that ESS is sufficient to eliminate the (R, R) equilibrium provided that some message is not sent in equilibrium. By way of contrast, we discussed an argument due to Matsui (1991) based on cyclically stable sets that eliminates the (R, R) equilibrium even with a fixed finite message space. As we noted, Matsui's argument implicitly supposes that players observe and respond to the strategy profile actually used by their opponent, including the parts of the profile that relate to off-path play. Once we recognize the extensive-form nature of a cheap-talk game, this is no longer a satisfactory assumption.

In this section we will sketch an argument similar to that of Noldeke and Samuelson that, unlike Matsui, supposes that players can only observe what actually happened in the course of play. Moreover we will see that the conclusions can depend on whether agents observe only the outcomes in their own matches, or instead can observe the outcomes in all of them, as in Noldeke-Samuelson. Another advantage of these arguments is that they each concern long-run behavior under a single dynamic and thus sidestep some of the interpretational questions posed by the Gilboa and Matsui (1991) definition of a cyclically stable set.

We begin with an extension of the Noldeke-Samuelson model of the previous section. Since each player moves twice along every path of play, instead of only once as assumed by Noldeke-Samuelson, their model is not immediately applicable to this game. To apply it, we will extend their independence assumption by adding the condition that observed play by a given player at a given information set is independent of that player's actions at all other information sets, even those which are successors of the information set in question. With this extension we can show that the limit of the long-run distributions assigns probability 1 to all players choosing the Pareto-optimal action L.

Here is a sketch of the argument, which we have not seen given elsewhere. We will argue first that, starting from any state in which all agents play R in the second stage given the prevailing distribution of messages, the system can move to a state where all agents play L at a "cost" of only three mutations. That is, the component in which all agents play R has a modified coradius (see chapter 5) of at most 3. To see this, let θ^{*R} be the state in which agents believe that all opponents will play R regardless of the first-period message, and all agents choose to both say and play R. If the current outcome is that all agents actually play R, given the prevailing distribution of messages, then all agents must believe that regardless of the message they send, their opponent is likely to play R. Consequently the state can move to θ^{*R} by a series of single mutations: Take each player who is currently saying L, and replace his conjectures by those of θ^{*R}. Since these conjectures are consistent with the observed distribution, each such single mutation leads to a new self-confirming equilibrium, and so to a new steady state of the unperturbed adjustment process. Thus the modified cost of this sequence of mutations is only 1. Next, from the state θ^{*R} two mutations are sufficient to shift the state to the basin of the equilibrium component in which all agents play L: Suppose that a single agent on each side mutates to the conjecture "all of my opponents will play L if I say L and will play R if I say R."[13] Suppose moreover that these two mutants are immediately matched with one another so that they both end up saying L and then playing L, and that this is followed by the event "all agents learn." (Recall that both of these events have positive probability in the unperturbed [no-mutations] dynamic.) Then with the assumption that beliefs are updated separately at each information set, the learning players have the new conjectures "everyone plays L if both messages were L, and plays R otherwise," and so all agents say and do L in the next period. Hence the modified coradius of "all play R" is at most 3.

However, the modified coradius of the component where all agents play L is proportional to the number of players and so is much larger if the population is large. For "learning" players to start choosing a message that leads to a significant chance of playing R, it must be that *both* messages have a substantial probability of leading to the opponent playing R. (Otherwise, the learning player would choose the message that made it likely his opponent will play L.) This is the key asymmetry between the strategies: Play shifts from R to L if *either* message is likely to result in (L, L), which can occur after only a single mutation onto an unsent message; while to induce players to choose R, some fraction of the population must mutate.

Note well that this asymmetry depends on the assumption that the event "all players learn at once" is much (infinitely) more likely than any single mutation. This can be seen by modifying the model so that agents learn only the distribution of outcomes induced by their own chosen strategy, but otherwise keeping the model the same.[14] Here two mutations are not enough to move from θ^{*R} to the basin of the component where all

---

13. The conjectures about play following "mismatched" messages are unimportant, as will be clear from the argument that follows.

14. If players only observe their own matches, the assumption that conjectures equal their most recent observation is not very sensible. For example, in the coordination game without cheap talk, the no-mutation process holds constant the numbers of agents playing L and playing R, so every state is in the support of the limit distribution.

agents play L, and agents will only choose to shift to sending L if a substantial fraction of agents mutates at the same time.

7.8 Experimentation and the Length of the Horizon

Basically the results of this chapter show that we should expect Nash rather than self-confirming equilibrium if there is enough experimentation. On the other hand, we argued, especially in chapter 4, that there is good reason for players to use a rule such as smooth fictitious play, which is random, and that there are many reasons to believe that players actually do randomize, including the random utility model of Harsanyi and the empirical research of psychologists. This raises the question of whether and why self-confirming equilibrium should be of interest.

To answer this question, we adopt Binmore and Samuelson's (1997) typology of the short, medium, long, and ultralong run. The short run is a period so short that players have no opportunity to learn and simply use their priors. In an experimental setting, Stahl and Wilson (1994) have explored models of prior formation that give some predictive power of play in the first round of an experiment, while falling far short of equilibrium of any kind. Nagel (1993) has examined how the transition from short to medium run takes place as people begin to best-respond to past play by opponents.

In the medium run, players have an opportunity to learn. In Binmore and Samuelson (1995) the medium run is identified with remaining for a long time near a component of steady states that is not dynamically stable, with the long run being long enough for the system to move away from unstable components and arrive at a stable one. We would prefer to emphasize instead that while experimentation may lead to Nash equilibrium in the long run, self-confirming equilibrium may be a good description of a system in the medium run. The point is that players accumulate data about the on-the-path play of their opponents much more rapidly than they generate data about their off-path play. Consequently we expect in the medium run that outcomes that are not self-confirming are unstable, but it only makes sense to believe that players will move away from self-confirming equilibrium to full Nash equilibrium (or one of its refinements) over a much longer horizon.[15] Unfortunately, we do not know of a way to make a formal distinction between these two horizon lengths.

---

15. This same point has been emphasized by Er'ev and Roth (1994).

Finally, in the very long run, we might expect the Kandori, Mailath, Rob and Young types of argument to become relevant, since the system spends most of its time near the particular steady state that is stochastically stable. As pointed out by Binmore, Samuelson, and Vaughan (1995), this distinction corresponds to two different orders of limits in evaluating the average behavior of the system: The case where mutations are very rare over the relevant horizon corresponds to the order $\lim_{t \to \infty} \lim_{\varepsilon \to 0}$, where ε is a measure of the size of the "noise," while the ultralong run is long enough for the noise to be nonnegligible, so the appropriate order of limits is $\lim_{\varepsilon \to 0} \lim_{t \to \infty}$.

In interpreting these results, it is important to think of the particular application. For example, in studying what happens in an experimental setting, the short and medium run seem most relevant, except for a few experiments running very simple games over fifty or more trials, where the long run may be relevant. In talking about rules of thumb, social norms, or customs in an economic setting, we imagine that these have evolved over a very long period of time, and so the long or ultralong run cases have greater relevance; this is the point of view taken by Young (1993).

Appendix: Review of Bandit Problems

In a multi-armed bandit problem, a single player with discount factor δ must choose from a finite set of "arms" or actions $a \in A$. The action chosen gives rise to a probability distribution over outcomes $\theta \in \Theta$; these outcomes are independently drawn each period from probability distributions $\sigma(a) \in \Delta(\Theta)$, which are unknown. Utility depends on the action and the outcome $u(a, \theta)$. Players' beliefs are given by prior distributions $\mu(a)$ over each probability distribution $\sigma(a) \in \Delta(\Theta)$. These priors are independent between actions so that learning the distribution corresponding to one action conveys no information about the distributions corresponding to others; the only way to learn about the distribution generated by a given action a is to play that action. After an action a is chosen in period t, beliefs $\mu_t(a)$ for the corresponding action are updated according to Bayes's law. For example, if $\mu_t(a)$ is a continuous density and a is chosen at time t with outcome θ, then

$$\mu_{t+1}(a)[\sigma] = \frac{\sigma(\theta) \cdot \mu_t(a)[\sigma]}{\int \sigma'(\theta) \cdot \mu_t(a)[\sigma'] \, d\sigma'}.$$

Because of the assumed independence, beliefs for actions not chosen are not updated at all.

Our discussion in this appendix follows Ross (1983). The problem is ordinarily analyzed by dynamic programming methods, that is, by postulating a value function $v(\mu)$ and using the Bellman relation

$$v(\mu) = \max_{a \in A} (1 - \delta)E_\mu u(a, \theta) + \delta E_{\mu', a} v(\mu'),$$

which says that the value of particular beliefs are equal to the greatest amount that can be earned by choosing an action that maximizes current expected utility plus the expected value of next period's beliefs. It may easily be shown that v is (weakly) convex in μ.

In the case of a multi-armed bandit problem, the solution of the dynamic programming problem was shown by Gittens (1979) to have a particularly simply form. Consider first the simple one-armed bandit problem where the option is to play the one arm or to drop out and receive a fixed utility U. Let $v(\mu, U)$ be the value function corresponding to this problem. This function may easily be shown to be continuous and nondecreasing in U. Let moreover $U(\mu)$ be the smallest value of U for which it is optimal to drop out. This is called the *Gittens index*. Then

$$U(\mu) = \min[U|v(\mu, U) = U]$$

The key fact in solving the multi-armed bandit problem is that the Gittens index for each individual arm can be used to determine which arm to pull. That is, the optimal plan is to compute for the current beliefs, and for each action a, the index $U_a(\mu(a))$, and to use the action for which this Gittens index is largest. Of course this result depends heavily on the assumption that the arms are independent, which means that the Gittens index is not so useful for analyzing extensive-form games.

A basic feature of the multi-armed bandit is that there is positive probability of stopping forever on the wrong arm. This is easy to see: Suppose that initially the Gittens index on the first arm is higher than that on the second arm. Then the first arm will be tried first. As long as the Gittens index on the first arm does not drop below the prior Gittens index on the second arm, the second arm will never be used even if it is actually more favorable.

On the other hand, we would not expect this phenomenon to be important if the player is patient, that is, if δ is near one. To see that it is not, observe that the strategy of experimenting with all arms for T periods, then switching to the most favorable arm forever, will, if δ is near one and T is sufficiently long, give nearly the same expected present value as knowing in advance which is the best arm. Consequently the optimal policy must also yield approximately the full-information payoff. This means that for δ near one there cannot be an appreciable chance of stopping on the wrong arm by mistake.

References

Binmore, K., and L. Samuelson. 1997. Muddling through: Noisy equilibrium selection. *Journal of Economic Theory* 74: 235–65.

Binmore, K., and L. Samuelson. 1995. Evolutionary drift and equilibrium selection. Mimeo. University College London.

Binmore, K., L. Samuelson, and K. Vaughan. 1995. Musical chairs: Modelling noisy evolution. *Games and Economic Behavior* 11: 1–35.

Boylan, R. 1995. Continuous approximation of dynamical systems with randomly matched individuals. *Journal of Economic Theory* 64: 615–25.

Diaconis, P., and D. Freedman. 1990. On the uniform consistency of Bayes estimates with multinomial probabilities. *Annals of Statistics* 18: 1317–27.

Er'ev, I., and A. Roth. 1996. On the need for low rationality cognitive game theory: Reinforcement learning in experimental games with unique mixed strategy equilibria. Mimeo. University of Pittsburgh.

Fudenberg, D., and D. K. Levine. 1993. Steady state learning and Nash equilibrium. *Econometrica* 61: 547–73.

Fudenberg, D., and D. M. Kreps. 1988. Learning, experimentation and equilibrium in games. Mimeo. Stanford University.

Fudenberg, D., and D. M. Kreps. 1995a. Learning in extensive games, II: Experimentation and Nash equilibrium. Mimeo. Harvard University.

Fudenberg, D., and D. M. Kreps. 1995b. Learning in extensive games, I: Self-confirming equilibrium. *Games and Economic Behavior* 8: 20–55.

Gilboa, I., and A. Matsui. 1991. Social stability and equilibrium. *Econometrica* 58: 859–67.

Gittens, J. 1979. Bandit processes and dynamic allocation indices. *Journal of the Royal Statistical Society* B14: 148–77.

Kohlberg, E., and J. Mertens. 1986. On the strategic stability of equilibria. *Econometrica* 54: 1003–37.

Matsui, A. 1991. Cheap-talk and cooperation in a society. *Journal of Economic Theory* 54: 245–58.

Myerson, R. 1978. Refinment of the Nash equilibrium concept. *International Journal of Game Theory* 7: 73–80.

Nagel, R. 1994. Experimental results on interactive competitive guessing. Mimeo, D.P. B-236. University of Bonn.

Noldeke, G., and L. Samuelson. 1993. An evolutionary analysis of backward and forward induction. *Games and Economic Behavior* 5: 425–54.

Ross, S. M. 1983. *Introduction to Stochastic Dynamic Programming*. New York: Academic Press.

Stahl, D. O., and P. W. Wilson. 1994. On players' models of other players: Theory and experimental evidence. *Journal of Economic Behavior and Organization* 25: 309–27.

Young, P. 1993. The evolution of conventions. *Econometrica* 61: 57–84.

8   Sophisticated Learning

8.1   Introduction

Throughout our discussion of evolutionary and learning models, we have emphasized our belief that people are relatively good at learning. However, the models we have examined so far imply that players are unable to detect simple cycles or other patterns in the data. Whether implicitly or explicitly, rules such as fictitious play and its variations, best response, and stimulus response are designed to perform well against an i.i.d. opponent; none attempts to detect cycles or other regularities in the data. In this chapter we examine learning rules that are more "sophisticated" in the sense that they explicitly attempt to detect patterns.

We consider three ways of modeling the idea that players may attempt to detect patterns in opponents' play. The most traditional starts from a set of opponents' strategies, possibly involving complex patterns of play over time, that are a priori viewed as possible. Supposing that players have prior beliefs over these strategies leads to a Bayesian model of learning. Such a Bayesian model is equivalent to specifying conditional probabilities over opponents' play conditional on particular events. A related approach is to specify the events that are to be conditioned on and then estimate the conditional probabilities directly. For example, rather than assuming that the probability distributions governing opponents' play are independent of the history, as in fictitious play, we can allow players to believe that the distributions are different in odd and even periods, or that they depend on the actions played in the last period. In this approach the primitive specification is not a set of opponent strategies that are viewed as possible but rather a method of classifying histories into categories within which conditional probabilities are assumed to be constant.

A third approach is to treat as primitive, not the opponents' strategies that are viewed as possible, but the set of the player's own strategies that are viewed as potential best responses. In the computer science literature these are referred to as *experts*, and the goal may be thought of as choosing the expert who makes the best recommendations for a course of play.

We begin in section 8.3 with the Bayesian learning model. Following Kalai and Lehrer (1993), we show that if these beliefs satisfy an absolute continuity condition with respect to one another, then play must converge to a Nash equilibrium. However, the absolute continuity condition can be difficult to justify because when opponents act as Bayesian learners, they may well follow strategies that were not a priori viewed as possible, in which case the assumption will fail. In section 8.4 we explore some of the difficulties with the absolute continuity assumption, including Nachbar's (1997) result providing conditions under which this assumption cannot be satisfied. Our conclusion is that it is important to use learning procedures that are robust in the sense that, unlike Bayesian learning, they continue to perform well even if none of the alternatives viewed as possible actually turn outs to be true.

The remainder of the chapter looks at learning procedures that are robust and that attempt to detect at least some patterns. In section 8.5 we examine procedures proposed in the computer science literature that make it possible to perform asymptotically as well as the best expert, even in the worst case. In section 8.6 we show how to extend the fictitious play idea, that players learn about frequencies, to the idea that they learn about conditional frequencies. The main result is that the conditional analogue of smooth fictitious play does about as well asymptotically as if the conditional frequencies are known in advance.

In general, we can say little about the relative performance of cautious fictitious play against alternatives such as best response or stimulus response. Despite the fact that cautious fictitious play has better theoretical properties, it may be outperformed by the other models in particular instances. In section 8.7 we show that this is due to the fact that the other procedures may inadvertently be conditioning on parts of the history that are ignored by cautious fictitious play. In fact, given any other procedure, we can design a particular conditional cautious fictitious play learning rule that regardless of whether the criterion is time average or discounted payoffs, and regardless of the discount factor, never does much worse than the other procedure, and sometimes does considerably better.

In section 8.8 we ask whether sophisticated learning is potentially destabilizing. Sonsino (1997) argues, for example, that sophisticated procedures may result in cycles where less sophisticated procedures would have converged. In section 8.9 we examine the converse question of whether sophisticated learning procedures can lead to convergence in cases where less sophisticated procedures cycle. Even if cycles can be successfully detected, is it possible that this generates even more complicated cycles that players are unable to detect, or is the system forced to convergence? The answer depends in an important way on players synchronizing the data they use from the past. Allowing the possibility that patterns more complicated than those contemplated in player's behavior rules may be generated, we observe one implication of this is that opponent's play may appear to be correlated with the player's own play. Put differently, a player's own choice may contain predictive power about what his opponents are going to do. In section 8.10 we examine the procedure developed by Foster and Vohra (1995) to take account of this extra information. If players do so, play in the long run must come to resemble a correlated equilibrium. However, there is still the theoretical possibility that the correlation, which is generated by a time dependence in behavior rules, is too complicated for players to anticipate; whether this is likely to happen in practice is currently unknown.

One important issue is that once we allow players to condition on histories of play, they may realize that opponents' future play depends on their own current play. If players are not myopic, this raises an important set of issues: First, players may try to manipulate their opponents' learning process. This possibility is discussed in section 8.11. Second, players may not be able to correctly infer the causal connection between their own play and that of their opponents. This possibility was explored in previous chapters examining extensive-form games. Finally, even if there is enough experimentation to reveal opponents' strategies, it is currently unknown whether or not there are analogues of conditional cautious fictitious play and other robust methods that are applicable in a nonmyopic setting.

8.2 Three Paradigms for Conditional Learning

Through most of this chapter we return to the simple setting of a fixed set of myopic players playing a static simultaneous-move game; as usual, this should be thought of as a convenient simplification of a model of a larger population. In the stage game the strategies are $s^i \in S^i$, and the utilities u^i. This game is repeated over time, and a finite history of play $h_t = (s_1, s_2, \ldots, s_t)$ is a list of how all players have played through period t. The play of all players except for player i is denoted by h_t^{-i}, an infinite history of play by h, and so forth. The set of all finite histories continues to be denoted by H.

We examine three behavioral paradigms for detecting patterns. The most traditional is a set of opponents' strategies, possibly involving complex patterns of play over time, that are a priori viewed as *plausible*. Adding a prior over these strategies will lead to a Bayesian model of learning. Specifically, let a *model* for player i be a map $m^i : H^i \rightarrow \Delta(S^{-i})$ from histories to correlated strategies in the repeated game for player i's opponents. Bayesian beliefs are then specified by a set of *plausible* models M^i and a prior over this plausible set.

Instead of focusing on models that are thought to be plausible, we can focus on strategies that are thought to be potential best responses. Specifically, as in the computer science literature we define an *expert* for player i to be a map defined on histories, $e^i(h_t) \in \Delta(S^i)$; this is simply a strategy in the repeated game. With this approach the goal of the learning rule is thought of as choosing the expert who makes the best recommendations for a course of play.

Given any model, we can consider the corresponding experts that are best responses to the model; given any expert, we can consider the models for which the expert would be a best response. While this is not a one-to-one correspondence between models and experts, there is a close link between the two. In particular, we can think of a player's beliefs about the possible dynamics of his opponents' play either in the form of a set M^i of *plausible* models or as a set E^i of *plausible* experts.

Instead of focusing on models, or on experts, we can attempt directly to estimate the probability of opponents' play conditional on particular categories. The essential element is the partitioning of histories into disjoint sets of events. Specifically, we suppose that there is a collection of categories Ψ^i into which observations may be placed. A *classification rule* is a map $\hat{\psi}^i : H \times S^i \rightarrow \Psi^i$.[1] The interpretation is that prior to observing s_t^{-i} the player knows h_{t-1}, s_t^i, and must choose a category $\hat{\psi}^i(h_{t-1}, s_t^i)$ based only on this information.

---

1. For notational simplicity we limit attention to deterministic classification rules.

8.3   Bayesian Approach to Sophisticated Learning

We begin by considering behavior rules ρ^i generated by playing a best response to a particular prior Γ^i that puts positive probability on each of a countable or finite set of *plausible* models M^i.[2] Our presentation is loosely based upon the work of Kalai and Lehrer (1993), who consider the more general case where players can be either patient or impatient.[3]

One desirable feature of Bayesian learning is that if priors are consistent with the true model, beliefs are consistent; that is, they converge to the true model. In the current context this will imply convergence to Nash equilibrium. To make this idea precise, we first define what we will mean by convergence to static Nash equilibria. Given behavior rules ρ^i for each player, there is a well-defined probability distribution D_ρ over histories, finite and infinite. If there exists a map from histories to Nash equilibria of the stage game $\hat{\sigma}_t(h_{t-1})$ such that $|D_\rho(s_t|h_{t-1}) - \hat{\sigma}_t(h_{t-1})(s_t)| \to 0$ almost surely with respect to D_ρ, we say that the rules *converge to static equilibrium*. This criterion for convergence requires convergence in every period, but it does not require convergence to a single static Nash equilibrium; deterministic movement between several static Nash is allowed. Since players are no longer assumed to believe that the world is stationary, there is no reason that they cannot, for example, engage in a cycle between different Nash equilibria.

Next we show that Bayesian rules do converge to the set of static equilibria whenever the beliefs satisfy an absolute continuity condition with respect to the path of play (and hence, implicitly, with respect to each other). Let $D^i_{\rho^i,\Gamma^i}$ be the probability distribution over histories induced by player i's behavioral rule and beliefs.

Definition 8.1   Beliefs Γ^i are *absolutely continuous with respect to the play path* if there exists some plausible model $m^i \in M^i$ such that $D^i_{\rho^i,m^i} = D_\rho$.

In other words, there should be some plausible model that is observationally equivalent to opponents' actual strategies in the sense that the probability distribution over histories is the same. However, the plausible model may generate different off-path play. In the current context of myopia, this is irrelevant, since players do not care about how their

---

2. Obviously there is no loss of generality in assuming positive weights; the set of plausible models is just the support of the probability distribution. We will comment on the case where the set of models is uncountably infinite below.
3. We discuss the issue of patience below.

deviation may effect opponents future play; in the context studied by Kalai and Lehrer of patient players, this means that we may have only a self-confirming equilibrium rather than a Nash equilibrium, since beliefs need be (asymptotically) correct only on the equilibrium path.

Proposition 8.1 (Kalai and Lehrer 1993)   If each p^i is a best responses to beliefs Γ^i which are absolutely continuous with respect to the play path, then the rules converge to static equilibrium.

Sketch of Proof   We will show that for large enough t each player's forecasts about opponents' date-t play are approximately correct. Since each p^i is a best response to that player i's beliefs, and the best-response correspondences have closed graph, the conclusion follows.

The fact that forecasts become approximately correct is essentially a result of Blackwell and Dubins (1962) which follows from the Martingale convergence theorem. To simplify, we suppose that for each player i the model m^i is such that $D^i_{p^i,m^i} = D_p$ specifies a pure-strategy profile at each history. This allows us to give a proof that mimics that in our (1989) paper on reputation effects.

Fix a player i and a model m^i such that $D^i_{p^i,m^i} = D_p$, and let ω denote the event (in player i's model of his opponents' play) that the opponents' play is generated by m^i. Let $\tilde{\omega}$ denote the complementary event that ω does not occur. We will use the following lemma:

Lemma 8.1   There is an $r < 1$ such that $p^i(h_{t-1})$ is a best response to m^i whenever the player i's posterior probability of opponents playing according to m^i is greater or equal to r.

This slight sharpening of the usual closed-graph result is a consequence of the assumption that there are finitely many strategies in the stage game and is shown, for example, in Fudenberg and Levine (1989).

Now, at any history consistent with h (the certain outcome under D_p), we can use Bayes's rule to determine player i's posterior probability of event ω,

$$\Gamma^i(\omega|h_t) = \frac{D_p(s_t^{-i}|h_{t-1},\omega)\Gamma^i(\omega|h_{t-1})}{D_p(s_t^{-i}|h_{t-1})}$$

so that

$$\frac{\Gamma^i(\omega|h_t)}{\Gamma^i(\omega|h_{t-1})} = \frac{D_p(s_t^{-i}|h_{t-1},\omega)}{D_p(s_t^{-i}|h_{t-1})}.$$

Thus the posterior probability of event ω increases by a factor of at least $1/r$ in any period in which player i fails to play a best response to the strategy prescribed by m^i, so there can be at most a finite number of periods where this is the case. Taking the maxima of these bounds over the finite number of players establishes the desired result, and in fact shows somewhat more: There is a finite time T after which play in every period is exactly that of a static Nash equilibrium.   ∎

It will not escape the careful reader that the hypothesis reads a lot like a definition of equilibrium: The rules are assumed to be best responses to beliefs that are plausible with respect to the play path generated by those rules. This "fixed-point" property makes the hypothesis somewhat difficult to interpret, but it is not so strong as to imply that play is a static Nash equilibrium from the first period on. To illustrate the condition further, consider an example from Kalai and Lehrer that shows how absolute continuity can be satisfied with respect to the sort of pure-strategy models we assumed in our proof of their result. The example also helps illustrate the "fixed-point" nature of the absolute continuity assumption.

Example 8.1 (Kalai and Lehrer 1993) Consider the following two-player stage game of "chicken" shown in figure 8.1 where the strategies are "yield" (Y) or "insist" (I). This game has two pure-strategy equilibria—one in which player one yields and two insists, and vice versa—and a mixed-strategy equilibrium. Following Kalai and Lehrer, we suppose that the plausible set consists of the pure-strategy models of the form "insist for the first n periods (possibly infinite), then yield forever." In addition we suppose that the prior puts exponentially declining weights on these models and that insisting forever has positive probability.

The best response for player i to this sort of prior beliefs is to insist for a finite period of time t_i and then yield if the other player has not done so already, since it becomes increasingly likely that the other player will never yield. Whether the resulting play path satisfies absolute continuity depends on how different the prior beliefs of the two players are. If player

	Y	I
Y	0, 0	1, 2
I	2, 1	−1, −1

Figure 8.1
Chicken

1, say, is much more pessimistic about his opponent yielding than vice versa, then player 1's best response will be to start yielding at an earlier time, so the play path will be that both players fight until t_1, and from this date on player 1 will yield and player 2 will fight. This path is the prediction of $D^1_{\rho^1,m^2}$ for any m^2 under which 2 fights past t_1 and is also the prediction of $D^2_{\rho^2,m^1}$ for the m^1 under which 1 stops fighting at exactly t_1, so both players' beliefs are absolutely continuous with respect to the path of play. And, as shown by the theorem, the outcome at all dates from t_1 on is a static Nash equilibrium.

Now suppose instead that the two players have symmetric prior beliefs (or nearly so) so that both will stop fighting at the same time. When this occurs, it is then optimal for both players to stop yielding, a path that has zero probability according to the original beliefs, so absolute continuity is violated.[4] This illustrates the problem in finding sets of plausible models that satisfy the absolute continuity assumption. It also raises the question of whether some more complicated beliefs might satisfy the absolute continuity assumption, an issue that we discuss more generally in the next section.

8.4   Interpreting the Absolute Continuity Condition

As we observed, the problem with interpreting the Kalai-Lehrer result as a favorable result about Bayesian learning lies in the fact that the prior beliefs must satisfy the absolute continuity condition. However, since absolute continuity is endogenous, finding beliefs in principle requires the same kind of fixed-point solution that finding an equilibrium does. One solution to this problem is to interpret this result as a new and weaker

---

4. The plausible sets in this example are reminiscent of equilibrium play in a "war of attrition" game, in which once a player yields she must yield forever afterward, so that the players' strategy space reduces to the choice of a time to yield if the "war" is still ongoing. This war of attrition has two pure-strategy equilibrium outcomes, "1 yields at the start and 2 insists," and vice versa. These outcomes correspond to equilibria of the repeated game in which one player always insists and the other always yields, which is why the associated asymmetric prior beliefs satisfy absolute continuity in the repeated game. The war of attrition also has symmetric equilibrium in mixed strategies, which corresponds to symmetric priors in the repeated game. However, this mixed equilibrium is not an equilibrium of the repeated game, for precisely the same reason that the associated beliefs do not satisfy absolute continuity: If the opponent's strategy is a randomization over strategies, all of which specify that once the player yields she will continue to do so, then a concession-time strategy will not be a best response. By definition all three of these equilibria of the war of attrition satisfy absolute continuity in the war of attrition itself, as noted by Kalai and Lehrer, but the war of attrition is not a repeated game.

equilibrium condition, rather than an answer to the question of "how do we get to equilibrium." That is, in this setup the "equilibrium" allows "substantial" disagreement among players about the likely course of play, but ultimately this disagreement disappears. In many ways this interpretation is similar to the model (and result) of Jordan (1991), who examines a full Bayesian Nash equilibrium of a repeated game, where players do not initially know what game they are playing. Here too the result is that play converges to Nash equilibria of the stage game.

Our interest here, however, is in models where the allowed priors are exogenously specified without reference to a fixed-point problem. Ideally the priors would have the property that the absolute continuity assumption is satisfied regardless of opponents strategies, but this is impossible: The space H^{-i} is uncountable, and therefore so is the set of all models. If we continue to restrict the set of plausible models to be countable, then necessarily it does not contain all possible models. If, on the other hand, we allow the set of plausible models to be uncountable, we must define absolute continuity by means of positive probabilities, and any probability distribution on an uncountable space must place probability zero on some points. If the opponents were to actually choose such a point, the absolute continuity assumption would be violated.

Instead, we will explore the weaker possibility that it is possible to specify a class of priors with the property that if all players pick from this class, the absolute continuity assumption is satisfied. Even this weaker goal can be difficult to achieve. In particular, the condition is less readily satisfied in the infinite horizon than in finite truncations of the game, as the example in figure 8.2 shows. We suppose that players' beliefs are that the opponent's play is independent of their own and that priors are "eventually equilibrium." By this we mean that the plausible sets of strategies are uncontingent strategies of the form $(s_1^{-i}, s_2^{-i}, \ldots, s_t^{-i}, s_t^{-i}, \ldots)$ with an arbitrary beginning but in which the opponent's play eventually converges to a particular pure strategy. Moreover all such sequences have positive probability, and only such sequences have positive probability.

	A	B
A	1, 1	0, 0
B	0, 0	1, 1

Figure 8.2
Pure coordination game

	H	T
H	1, –1	–1, 1
T	–1, 1	1, –1

Figure 8.3
Matching pennies

As an example of such beliefs, suppose that player 1 believes A is 90% likely in period 1, while player 2 believes B is 90% likely. Moreover both players beliefs are that if the other opponent played $(s_1^{-i}, s_2^{-i}, \ldots, s_{t-1}^{-i})$ in the past, there is only a $(0.1)^t$ probability that he will fail to play s_{t-1}^{-i} in period t. Then each player always plays the way his opponent did last period, but player 1 initially plays A and player 2 plays B. So play alternates deterministically between (A, B) and (B, A), an event that was thought a priori to have probability zero. The two players never manage to coordinate. The absolute continuity assumption is satisfied with respect to any finite truncation of the game; the problem is that it is not satisfied asymptotically.

Of course it may be argued that players should place positive a priori weight on two cycles. But there is still no guarantee that this will not result in three cycles. We must check that when each player optimizes against his prior over the plausible set, the resulting play lies with probability one in the set considered plausible by his opponent. The problem in the example above was that it did not.

Our further discussion of this problem is based loosely on Nachbar (1997). For simplicity we will limit the discussion to the game of matching pennies shown in figure 8.3. Recall that a *model* for player i is a map $m^{-i}(h_t) \in \Delta(S^{-i})$ from histories to strategies in the repeated game for player i's opponent and that the set of models viewed as plausible by player i is denoted by M^i. If a model puts probability one on a single strategy for player i's opponent, we refer to it (by analogy to a pure strategy) as a pure model. For any pure model m^{-i} we denote by $\tilde{m}^i(m^{-i}) = BR^i(m^{-i})$ the pure model that yields a payoff of 1 in every period against m^{-i}. Following Nachbar, we assume that if a pure model $m^{-i} \in M^i$ is viewed as plausible by player i, then the pure model $\tilde{m}^i(m^{-i})$ is viewed plausible by player $-i$; that is, $\tilde{m}^i(m^{-i}) \in M^{-i}$.

Suppose that there exist best responses ρ such that the resulting play with probability 1 is plausible for each player i and such that some pure model m^i has positive probability. Then, by assumption, this means the model $\tilde{m}^{-i}(m^i)$ must be viewed as plausible by player i and so has positive weight in his prior. By proposition 8.1 this implies that eventually player i

must learn that player $-i$ is playing $\tilde{m}^{-i}(m^i)$. Once player i learns this fact, he will no longer play according to m^i, contradicting the fact that ρ^i is a best response to i's prior.

The difficulty in this line of argument is that it shows only that best responses cannot be plausible if they put a positive weight on a pure model. However, if the best responses are sufficiently mixed (e.g., an independent 50-50 coin flip in each period, which is an obvious way to play matching pennies), then they may not put positive weight on any pure model. Consequently the question of whether there exist plausible sets for all players such that the best responses lead to plausible outcomes remains incompletely answered. Nachbar (1997) shows that if we insist that all best responses to plausible sets are plausible (rather than just some, as we do here), then this impossibility result can be extended to mixed strategies and trembles, as well as many other games. In a loose way this suggests that the absolute continuity assumption is difficult to satisfy.

8.5 Choosing among Experts

The problem with the Bayesian approach is that the true process, which is endogenously determined, may not be in the set of processes initially considered to be possible, and that Bayesian updating can have odd consequences when the support of the prior does not contain the process generating the data. Bayesian updating does minimize a certain measure of logarithmic distance to the "true model," but this is no guarantee that the player will obtain a reasonable payoff; in particular, the Bayesian optimal decision rule can give the player less than the minmax payoff against some unanticipated play by the opponent.

For this reason we are interested in learning rules that are robust to the possibility that the process generating the data may not be in the support of the prior. That is, we seek rules that do reasonably well even if the true process generating the data is different than those initially contemplated. Since our measure of success is the utility achieved by the learning rule, it is convenient at this point to abandon the Bayesian point of view, and instead focus on directly on strategies that are thought to be potential best responses. In this section we will adopt the computer science terminology approach introduced earlier in the chapter and recast the learning problem as that of choosing the expert who makes the best recommendations for a course of play. Our goal is to demonstrate that a relatively simple procedure of rating experts by their historical performance does about as well asymptotically as the best expert does. In other words, while none of the experts (or models) necessarily does as well as would be possible if the "true" model or expert were considered a priori plausible, there is no need to do worse than the expert who is closest to the "true" expert in the sense of getting the highest time average utility among all experts thought to be a priori plausible.

To demonstrate this fact, let us recall the results in chapter 4 about cautious fictitious play; the results about experts can be derived as a corollary of this basic result. We will employ the version of the result for time-varying utility functions. Define

$$\bar{u}_t^i(e^i) = \frac{1}{t} \sum_{\tau=1}^{t} u^i(e^i(h_{\tau-1}), s_\tau^{-i})$$

to be the utilities that would be realized if the expert e^i played on behalf of player i. Note that while the game played by choosing actions is stationary, the game played by choosing experts is time and history dependent, since utility corresponding to choosing a particular expert will depend on the action that expert recommends given the history. By analogy with the construction in chapter 4, we define a rule $\overline{BR}_e^i(\bar{u}_t^i)$ mapping histories to probability distributions over experts by solving the optimization problem

$$\max_{\vartheta^i} \ \vartheta^i \cdot \bar{u}_t^i + \lambda v^i(\vartheta^i).$$

where $\vartheta \in \Delta(E^i)$ is a probability distribution over the set of plausible experts, v^i is a smooth function that becomes large at the boundaries of the simplex, and λ is a small positive real number.

We also can define a learning rule in the more ordinary sense by first applying $\overline{BR}_e^i(\bar{u}_t^i)$, then letting the (randomly chosen) expert choose the action; denote this by $\overline{BR}^i(\bar{u}_t^i)$.

In this context, and with this notation, we can define an analog of universal consistency:

Definition 8.2 A rule ρ^i (mapping histories to mixed actions) is ε-*universally expert* if for any ρ^{-i}

$$\limsup_{T \to \infty} \ \max_{e^i \in E^i} \ \bar{u}_T^i(e^i) - \frac{1}{T} \sum_{t=1}^{T} u^i(\rho_t(h_{t-1})) \le \varepsilon$$

almost surely with respect to (ρ^i, ρ^{-i}).[5]

---

5. Note that $u^i(\rho_t(h_{t-1}))$ does not need a time subscript, since the rule $\rho_t(h_{t-1})$ is still by definition a choice of action, not a choice of expert. Equivalently we could define the learning rule to be a choice of expert, in which case utility would depend on the history. Naturally both ways of computing the utility actually realized yield the same answer.

This says that the best expert does no more than ε better than the utility actually received.

With this notation, we may restate proposition 4.5 as follows:

Proposition 8.2 Suppose that v^i is a smooth, strictly differentiably concave function satisfying the boundary condition that as ϑ^i approaches the boundary of the simplex, the slope of v^i becomes infinite. Then for every ε there exists a λ such that the $\overline{BR}^i$ procedure is ε-universally expert.

Notice also that we may equally easily derive proposition 4.5 from proposition 8.2: We suppose that among the plausible experts each recommends playing a fixed action in every period, and every action is represented by some expert. Thus the best expert gets the payoff of playing the action that is optimal against the time average of play, so a universally expert rule is universally consistent.

In the case where $v^i(\sigma^i) = - \sum_{s^i} \sigma^i(s^i) \log(\sigma^i(s^i))$ (which is the negative of entropy defined in chapter 3) the scheme for choosing among experts picks them with a frequency proportional to the exponential of the historical utility. This type of exponential weighting scheme was introduced in computer science by Littlestone and Warmuth (1994), Desantis, Markowski, and Wegman (1992), Feder, Mehrav, and Gutman (1992), and Vovck (1990). Vovck (1990) gives a proof of proposition 8.2 in a special case, while the complete theorem is shown by Chung (1994) and Freund and Schapire (1995). Freund and Schapire (1995) are especially attentive to the rate of convergence. There are also various extensions, such as that of Kivinen and Warmuth (1993), to the case of continuous outcomes. A nice review of this literature can be found in Foster and Vohra (1996).

8.6 Conditional Learning[6]

An alternative way to develop rules that do well in a broad class of learning environments is to focus directly on estimating the set of conditional probabilities of opponents' play given the history of all players' play. That is, we will divide the sample into subsamples and ask if the player could do as well as if she knew the frequencies of opponents' play in each of the subsamples and was told in advance which subsample each observation was going to be drawn from. Thus the universal consistency condition is the special case of this robustness criterion where there is only a single subsample.

---

6. The discussion in this section follows Fudenberg and Levine (1995).

To make this precise, suppose that there is a collection of categories Ψ^i into which observations may be placed. A *classification rule* is a map $\hat{\psi}^i : H \times S^i \rightarrow \Psi^i$. Prior to observing s_t^{-i}, the player knows h_{t-1}, s_t^i and must choose a category $\hat{\psi}^i(h_{t-1}, s_t^i)$ based only on this information; this category is then the basis for the player's forecast of play at date t. At this point it may seem odd that the category chosen can depend on s_t^i as well as on the history h_{t-1}; since our first results will concern rules that do not condition on s_t^i, we will defer explanation of this possibility until it becomes important. For simplicity our presentation here restricts attention to the case of finitely many categories. Fudenberg and Levine (1995) allow for countably many categories provided that the number of "effective categories" does not grow too quickly.[7]

Arbitrary methods of dividing the sample into subsamples do not make sense—only classification *rules* that assign outcomes to categories based on information available prior to the observation being made do. For example, if a player suspects that the outcome may be following a deterministic two cycle, he can use two categories according to whether the period is odd or even. Or, if the player is concerned that the outcome may be generated by a first-order Markov process, he could use the previous period's outcome to define categories.[8]

Fix a classification rule $\hat{\psi}$. Given a history h_t, we define $n_t^i(\psi)$ to be the total number of times the category ψ has been observed. We define $D_t^{-i}(\psi)$ to be the vector whose components are the frequency with which each strategy profile of i's opponents has appeared when ψ has been observed. For example, the category might correspond to the previous period's play, so the distribution $D_t^i(s^2)$ is simply the empirical distribution of outcomes conditional on the previous period's play having been s^2.[9] Also we denote the average utility received in the subsample ψ by $u_t^i(\psi)$. For each subsample we can define the difference between the utility that might have been received and the utility that actually was obtained as

---

7. In the literature on nonparametric statistics, this case of countably many categories is known as the method of sieves; for example, see Grenander (1981).

8. Note that the requirement that each partial history be assigned to only one category is less restrictive than it might appear, since given two categorization schemes with a finite number of categories (e.g., one that distinguishes even vs. odd periods, and a second that looked at the previous period's play) one can construct a new scheme that corresponds to the coarsest common refinement (i.e., the meet) of the two partitions.

9. The rules considered by Ayoyagi and Sonsino correspond to categorization by the opponent's play in the "recent" past.

$$
c_t^i(\psi) = \begin{cases} n_t^i(\psi)[\max_{s^i} u^i(s^i, D_t^{-i}(\psi)) - u_t^i(\psi)], & \text{if } n_t^i(\psi) > 0, \\ 0 & \text{if } n_t^i(\psi) = 0. \end{cases}
$$

This is the difference between the realized payoff in this category and the payoff from playing the constant strategy that is a best response to the empirical distribution in the category. (Note that in some histories the "loss" in a category can be negative—this happens if the player has "been lucky" or "guessed well.") We define the total cost to be $c_t^i = \sum_{\psi \in \Psi^i} c_t^i(\psi)$. Our analogue to universal consistency relative to the rule $\hat{\psi}$ for choosing subsamples is that the time average cost c_t^i/t should be small. Thus the player does as well as if she knew the frequency of play in each subsample.

Definition 8.3 A behavior rule $\rho^i : H \to \Sigma^i = (\Delta(S^i))$ is *ε-universally consistent conditional on* $\hat{\psi}$ if for every behavior rule $\rho^{-i} : H \to \Sigma^{-i}$, $\limsup_{t \to \infty} c_t^i/t \le \varepsilon$ almost surely with respect to the stochastic process induced by $\rho = (\rho^1, \rho^2)$.

When the classification rule is fixed, we simply refer to a strategy being *ε-universally conditionally consistent*.

As with universal consistency this criterion measures the rule's effectiveness in optimizing against an exogenous distribution of opponents' play. Note that it does *not* require that players experiment in order to learn how their opponent's play varies with their own, nor does it require that the rule do a good job of influencing their opponents' play. Thus the condition seems most natural in settings of anonymous random matching. To illustrate this point, it is worth considering a repeated prisoner's dilemma game in which player two plays tit-for-tat. If player 1 cheats in every period, this is "optimal" in the sense used here: given the empirical distribution of player 2's play (cooperate in period 1, cheat in every other period), a best response is in fact always to cheat. Of course it would be much better for a patient player 1 to cooperate in every period.

We now temporarily restrict attention to rules of the form $\hat{\psi}^i(h_{t-1})$ so that the category chosen does not depend on the player's own intended action. Let ρ^i be a learning rule. Given any such rule, we create a conditional analogue $\rho^i(\hat{\psi})$ in the following simple way: For any history h_{t-1} we can define another history $h_{t-1}(\hat{\psi})$ to be the sequence of past outcomes that were assigned to category ψ. (This subhistory will in general have length less that $t - 1$.)

We then define $\rho^i(\hat{\psi})(h_{t-1}) = \rho^i(h_{t-1}(\hat{\psi}))$; that is, we apply the original rule to the subhistory corresponding to the category ψ. The essential feature of such a conditional rule is that if the original rule is universally consistent, then the extended rule is universally conditionally consistent.

Proposition 8.3 If ρ^i is ε-universally consistent, then $\rho^i(\hat{\psi})$ is ε-conditionally universally consistent.

Proof We examine the cost in the definition of conditional universal consistency

$$\frac{c_t^i}{t} = \sum_{\psi \in \Psi^i} n_t^i(\psi) \frac{[\max_{s^i} u^i(s^i, D_t^{-i}(\psi)) - u_t^i(\psi)]}{t}$$

If $n_t^i \to \infty$, then $\max_{s^i} u^i(s^i, D_t^{-i}(\psi)) - u_t^i(\psi) \le \varepsilon$ because ρ^i is ε-universally consistent. On the other hand, if $\lim n_t^i < \infty$, $n_t^i/t \to 0$. So clearly $\limsup c_t^i/t \le \varepsilon$. ∎

We should note that Aoyagi's (1994) model of conditional but exact fictitious play is closely related to the conditional learning rules of this section. In this model, histories are categorized according to the outcome during the most recent L periods of the history where L is a fixed number. That is, each category corresponds to a sequence of L outcomes, and the rule for assigning histories to categories is to assign a history to the category that corresponds to the most recent L outcomes of the history. As in conditional smooth fictitious play a separate frequency of opponent's play is tracked for each category. However, the Aoyagi model differs in assuming that following each history, a player plays an exact best response to the frequency for the category, rather than a smoothed best response. In this model Aoyagi shows that strict Nash equilibria are stable and that, in a zero-sum game with a unique equilibrium, the marginal frequencies converge to that equilibrium. The analysis of mixed equilibria in this model is more delicate; we discuss it in section 8.8 below.

Even if stability properties are preserved by sophisticated learning procedures, it is possible that cycles will be introduced when without such sophisticated procedures there were no cycles. This is particularly true since play in the early periods will tend to be relatively random, and this may accidentally establish a pattern or cycle that will then take hold. Although this possibility should hold more generally, it has been studied in the context of models in which players follow relatively unsophisticated procedures until a cycle is detected (or thought to be detected), and then a more sophisticated procedure is introduced. In such a variation on conditional ordinary fictitious play, Aoyagi shows that the stability of mixed equilibrium is reversed due to constant switching back and forth between sophisticated and unsophisticated procedures.

8.7 Discounting

So far our discussion of learning has been cast in terms of time averages of utility. This reflects the idea that a "good" learning rule ought to do well in the long run. However, economists generally regard people as impatient and view discounting as a better model of intertemporal preference. In general, we can say little about how well learning rules do in terms of the discounted present value of the players' payoffs. Early in the game, before there are much data to learn from, the player is essentially guessing what the outcome will be. Regardless of whether "learning" is effective or ineffective, a rule that happens to guess well early on can outperform a rule that guesses poorly. Moreover, in addition to guessing the outcome, the player must guess which patterns of data are most likely. With a small amount of data, only a relatively small number of conditional probabilities can be estimated. If other players switch strategies every other period, a player who guesses this is likely to be the case will outperform a player who is more focused on the possibility of two cycles.

As a result of these considerations, we cannot hope to compare two arbitrary learning rules and determine that one rule is "better" from a discounted point of view. What we can hope to do is to compare classes of learning rules broad enough to incorporate various possibilities of "guessing." What we will show in this section is that the class of conditional smooth fictitious play rules has a kind of dominance property. Given an arbitrary rule ρ^i and any $\varepsilon > 0$, we can design a conditional smooth fictitious play rule that never does more than ε worse than ρ^i regardless of the discount factor.

To illustrate this result, considering the example of the best-response learning rule and the Jordan three-player matching pennies game. In this game player 1 wins if he plays the same action as player 2, player 2 wins if he matches player 3, and player 3 wins by *not* matching player 1. If all players follow a fictitious play, then play cycles. However, each player, in a certain sense, waits too long before switching: For example, when player 1 switches from H to T, player 3 does not switch from T to H until player 1 has switched for a sufficiently long time that the average frequency with which he has played H drops to $1/2$. Smooth fictitious play performs similarly. However, a player who plays the best-response rule will switch one period after his opponent does and as a result will get a much higher payoff (even in the time average sense) than a player using a smooth fictitious play. The reason that the best-response rule does better is that it guesses correctly both that opponents' last period play is a good predictor of this period's play and that the correlation is positive. If in fact the correlation were negative, for example, if the opponents alternated deterministically between H and T, then best response would do considerably worse than a smooth fictitious play.

The basic idea we develop in this section is that it is possible (with a small cost) to have the best of both worlds by using a conditional smooth fictitious play, conditioning on the opponents' play last period with a strongly held prior that this periods play is the same as next period's play. In the short run such a rule does exactly the same thing as best response. In the long run, if the correlation is actually positive as it is in the Jordan example, the rule continues to behave like the best-response function. However, if the correlation is negative, as is the case when the opponent alternates deterministically between heads and tails, eventually the data overwhelm the prior, and the conditional smooth fictitious play begins to match the opponents moves, so it does better than best-response and even ordinary smooth fictitious play.

To establish the basic result, it is helpful to begin with a simple case. We consider an ordinary smooth fictitious play against a particular guess σ^{-i} about how opponents will play. We first show that for any such guess we can design a smooth fictitious play whose present value is no more than ε lower than that of the guess, regardless of the discount factor. Since the smooth fictitious play is universally consistent, for discount factors close to one, its present value is not much below that of a best response to the limiting value of the empirical distribution of opponents' play, while a particular guess may well be.

Lemma 8.2 For any fixed strategy σ^i and any $\varepsilon > 0$ there exists a smooth fictitious play ρ^i such that for any strictly decreasing positive weights β_t summing to one and any ρ_t^{-i}

$$\sum_{t=1}^{\infty} \beta_t u^i(\sigma^i, \rho_t^{-i}) \le \sum_{t=1}^{\infty} \beta_t u^i(\rho_t) + \varepsilon.$$

A proof can be found in Fudenberg and Levine (1995) and is along much the same lines as the proof of proposition 4.5. The key observation is that careful use of the argument in proposition 4.5 makes it possible to bound the time average loss uniformly regardless of the length of the horizon. Since the average present value can be written as a convex combination of time averages over all different possible time horizons, this uniform bound gives the desired result in the discounted case.

The rule that is being outperformed, that of guessing the opponent will always play a single action, is not very interesting. However, let ρ^i be an arbitrary deterministic learning rule,[10] and let $\varepsilon > 0$ be given. Take a set $\Psi^i = S^i$ to be strategies for player i. Define the classification rule $\hat{\psi}^i(h_t) = \rho^i(h_t)$, that is, classify histories according to the way in which ρ^i is going to play. For each s^i choose a smooth fictitious play $\overline{BR}^i(\varepsilon, s^i)$ so that lemma 8.2 is satisfied with respect to ε, and define a rule

$$\hat{\rho}^i(\rho^i, \varepsilon)(h_t) = \overline{BR}^i(\varepsilon, \hat{\psi}(h_t))(h_t(\hat{\psi}))$$

by applying the appropriate smooth fictitious play to the subhistory of the chosen category. Since we showed that lemma 8.2 held even for non-stationary discounting (corresponding to skipping periods when a rule is not used), we have the immediate corollary

Proposition 8.4 For any rule ρ^i and any $\varepsilon > 0$ there exists a conditional smooth fictitious play $\hat{\rho}^i$ such that for any discount factor $\delta > 0$ and any ρ^{-i},

$$(1 - \delta) \sum_{t=1}^{\infty} \delta^{t-1} u^i(\rho_t^i, \rho_t^{-i}) \leq (1 - \delta) \sum_{t=1}^{\infty} \delta^{t-1} u^i(\hat{\rho}_t^i, \rho_t^{-i}) + \varepsilon.$$

This shows that even when discounting is considered, the "extra cost" of using a universally consistent rule can be made arbitrarily small, and moreover the loss can be bounded uniformly over the discount factor. From a normative point of view this result provides an argument that rational agents "should" use universally consistent rules. Whether this implies that real people will tend to use such rules is a more complicated question, but the result certainly does not make that prediction *less* plausible.

8.8 Categorization Schemes and Cycles

Since categorization schemes are intended to allow players to detect cycles, it is natural to ask whether cycles can in fact occur when both players use categorization schemes. In this section we consider categorization schemes that are do not depend on the player's own anticipated action; we consider endogenous categorization in the following section. To begin, consider the behavior of Aoyagi's model of exact conditional

---

10. The extension to random rules is straightforward.

	L	M	R
U	0, 0	0, 1	1, 0
M	1, 0	0, 0	0, 1
D	0, 1	1, 0	0, 0

Figure 8.4
Shapley game

fictitious play (discussed in section 8.6) near a mixed-strategy equilibrium. Since players are assumed to use exact fictitious play given the conditional frequencies rather than a smooth fictitious play, they will not use randomized strategies but instead vary their play over time. If each player is trying to detect such deterministic variation by his opponent, patterns more complicated than conditioning on all histories with a fixed lag must be introduced to preserve the equilibrium. By way of contrast, we would expect a smooth conditional fictitious play to be relatively robust: "Near" (in the appropriate space) a mixed equilibrium that is stable with respect to unconditional smooth fictitious play we would expect that players randomize with approximately the equilibrium probabilities, so the frequencies in any category that players might consider would tend to remain near the equilibrium level. In other words, with a smooth conditional fictitious play, there would be no patterns to detect.

Next, suppose that both players use logistic fictitious play with a single category in the "Shapley game," the two-player, three action per player game with payoffs as shown in figure 8.4. We know that play can asymptote to any stable best-response cycle. Recall that in this game, such a cycle begins at (U, M). Player 1 then wishes to switch to D. At D, M, player 2 wishes to switch to L, then from D, L to M, L to M, R to U, R, then back to the start at U, M. It can be shown that this cycle is asymptotically stable in both the best response and approximate fictitious play dynamic.

In the case of interest to us, approximate fictitious play, the cycles are of ever-increasing length. Thus holding opponent's behavior fixed, each player could do better by conditioning on the profile played last period. Suppose that *both* players do so. Then within each of the nine categories, play is again an approximate fictitious play, and (for some initial conditions) play will simply follow the Shapley cycle within each category. Of course players might notice this and introduce even more sophisticated conditional cycle detection, but as long as they both condition on exactly the same histories, there will still be a Shapley cycle within each category.

Intuitively the use of a common categorization scheme is much like a public randomization between initial conditions of the fictitious play.

Suppose, however, that the two players are not conditioning on exactly the same histories. This raises the possibility that the players may not be able to "accidentally" correlate their play, as they do when they use exactly the same conditioning procedure. To understand this possibility better, let us consider the case where each player conditions only on his opponent's last action (but not his own) in the Shapley game.[11] The resulting dynamical system has 18 dimensions, since each player must keep track of the number of occurrences of three outcomes for each of three categories corresponding to opponent's last period play. Since it is difficult to analyze such a high-dimensional system analytically, Fudenberg and Levine (1995) used a simulation. Each player was assumed to use a smoothing function of the form $v^i(\sigma^i) = -(1/\kappa) \sum_{s^i} \sigma^i(s^i) \log \sigma^i(s^i)$, where $\kappa = 10$, so that within categories the players use a logistic fictitious play. The payoffs are those for the Shapley game given above. To initialize the system, each player was endowed with 12 initial observations independent of category. Player 1 was endowed with the initial sample (1, 1, 10), and player 2 with (10, 1, 1). Given these frequencies, it was optimal for player 1 to play to play U and player 2 to play M, which is an initial condition that starts the Shapley cycle. The graph in figure 8.5 reports the time average of the joint distribution of outcomes. Each line in the graph represents the time average frequency of a single outcome, for example, the line that is nearly 1 for the first 6 periods corresponds to the outcome U, M. The thick horizontal line represents the common frequency in the unique Nash equilibrium of 1/9. Note that the horizontal axis is measured in logarithmic units, since this is the time scale over which the Shapley cycle occurs. In this simulation the system does not cycle but has essentially converged to the Nash equilibrium after 1,000 periods.

By way of contrast, Fudenberg and Levine also did a simulation in which players did not condition on the history at all. That is, each player used a single category, and play corresponded to ordinary logistic fictitious play. All the other parameters including the initial conditions were held fixed at the values given above. The results of the simulation are shown in the figure 8.6. As we can expect, the system cycles, settling into

---

11. Aoyagi (1994) also considers an example where two players classify observations using different categories. However, in his example players are using exact fictitious play within categories, so the player with a more refined category scheme can exploit the player with the less refined scheme. This cannot happen with logistic fictitious play.

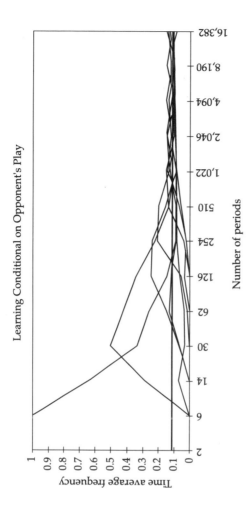

Figure 8.5
Simulated play conditioning on opponent's last period action

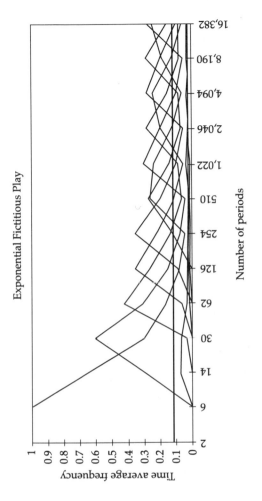

Figure 8.6
Simulated Shapley cycle for exponential fictitious play

a relatively stable cycle after about 500 periods. A significant feature is that the frequencies corresponding to the diagonal (U, L), (M, M) and (D, R) remain close to zero. This is not the case when players condition on each other's previous actions.

In general, we do not know to what extent the "noise" introduced by different players' conditioning on different histories ultimately causes correlation to break down. If it does, then in the long-run learning will lead to Nash equilibrium. Although we have seen that this happens in a particular example, whether it is generally the case remains an open question for future research.[12]

8.9 Introspective Classification Rules, Calibration, and Correlated Equilibrium

The general categorization framework we developed in section 8.6 allows players to condition on the action he is about to play as well as on the history itself. Until now we have avoided discussing the possibility of such "introspective" rules, and it is not covered by the formal results in earlier sections. We now wish to suggest that there are cases where introspective rules may be sensible. Note that in the Shapley cycle player gets less utility than if he conditioned on his own intended action. Suppose that players condition on their own anticipated actions in the sense that no category can ever be assigned two observations in which the player's own action is different. This has two implications. First, the two players are not conditioning on exactly the same histories, since each player can anticipate his own action but not that of his opponents. This raises the possibility that players cannot "accidentally" correlate their play leading to Nash equilibrium in much the same way that conditioning only on the opponent's previous action did in the discussion above.[13] Second, the empirical joint distribution of action profiles must come to approximate a correlated equilibrium.[14] This follows immediately, since each player,

---

12. Recent papers by Sanchirico (1996) and Sonsino (1997) have stressed another implication of noise: It can help ensure that long-run play ends up in one of the "minimal CURB sets" of the game (see chapter 4). This is an interesting fact, but rather different than what we are discussing here, because the minimal CURB set in the Shapley game is the entire game.
13. Foster and Vohra (1995) examine the case of conditioning only on a player's own anticipated action and give simulation results with convergence to Nash equilibrium very much like those described above in the case where players condition on their opponent's previous action.
14. However, unless the correlated equilibrium is actually a Nash equilibrium, the empirical joint distribution cannot converge and must shift from one correlated equilibrium to another.

conditional on his own action, is playing an approximate best response to the distribution of opponents play.

The resemblance of the empirical joint distribution of action profiles to a correlated equilibrium is closely related to a point originally made by Foster and Vohra (1993) who consider best responses to beliefs that are *calibrated*. This means that if we categorize periods according to forecasts of the opponent's play, the frequency distribution of actual play of the opponent converges to the forecast. For example, we would say that a weather forecaster is calibrated if on those occasions on which a 50% chance of rain was announced, it actually rained 50% of the time.[15] From our perspective, the important feature of calibration of beliefs is that it implies that actions are *calibrated*. By this we mean that each player conditional on his own action, is playing an approximate best response to the distribution of opponents play, the condition that leads directly to correlated equilibrium.

However, even the use of calibrated rules leaves open the possibility that opponents "accidentally" correlate their play. If they did not do so, then we would have the stronger result that play would eventually come to resemble a Nash equilibrium. What we should point out is that calibration guarantees no such thing. The easiest way to make this point is to observe that calibration of actions does not actually require that players condition on their own actions; it is sufficient that no category can ever be assigned two periods with more than two distinct values of the player's own action. The essential point is that if a joint distribution over two actions and all outcomes has the property that the realized utility is at least that that can be obtained by playing a single best response to the marginal distribution over outcomes, then each action must actually be a best response conditional on that action.[16] In particular, if each player has only two actions, then his strategy is calibrated even if he uses only a single category; for example, logistic fictitious play is calibrated in this case, yet logistic fictitious play need not converge to Nash equilibrium in games with two actions per player.

---

15. This notion of calibration lumps together all histories in which the forecaster's prediction was the same. Refining this by conditioning on all histories leads to a notion very close to the statistical concept of consistency. This connection is examined in detail in Kalai, Lehrer and Smorodinsky (1996).

16. More generally, it follows from straightforward algebra that if a joint distribution over all actions and all outcomes has the property that the realized utility is at least the amount that can be obtained by playing a best response to the marginal distribution over outcomes, then no action that has positive probability is a worst response to the distribution of outcomes conditional on that action.

Consider, for example, the three-player, two-action per player game of matching pennies introduced by Jordan (1993). In this game player 1 wishes to match player 2, who wishes to match player 3, who wishes to avoid matching player 1. Again we can apply the results of Benaim and Hirsch (1994) and, supposing that players use logistic fictitious play,[17] focus on best-response cycles. The key is that in every pure-strategy profile exactly one player can gain by deviating. Once he does so, one opponent wishes to switch, and so on, in a cyclic fashion. Jordan also shows that this cycle is asymptotically stable under exact fictitious play; Benaim and Hirsch extend this to stochastic smoothed versions. Moreover, since each player has only two actions, it follows that this cycle takes place (approximately) through the set of correlated equilibria. Despite the fact that players are calibrated and play resembles a correlated equilibrium, this cycle is just as disturbing as the Shapley cycle: Players observe long sequences of their opponent repeatedly playing the same action yet fail to anticipate that it will happen again. If they (all) introduce schemes conditioning on the last period's play, then the cycle simply takes place independently in each category, and so on. Consequently the issue in cycling is not calibration per se but rather how the players' categorization rules fit together.

We next present Foster and Vohra's result that it is possible to design learning rules that condition on a player's own anticipated action. For simplicity we suppose that this is the only part of the history to be conditioned on. In other words, we take the categories to be $\Psi^i = S^i$, the players own strategies, and the categorization scheme to be $\hat{\psi}^i(h_{t-1}, s_t^i) = s_t^i$. Formally we refer to the notion of universal consistency in this case as *calibration*.

Definition 8.4 A behavior rule $\rho^i : H \to \Sigma^i$ is *ε-calibrated* if for every behavior rule $\rho^{-i} : H \to \Sigma^{-i}$ $\limsup_{t\to\infty} \sum_{s^i} n_t^i(s^i)[\max_{\sigma^i} u^i(\sigma^i, D_t^{-i}(s^i)) - u_t^i(s^i)]/t \le \varepsilon$ almost surely with respect to the stochastic process induced by ρ.

Instead of following Foster and Vohra's (1995) proof, we give a simplified construction based on an arbitrary universally consistent rule. Let ρ^i be any ε-universally consistent learning rule. Suppose that player i is

---

17. Implicitly we assume that when there are more than two players, the profile of opponents' actions is treated as a single outcome. This means that each player tracks a joint distribution of opponents' play. Jordan actually supposes that players do fictitious play by keeping a separate distribution for each opponent, assuming that opponents' play is independent. However, in this particular game, there is no distinction between the two procedures, since each player cares only about the play of one opponent.

contemplating playing s^i. Then he ought to try to apply ρ^i to $h_t(s^i)$. The only problem with this is that ρ^i does not put probability one on playing s^i. Suppose, however, that player i is contemplating playing σ^i. Then with probability $\sigma^i(s^i)$ he will play s^i and should therefore play $\rho^i(h_t(s^i))$. Consequently he will actually wind up playing according to $\sum_{s^i} \sigma^i(s^i)\rho^i(h_t(s^i))$. If in fact

$$\sigma^i = \sum_{s^i} \sigma^i(s^i)\rho^i(h_t(s^i)),$$

then his contemplated play and desired play wind up being the same. Notice that $\sigma^i = \sum_{s^i} \sigma^i(s^i)\rho^i(h_t(s^i))$ is a simple fixed-point problem based on a linear map from the nonnegative orthant to itself. So it may easily be solved by linear algebra. Denote the solution $\hat{\rho}^i(h_t)$.

Proposition 8.5 If ρ^i is ε-universally consistent, then $\hat{\rho}^i$ is ε-calibrated.

Proof We examine the asymptotic average cost

$$\frac{\sum_{s^i} n_t^i(s^i)[\max_{\sigma^i} u^i(\sigma^i, D_t^{-i}(s^i)) - u_t^i(s^i)]}{t}$$

$$= \frac{\sum_{s^i}(n_t^i(s^i)[\max_{\sigma^i} u^i(\sigma^i, D_t^{-i}(s^i))] - \sum_{\tau \le t | \hat{\psi}_\tau^i = s^i} u^i(s^i, s_\tau^{-i}))}{t}$$

$$= \frac{\sum_{s^i}(n_t^i(s^i)[\max_{\sigma^i} u^i(\sigma^i, D_t^{-i}(s^i))])}{t} - \frac{\sum_{\tau=1}^t u^i(s_\tau^i, s_\tau^{-i})}{t}.$$

By the strong law of large numbers for orthogonal sequences, $\sum_{\tau=1}^t u^i(s_\tau^i, s_\tau^{-i})/t$ almost surely has the same in the limit as

$$\frac{\sum_{\tau=1}^t u^i(\hat{\rho}_\tau^i, s_\tau^{-i})}{t} = \frac{\sum_{\tau=1}^t \sum_{s^i} u^i(\rho^i(h_\tau(s^i)), s_\tau^{-i})\rho^i(h_\tau(s^i))(s^i)}{t}$$

$$= \frac{\sum_{\tau=1}^t \sum_{s^i} u^i(\rho^i(h_\tau(s^i)), s_\tau^{-i})\rho_\tau^i(s^i)}{t},$$

where we have used the defining equation for $\hat{\rho}^i$. Again applying this strong law of large numbers for orthogonal sequences, this almost surely has the same limit as

$$\frac{\sum_{\tau=1}^t u^i(\rho^i(h_\tau(s_\tau^i)), s_\tau^{-i})}{t} = \frac{\sum_{s^i} \sum_{\tau \le t | \hat{\psi}_\tau^i = s^i} u^i(\rho^i(h_\tau(s^i)), s_\tau^{-i})}{t}.$$

Substituting back in the expression for average cost, we find that

$$\frac{\sum_{s^i} n^i_t(s^i)[\max_{\sigma^i} u^i(\sigma^i, D^{-i}_t(s^i)) - u^i_t(s^i)]}{t}$$

$$= \frac{\sum_{s^i} \left(n^i_t(s^i)[\max_{\sigma^i} u^i(\sigma^i, D^{-i}_t(s^i))] - \sum_{\tau \le t | \hat{\psi}^i_\tau = s^i} u^i(\rho^i(h_\tau(s^i)), s^{-i}_\tau) \right)}{t}$$

$$= \sum_{s^i} \frac{n^i_t(s^i)}{t} \left(\left[\max_{\sigma^i} u^i(\sigma^i, D^{-i}_t(s^i)) \right] - \frac{1}{n^i_t(s^i)} \sum_{\tau \le t | \hat{\psi}^i_\tau = s^i} u^i(\rho^i(h_\tau(s^i)), s^{-i}_\tau) \right).$$

However, since ρ^i is ε-universally consistent, either

$$\limsup \left(\left[\max_{\sigma^i} u^i(\sigma^i, D^{-i}_t(s^i)) \right] - \frac{1}{n^i_t(s^i)} \sum_{\tau \le t | \hat{\psi}^i_\tau = s^i} u^i(\rho^i(h_\tau(s^i)), s^{-i}_\tau) \right) \le \varepsilon,$$

or $n^i_t(s^i)/t \to 0$, which gives the desired result.   ∎

It is useful to note (and this follows from the results of Hart and Mas-Colell 1996) that instead of using the rule $\sigma^i = \sum_{s^i} \sigma^i(s^i)\rho^i(h_t(s^i))$, which involves solving a fixed-point problem, it suffices to use the recursive rule

$$\hat{\rho}^i(h_t) = \sum_{s^i} \hat{\rho}^i(h_{t-1})\rho^i(h_t(s^i)),$$

since $\hat{\rho}^i(h_t)$ is approximately the same as $\hat{\rho}^i(h_{t-1})$ anyway and so approximately solves the fixed-point problem. We should emphasize that there are many learning rules that lead to correlated equilibrium in the long run. For example, Hart and Mas-Colell (1996) consider playing strategies in proportion to the positive part of $(1/t)\sum_{\tau=1}^t [u^i(s^i, D^{-i}_t) - u^i_t]$. Using Blackwell's (1956) approachability theorem, they show that this rule is universally consistent. It follows that the corresponding rule $\hat{\rho}^i$ is universally consistent. They consider a further variation on this such that the player either plays the same action as the last period or plays another action with probability proportional to how much better that alternative would have done conditional on the history corresponding to the action played the last period. They show that if all players use rules of this type, then each rule can be calibrated against a class of outcomes that have probability 1 in this environment.

The final rules considered by Hart and Mas-Colell are not *universally* *calibrated*; that is, they are not calibrated against all opponents' play. For example, suppose that the probability of playing the same action as the last period is bounded below by 3/4 and that the game is matching pennies. Clearly a clever opponent will always play the opposite of what a player using this rule used last period, since this wins at least 3/4 of the time, and so in this case the Hart and Mas-Colell rule loses 3/4 of the time. Since the universally calibrated rule $\hat{\rho}^i$ from which they derive this final rule is not especially more difficult to compute, it is not transparent why players should settle for using rules that are only sometimes calibrated.

8.10   Sonsino's Model of Pattern Recognition

Sonsino (1997) develops an alternative model of "pattern recognition" that supposes players switch between unsophisticated and sophisticated behavior depending on whether patterns have been identified in the past. Patterns are restricted to be sequences of pure Nash equilibria, which has the unfortunate implication that players must know one another's payoffs, but this assumption is probably not essential. Sonsino restricts attention to games that have generic payoffs and satisfy the condition that every strategic-form "subgame" that is closed under the best-response correspondence contains a pure-strategy Nash equilibrium.[18] The assumed form of "unsophisticated behavior" is similar to that of Sanchirico (1996) and Hurkens (1995) in that players are assumed to have at least some chance of following the best-response dynamic. Sonsino makes a number of other highly specialized assumptions about the learning procedure and shows that the system converges globally to a cycle through the pure Nash equilibria. If there is enough initial randomness, then there is positive probability that a nontrivial cycle is established.

Unlike the methods discussed above using either experts or conditional smooth fictitious play, Sonsino deals with the exact detection of cycles. That is, either a cycle is "detected" with probability one or it is not detected at all. This creates some complications that are worth noting. One method of detecting cycles is to assume that a cycle $ABAC$, for example, is detected if it is repeated a sufficient number of times. However, there may be no cycles early in the game, with cycles only emerging

---

18. Here a "subgame" of a strategic-form game is obtained by restricting each player to some subset of the original strategies. A "subgame" is closed under the best-response correspondence if all best responses to profiles in the set lie in the set, which is the definition of a CURB set (see chapter 4). However, not all CURB sets are "subgames" in Sonsino's sense, since a CURB set need not be a product set; for example, a set consisting of two strict Nash equilibria is a CURB set but not a subgame.

after play has gone on for some time. We would like players to be able to detect these cycles also, so it seems reasonable to assume that a cycle is "detected" if it has occurred a sufficient number of times in the recent past. There are complications with this as well: Suppose, in particular, that the sequence of events $ABABABAC$ repeats three times followed by $ABABABA$. Let the rule for cycle detection be that if a pattern has repeated three times at the end of the history, it is "recognized." In this example, the pattern $ABABABAC$ has repeated three times at the end of the history, so following $ABABABA$, the player should expect C. However, the pattern AB has also repeated three times at the end of the history, so following the final A, the player should expect B. In this example two patterns are "recognizable," and each leads to a different conclusion. Sonsino proposes restrictions on cycle recognition procedures that eliminate this ambiguity.

Note that in conditional fictitious play, either the smooth type discussed in Fudenberg and Levine (1995) or the exact type discussed in Aoyagi (1994), this type of issue need not arise, since these models consider more general rules for classifying histories. For example, if, following Aoyagi, we categorize histories according to the final L outcomes, and simplify by setting $L = 1$, then following A the frequency is 80% B and 20% C, so in effect this is what is "expected" to happen next. More generally, the model of conditional fictitious play allows for any arbitrary rules for assigning histories to categories, and the play observed in a given category need not be the same each time the category is observed. Thus Sonsino's paper can be viewed as exploring the difficulties that arise with a special sort of assignment rules.

Another issue in exact pattern recognition arises when we have a sequence such as $ABCAABCDABCADABCDCCAB$ in which AB is always followed by C, even though there is not an ABC cycle per se. It seems sensible that this pattern might be recognized, although it would not be recognized by Sonsino's method. Notice that a conditional (smooth or exact) fictitious play will detect this pattern provided that $L \geq 2$.

8.11 Manipulating Learning Procedures

The focus of attention in this book, as well as in the recent game theory literature, has been on myopic learning procedures, not in the sense that players do not care about the future but in the strategic sense of lacking concern about the consequences of current play for opponents' future action. We have justified this by sometimes casual reference to large populations.

This section discusses two related points. First, although the idea of extrapolation between "similar" games suggests that the relevant population may be large even when there are few people playing *precisely* the game in question, there are also situations of interest in which the relevant population must be viewed as small, so it is of some interest to consider the case of a small population. This raises an important issue: A player may attempt to manipulate his opponent's learning process and try to "teach" him how to play the game. This issue has been studied extensively in models of "reputation effects," which typically assume Nash equilibrium but not in the context of learning theory. A second issue has been raised by Ellison (1994) who considers the possibility of contagion effects in the type of large-population anonymous random matching model we have used to justify myopia. Under certain conditions Ellison shows that even in this setting there is a scope for a more rational player to teach his opponents how to play. In particular, this is true if the more rational player is sufficiently patient relative to the population size but not if the population size is large relative to his patience (i.e., the order of limits matters).

8.11.1 A Model of Reputation

A simple setting in which to begin to understand teaching an opponent to play the game is to imagine that one player is myopic and follows the type of learning procedure we have discussed in this book, while another player is sophisticated and has a reasonably good understanding that his opponent is using a learning procedure of this type. What happens in this case? This has been studied extensively in the context of equilibrium theory, where models of this type are called "reputational," but not in the context of learning theory. However, much as Kalai and Lehrer (1993) show that the results of Jordan (1991) on equilibrium learning carry over to the case of nonequilibrium learning, so we expect that the lessons of the literature on reputation will carry over also to the case of nonequilibrium learning.

In order to introduce learning into an equilibrium context, it is necessary, as in the case in the Jordan model, to introduce uncertainty on the part of the players about the game that is being played. That is, while

Nash equilibrium and its refinements suppose that players know one another's strategies, they are allowed to have doubts about their opponents' preferences, which in many ways is the same thing as having doubts about their strategies. Suppose, as in many papers on reputation effects, that there are two players, a long-run player and a short-run player. The short-run player is myopic and is the "learner." The long-run player has many possible different types, the type remaining fixed as the game is repeated, and each type corresponding to different preferences. Consequently the short-run player wishes to learn the type of long-run player in order to play a best response to the actions of that type. Because of the fact that this is an equilibrium theory, if the short-run player is to have relatively diffuse priors about the strategy of the long-run player, it is important that in equilibrium different types of long-run player really play different strategies. To solve this problem Kreps and Wilson (1982) and Milgrom and Roberts (1982) introduced the idea of committed types with preferences that force them to play a particular strategy regardless of the particular equilibrium.

The second issue that must be addressed is the long-run consistency of the learning procedure used by the short-run player. Fudenberg and Levine (1992) show that the beliefs of the short-run player converge to something observationally equivalent to the truth at a *uniform* rate, using an argument based on up-crossing numbers of supermartingales. Essentially the reputational literature introduced the idea of committed types, precisely so that Blackwell and Dubins absolute continuity assumption would be satisfied.

If we now assume that the long-run player is relatively patient, then Fudenberg and Levine (1989) show that he can get almost as much utility as he could get in the Stackelberg equilibrium of the stage game. The idea is that the long-run player can guarantee himself at least this much by playing the optimal precommitment strategy forever. The basic argument carries over in a straightforward way to the case of nonequilibrium learning:[19] If the long-run player plays the optimal precommitment strategy forever, the short-run player will eventually learn this and begin to play a best response to it. Since the long-run player is very patient, this means that the average present value received will be nearly that of playing the optimal precommitment strategy with the short-run player playing a best response to it. Moreover, since the short-run player is always

---

19. Essentially this point is made in Watson (1993) and Watson and Battigalli (1997), who weaken Nash equilibrium to rationalizability.

	A	B
A	10, 10	0, 0
B	0, 0	1, 1

Figure 8.7
Coordination game

playing a best response to some beliefs about the long-run players strategy, the long-run player cannot really hope to do better than this. The point is that if your opponent is playing myopically, rather than do the same, you should play as a Stackelberg leader and "teach" him how to play against you.

8.11.2   Teaching in a Large Population

The key ingredient in the reputation model is that the patient (or rational) player can change the behavior of his opponents in a significant way through his own action. It is natural to conjecture that this would not be true in the type of large-population anonymous random matching model we have been using to justify myopic play. However, Ellison (1994) has pointed out that this need not be true, due to contagion effects.

This point is best understood in the following example taken from Ellison. Suppose that there is a homogeneous population of N agents playing the 2×2 pure coordination game with anonymous random matching shown in figure 8.7. Note that there are two pure Nash equilibria in this game at (10, 10) and (1, 1). One of these, the Pareto-efficient equilibrium at (10, 10) is also the Stackelberg equilibrium. In other words, a player who can teach his opponents how to play would like to teach them to play A.

Suppose first that every player follows the behavior prescribed by exact fictitious play, with prior weights (0, 1). Then all players choose B in period 1, and the result is that all players choose B in every period. Suppose next that for some reason, player N plays A in period 1 and follows fictitious play in all future periods, while players 1 through $N - 1$ continue to follow fictitious play in every period. Then whoever is matched with player N in period 1 has weights (1, 1) in period 2, and so must play A until at least period 10; call this player 1. Then suppose that player 1 is not matched with player N in period 2 but with some other player 2; this player 2 will also play A at least until period 10. If moreover 1 and 2 are matched with 2 new players 3 and 4 in period 3, and not with themselves or with player N, then there will be 4 players who play A in period 4. At each period until period 10, there is a positive probability that the number of A-players doubles, so that if N is small enough, there is a positive probability that every player plays A in period 9, so that only A is played from that period on.

Now suppose that player N is rational and knows that all other players follow fictitious play. Then player N knows that by playing A in the first period only and following fictitious play thereafter, there is a nonzero probability that the entire population will move permanently to the Pareto-preferred equilibrium (10, 10) in 10 periods.[20] For a small discount factor the short-run cost of inducing this shift might exceed the expected present value of the benefit. Indeed, for any fixed discount factor the expected present value becomes small as the population size grows, since it must take at least $\log(M)$ periods to change the play of M other agents. However, changing the order of limits changes this conclusion: For any fixed population there is some time T such that there is a positive chance that all agents will be playing A from period T on if the rational agent plays A in the first period. Thus the benefit from playing A outweighs its cost if the rational player's discount factor is sufficiently close to 1. Ellison computes that this simple but nonmyopic strategy improves on the naïve one in a population of 100 if the discount factor exceeds 0.67 and that even in a population of 5,000 the nonnaïve play yields a higher payoff if the discount factor exceeds 0.94.[21]

Note moreover that *regardless* of the discount factor, the rational player has no incentive for nonnaïve play if naïve play would yield his preferred equilibrium. Ellison shows that the converse is not true: In general, 2×2 coordination games, even when the rational player would prefer the other equilibrium, he cannot steer play in that direction unless the "preferred" equilibrium is also risk dominant: Players defect from a risk-dominated equilibrium too quickly for "contagion" to take hold.

It is also worth noting that the incentive to "teach" opponents in a large population in the example is not robust to noisy play by the players. If players randomize, then the contagion is likely to occur even without the intervention of a rational "teacher," and so the incentive to intervene

---

20. If the shift does not occur in the first ten periods, players who have seen A only once will return to playing B in period 11, but there is still a chance that the contagion will resume from the base of players who saw two or more A's in the first ten periods.

21. In some sense these calculations may overstate the case, since using a game with less extreme payoff differences would yield less striking numbers. On the other hand, the incentive to "teach" opponents is even greater than in the calculations if players attach greater weight to more recent observations, as with exponential weighting.

	A	B
A	a, a	0, 0
B	0, 0	1, 1

Figure 8.8
General coordination game

is reduced. The following example indicates the extent to which contagion is likely to occur with even a "small" amount of noise. Consider the
general coordination game (Ellison's example corresponding to $a = 10$)
shown in figure 8.8. Here we assume that $a > 1$, so that A, A is the
Pareto-preferred equilibrium. Suppose that players, rather than using
the usual deterministic fictitious play, use a smooth fictitious play. If
the smoothing function is

$$v^i(\sigma^i) = \sum_{s^i} -\sigma^i(s^i) \log \sigma^i(s^i),$$

as we saw in chapter 4, the smoothed best response is

$$\overline{BR}^i(\sigma^{-i})[s^i] \equiv \frac{\exp((1/\lambda)u^i(s^i, \sigma^{-i}))}{\sum_{r^i} \exp((1/\lambda)u^i(r^i, \sigma^{-i}))}.$$

If players' play converges to a symmetric deterministic steady state in
which each player plays A with probability σ_A, then by a standard extension of the strong law of large numbers, the empirical distributions will
converge to the same limit with probability 1.[22] Asymptotic empiricism
implies that the assessments converge to this limit value along every path
so that at the steady state

$$\sigma_A = \overline{BR}^i(\sigma_A) = \frac{\exp((1/\lambda)a\sigma_A)}{(\exp((1/\lambda)a\sigma_A) + \exp((1/\lambda)\sigma_B))}.$$

This corresponds to the "quantal response equilibrium" of McKelvey and
Palfrey (1995). A calculation shows that for each $a > 1$ there is a sufficiently large λ (i.e., enough noise) that this equation has a unique solution
and that this solution satisfies $\sigma_A > 0.5$; that is, the Pareto-preferred
action is more likely.

To report on the quantitative significance of noise for the steady state,
we measure the size of the noise by $b_A(\lambda) = \overline{BR}^i(\sigma_A = 0)$, that is, the

---

22. See, for example, Fudenberg and Kreps (1993). The only way that this differs from the
standard form of the strong law is that the distribution at each date t may depend on the
history to that date.

Table 8.1
Impact of Noise on the Steady State

a	$b_A(\lambda)$	σ_A
1.1	10.0%	85%
1.3	8.3%	95%
1.5	6.3%	99%
2	4.7%	100%
3	2.9%	100%
4	2.2%	100%
6	1.5%	100%
7	1.2%	100%
10	1.0%	100%

probability that the action A is used when the assessment is that the probability of B is one. (In the usual fictitious play, this probability is zero.) For each a we can calculate the least value of $b_A(\lambda)$ for which there is a unique symmetric steady state, together with the steady state value of σ_A. This is reported in the table 8.1. In Ellison's example, even 1% noise is enough to guarantee a unique steady state in which (to the limit of computer precision) 100% of the time A is played. However, the table indicates how remarkably strong the contagion effect is: When the Pareto-preferred equilibrium is only a 10% improvement ($a = 1.1$), a 10% noise ratio leads to a unique equilibrium in which A is played 85% of the time. If the system is going to converge to a favorable steady state anyway, then there is little incentive for intervention by a rational player.

This example shows several things. First of all, the incentive to "teach" opponents is diminished in noisy environments, and it becomes more reasonable for players to behave myopically. This is not to say that the outcome in a noisy model with one rational player is the same as that in the standard fictitious play model without noise where all players are myopic. Rather, the second point to be drawn from the example is that once again small amounts of noise can serve to select between the long-run outcomes of the noiseless model.

References

Aoyagi, M. 1994. Evolution of beliefs and the Nash equilibrium of normal form games. *Journal of Economic Theory* 70: 444–69.

Benaim, M., and M. Hirsch. 1994. Learning processes, mixed equilibria and dynamical systems arising from repeated games. Mimeo. University of California at Berkeley.

Blackwell, D. 1956. An analog of the minmax theorem for vector payoffs. *Pacific Journal of Mathematics* 6: 1–8.

Blackwell, D., and L. Dubins. 1962. Merging of opinions with increasing information. *Annals of Mathematical Statistics* 38: 882–86.

Chung, T. 1994. Approximate methods for sequential decision making using expert advice. *Proceedings of the 7th Annual ACM Conference on Computational Learning Theory*, 183–89.

Desantis, A., G. Markowski, and M. Wegman. 1992. Learning probabilistic prediction functions. *Proceedings of the 1988 Workshop of Computational Learning*, 312–28.

Ellison, G. 1994. Learning with one rational player. Mimeo. Massachusetts Institute of Technology.

Feder, M., N. Mehrav, and M. Gutman. 1992. Universal prediction of individual sequences. *IEEE Transactions on Information Theory* 38: 1258–70.

Foster, D., and R. Vohra. 1993. Calibrated learning and correlated equilibrium. Mimeo. Wharton School.

Foster, D., and R. Vohra. 1995. Asymptotic calibration. Mimeo. Wharton School.

Foster, D., and R. Vohra. 1996. Regret in the on-line decision problem. Mimeo. Wharton School.

Freund, Y., and R. Schapire. 1995. A decision theoretic generalization of on-line learning and an application to boosting. *Proceedings of the Second European Conference on Computational Learning*. New York: Springer, pp. 23–27.

Fudenberg, D., and D. K. Levine. 1989. Reputation and equilibrium selection in games with a patient player. *Econometrica* 57: 759–78.

Fudenberg, D., and D. K. Levine. 1992. Maintaining a reputation when strategies are imperfectly observed. *Review of Economic Studies* 59: 561–79.

Fudenberg, D., and D. K. Levine. 1995. Conditional universal consistency. Mimeo. University of California at Los Angeles.

Fudenberg, D., and D. Kreps. 1993. Learning mixed equilibria. *Games and Economic Behavior* 5: 320–67.

Grenander, U. 1981. *Abstract Inference*. New York: Wiley.

Hart, S., and A. Mas-Collel. 1996. A simple adaptive procedure leading to correlated equilibrium. Mimeo. Hebrew University.

Hurkens, S. 1995. Learning by forgetful players: From primitive formations to persistent retracts. *Games and Economic Behavior* 11: 301–29.

Jordan, J. 1991. Bayesian learning in normal form games. *Games and Economic Behavior* 5: 368–86.

Jordan, J. 1993. Three problems in learning mixed strategy equilibria. *Games and Economic Behavior* 5: 368–86.

Kalai, E., and E. Lehrer. 1993. Rational learning leads to Nash equilibrium. *Econometrica* 61: 1019–45.

Kalai, E., E. Lehrer,and R. Smorodinsky. 1995. Calibrated forecasting and merging. Mimeo, MEDS 1144. Northwestern University.

Kivinen, J., and M. Warmuth. 1993. Using experts in predicting continuous outcomes. *Computational Learning Theory: EURO COLT*. New York: Springer, 109–20.

Kreps, D., and R. Wilson. 1982. Reputation and imperfect information. *Journal of Economic Theory* 27: 253–79.

Littlestone, N., and M. Warmuth. 1994. The weighted majority algorithm. *Information and Computation* 108: 212–61.

Loeve, M. 1978. *Probability Theory II*. Berlin: Springer.

McKelvey, R., and T. Palfrey. 1995. Quantal response equilibria for normal form games. *Games and Economic Behavior* 10: 6–38.

Milgrom, P., and J. Roberts. 1982. Predation, reputation and entry deterrence. *Econometrica* 50: 443–60.

Nachbar, J. 1997. Prediction, optimization and learning in repeated games. *Econometrica*, 65: 275–309.

Sanchirico, C. 1996. A probabilistic model of learning in games. *Econometrica* 64: 1375–93.

Sonsino, D. 1997. Learning to learn, pattern recognition and Nash equilibrium. *Games and Economic Behavior* 18: 286–331.

Vovck, V. 1990. Aggregating strategies. *Proceedings of the 3rd Annual Conference on Computational Learning Theory*, 371–83.

Watson, J. 1993. A "reputation" refinement without equilibrium. *Econometrica* 61: 199–205.

Watson, J., and P. Battigalli. 1997. On "reputation" refinements with heterogeneous beliefs. *Econometrica* 65: 363–74.

Index